The End of Exceptionalism
in American Education

The End of Exceptionalism in American Education

The Changing Politics of School Reform

Jeffrey R. Henig

Harvard Education Press
Cambridge, Massachusetts

Library of Congress Control Number 2012948703

Paperback ISBN 978-1-61250-511-4
Library Edition ISBN 978-1-61250-512-1

Published by Harvard Education Press,
an imprint of the Harvard Education Publishing Group

Harvard Education Press
8 Story Street
Cambridge, MA 02138

Cover Design: Deborah Hodgdon

The typefaces used in this book are Bembo and ITC Symbol.

CONTENTS

ONE

1   Education and Single-Purpose Governance

TWO

33   The New Education Executives

THREE

79   An Expanded Role for Legislatures and the Courts

FOUR

119   Changing Actors, Issues, and Policy Ideas

FIVE

161   The End of Exceptionalism: Implications for the Future

181   *Notes*

207   *References*

225   *Acknowledgments*

227   *About the Author*

229   *Index*

CHAPTER ONE

EDUCATION AND SINGLE-PURPOSE GOVERNANCE

And something is happening here
But you don't know what it is
Do you, Mister Jones?

—Bob Dylan, *Ballad of a Thin Man*

IMPORTANT THINGS are happening in the way we deal with education policy in the United States, but most accounts fail to capture the underlying nature of the change. Conventional portrayals hint at a new dynamism in what has traditionally been a hidebound and bureaucratically entrenched system. But the elements of change are treated as a series of disconnected reforms. Charter schools. Vouchers. High-stakes testing. So-called education governors and education presidents. Educational adequacy legal cases that involve state courts and legislatures in determining what constitutes a sound basic education. Mayoral control. A new federal role via No Child Left Behind. Contracting with private education providers. Portfolio management models of urban school district reform. Each of these innovations has its own institutional settings, its own champions, its own underlying rationale. And each, for the most part, is studied in isolation from the others, by researchers who specialize in a particular level of government (federal, state, local), a particular branch of government (executive, legislative, judicial), a

1

particular kind of reform (curriculum, governance, delivery systems), or a particular scholarly lens.

This image of chaotic and cycling change makes sense in light of the recent history of educational reform. Decision making for urban school systems has been like a series of spinning wheels.[1] In a seeming contradiction, school systems are portrayed both as rigidly resistant to new ideas and as fickle consumers that embrace every latest trend. Philanthropist Eli Broad, who has put millions of dollars into the task of changing American education, expresses the "stagnant systems" view as follows: "A classroom today in America, and the school day today in America, is not different than it was 50 or 100 years ago. You still have a 10- to 12-week summer recess or vacation, which goes back to an agrarian era. You still teach the same way. The classroom looks the same. The only difference is in some classrooms instead of blackboards you've got whiteboards with marker pens."[2] Anthony Bryk et al. express the view of schools as fickle consumers of the fad du jour. Discussing Chicago school reform, they refer to the tendency of some to become "Christmas tree" schools, loaded down with a boxful of programs with varying and often inconsistent methods and rationales: "The addition of new programs on top of old ones may result in a disjointed and fragmented set of experiences for students . . . Much of school life seems to follow an endless cycle of soliciting funds, implementing new initiatives, and then going out to solicit more funds for even newer initiatives to replace the current ones."[3]

The contradiction might be illusory, though, because the dynamism of school systems might be merely superficial. Change, say some critics, typically takes place on a symbolic level only. A turbulent surface can mask bland consistency at deeper levels where things really matter.

If the various aforementioned reforms *are* simply a matter of spinning wheels, it would be right to regard them with a jaundiced eye. There are too many serious matters to attend to, and our financial resources, political capacity, and emotional reserves are too thin to invest them in every passing fashion. But while it is true that educational decision making in the U.S. has often been frivolous and superficial, it is a mistake to think of these reform initiatives as just the latest in a string of disparate, ephemeral, and herky-jerky enthusiasms that will come and go, leaving behind little of consequence. It is right to regard them as symptoms—not of a chronic disease but rather of a structural shifting of plates and the consequent conflict, turmoil, and uncertainty that structural change frequently entails.

I argue in this book that these seemingly unconnected initiatives stem from a common root: broad changes, still under way, in how collective decisions are made about what schools should do and how schooling should be organized, funded, and evaluated. Compared to how we make decisions about most other important areas of domestic policy—the economy, welfare and income support, family policy, civil rights, and most questions relating to environment, transportation, and crime—decisions about public schools historically have been highly localized, consigned to special, single-purpose governance structures, and dominated by a smaller array of highly focused interest groups. "Earlier than any other public service in America," Laurence Iannacone observed in 1967, "education acquired special legal protections against the operations of 'normal' politics."[4] This set of special governance arrangements, he argued, made education a closed system "encased in a network of extra-governmental friends and allies," providing elevated status to "schoolmen" wielding a claim to pedagogical expertise, and resistant to intellectual challenge and new policy ideas.[5] I believe that this special status has been eroding, and that we are witnessing the gradual reabsorption of educational decision making into multilevel, general-purpose government and politics.[6]

The sharpest manifestation of the reabsorption is the movement toward mayoral control of public schools, with a number of large cities eliminating or substantially weakening elected school boards to give increased power to the mayor. Mayoral control is usually undertaken in the belief that a clearly identified central leader can better plow through obstacles to reform, mobilize broader coalitions of support, coordinate education with services provided by other agencies, and stand up to teacher unions. But the phenomenon I'm describing is much broader than this. For example, rather than being limited to mayors, the expanded role of general-purpose decision makers is also reflected in the increasingly proactive involvement of executives at other levels of government—so-called education governors and education presidents.[7]

3

Nor is the reabsorption of education into general-purpose government and politics just a by-product of increasingly muscular executives. It also involves the other branches of general-purpose government. At the federal and state levels, the judiciary arguably was the leading wedge for breaching the traditional autonomy of local school districts. As presidents, governors, and mayors have extended their involvement in education, so too have Congress, state legislatures, and city councils.

The broad changes under way constitute the end of education exceptionalism in the United States. There is an extended literature about "American exceptionalism," which focuses on the ways in which institutions, norms, and political practices in the United States differ from those in other nations.[8] While the U.S. system of education governance is indeed unusual when compared to other developed nations, in referring to education exceptionalism I'm focusing not on the differences between the U.S. and other countries, but on the differences between the handling of education and the handling of other major domestic policies. Education policy in the U.S has traditionally been seen—and treated—as different and distinct, a thing apart. "Although few Americans realize it, the nation long has maintained one government for schools—[composed] mainly of local and state boards of education and superintendents—and another for everything else," wrote Michael Kirst. He traced this to 1826, "when Massachusetts created a separate school committee divorced from general government, a practice that spread nationally."[9]

The end of education exceptionalism means that education is becoming more like other domestic policy areas. This, I will argue, has implications for how theorists and researchers should think about education and for how politicians, parties, interest groups, and citizens should act if they hope to shape effective and sustainable reform.

SHIFTING FAULT LINES IN THE INSTITUTIONAL LANDSCAPE OF AMERICAN EDUCATION

The erosion of single-purpose institutions for educational decision making is the least understood of three broad areas of institutional alignment that are changing the landscape of American education policy.

4

There are other important lines of cleavage, but it is along these three dimensions that many of the key controversies around school reform have bubbled to the surface.[10] And because these seismic shifts are both extremely consequential and not well understood, it is around these lines that some of the most high-stakes political battles are taking place.

The other two shifting fault lines are centralization versus decentralization and public sector versus private sector. I devote less attention to these two dimensions because these are likely to be familiar to most readers, and because they have been written about elsewhere, and well.[11] But there are good reasons to draw the links among these broad kinds of institutional change. Besides alerting us to how the politics engendered by such institutional shifts are similar, movements along the three fault lines are interconnected in ways that contemporary debates about education policy generally ignore.

Centralization Versus Decentralization in a Federal System

For many decades, public education in the United States was very much a local affair. Nominally, the states were in charge. Constitutionally, education was a "reserved power"—limiting the potential role of the national government—and local governments, including school districts, were creations of the states, which delegated authority to them but could also take that authority away.[12] The states, however, had neither the inclination nor the capacity to directly intervene. Partly this was a matter of culture and expectations: that a state might "meddle" in local education decisions was seen by many, including state officials, as something that just was not done. Partly it was deference to the idea of localism, and partly to the sense that education decisions should be made by educators, who themselves were primarily situated at the district level. It was also a matter of capacity: state education agencies remained rather flimsy things, lacking the ability as well as the mandate to do much more than collect very basic data.[13] As of 1890, the median number of employees in state departments of education was two, and that included the state superintendent.[14] And when states challenged local prerogatives—for example, by attempting to whittle down cross-district

5

inequities in race or class—they often found that resistance by local leaders and citizens was intense and politically too much for them to stand their ground.[15]

For most of the nineteenth and well into the twentieth century, the key unit of decision making was the school district. Early on, these were rather intimate venues in which local families and community leaders could easily gain access. "What the colonial period bequeathed nineteenth-century school reformers was a tradition of democratic localism and individualism that was viscerally opposed to state centralization . . . As such, schools were the products of individual teachers, churches, philanthropic societies, town, and districts without connection to a 'state interest.'"[16]

Although neither smooth nor continuous, the general arc of institutional development within American education has been toward greater centralization. The first strong wave of centralization was a matter of increasing scale driven by the consolidation of school districts. In 1939 there were 117,108 school districts in the nation; with about 30.1 million five to seventeen-year-olds enrolled, the average district contained fewer than two schools and served only 257 students.[17] The scale of governance was much like the scale we associate with a single charter school today. Forty years later, in 1979, the number of districts had dropped to 15,994, and the ratio of students per district had increased over 1,000 percent, to about 3,020.

The number of districts continued to decline after 1979, albeit at a much-diminished rate (in 2007, there were 13,838 districts), but localism also began to be attenuated in other and even more dramatic ways. While centralization prior to 1980 was largely confined to institutional changes at the district level, subsequently the shifts have implicated the structure of federalism itself. The first wave involved more forceful action on the part of the states. During the 1960s and 1970s, some individual governors, mostly from the South, began to focus more on education as a tool for economic development. During the 1980s this gubernatorial interest spread and found collective expression through the National Governors Association (NGA). James Hunt, who had made education his signature issue during his tenure as governor of North Carolina, used an NGA meeting in 1983 as an opportunity to urge his colleagues to make education their top priority, on the heels of the *A Nation at Risk* report from the National Commission on Excellence in Education.[18] Two years later, an article in *Education Week* observed that it was "the rare governor who has not, in the past two years, devoted a large portion of his or her time, energy, and political capital . . . to nuts and bolts questions of education policy."[19]

The growing role of the states was followed by a growing role of the national government. In chapter 2, I discuss in greater detail the rise of both "education governors" and "education presidents" as a manifestation not only of centralization but also of the reabsorption of education decision making into general-purpose government and politics. For now it is enough to note that *A Nation at Risk* provides a convenient road marker for growing readiness on the part of state and national leaders to get more directly involved in the mechanics of school reform. This greater interest in schools did not immediately translate into direct involvement.[20] As Susan Fuhrman observed, "as the 1990s began, it was clear that some resurgence in federal leadership would follow, but the shape of a revitalized federal role was not yet apparent." By 1994, she concluded, "a more vigorous federal presence in education was evident."[21]

The increasing importance of education in presidential elections and the subsequent enactment of the No Child Left Behind Act (NCLB), signed into law by George W. Bush on January 8, 2002, represented such a sharp escalation of the federal role that it has been tempting to see it as the culmination of an inevitable expansion. Political scientists, borrowing from evolutionary biology, describe cases like this as "punctuated equilibrium"; the rapid unseating of a long-standing regime is followed by the institutionalization of a new political regime, with the process unlikely to be reversed.[22] The subsequent election of Barack Obama, despite marking a change in partisan control of the White House, saw the arc of centralization continue with Obama's Race to the Top program, which used competitive federal grants to leverage changes in state education policy that were more direct, and arguably larger, than those sparked by NCLB.[23]

7

Public Versus Private Sector

A second major institutional dimension involves the allocation of authority between the public and private sector: between government on the one hand, and either market systems or civil society (nonprofit organizations, community groups, family, and organized religion) on the other. The contemporary manifestation of the public versus private debate has been a high-profile, hotly contested battle centered on vouchers, charter schools, and the growth of both a for-profit and nonprofit education sector.[24]

The basic tension between reliance on government as opposed to private provision has existed since the middle of the nineteenth century, when early proponents of public education began their quest to create a government-based, mandatory public education system rather than leaving it to the instincts and whims of families. The creation of a system of public education is often portrayed as an inevitable step in the development of a strong economic and civil society, with leaders like Horace Mann in the role of heroic midwives of modernity. But it also represented a wresting of authority away from families and religious organizations, which led to much resistance. As Michael Katz has chronicled, some regarded this change as illegitimate usurpation at the time, and even though the idea that we should have a publicly supported and delivered education system has won broad acceptance, the borderline between government and family responsibility remains fluid and contested.[25]

The tension between public and private also came to the fore in battles surrounding school desegregation. Among political elites, the dominant framing of those battles was along the centralization versus decentralization fault line, with "states' rights" and "local control" serving as rallying cries for those opposed to mandated desegregation. But at the street level, where the changes were felt more viscerally, resistance to desegregation was premised less on theoretical models of federalism than on the issue of parent rights versus government intrusion, and private academies played an early key role as a vehicle for exit by those unwilling to have their children attend integrated schools.[26] A combination of demographic, political, and judicial factors has caused desegregation to recede as an issue of open contention, but the government versus family fault line has been more active again, of late, around issues such as home schooling and the teaching of traditional and religious values. Rick Santorum, on the 2012 presidential primary trail, rallied some and appalled others when he questioned whether the governmental role in schooling had gone much too far. "Where did they come up that public education and bigger education bureaucracies was the rule in America?" he asked while campaigning in Ohio. "Parents educated their children, because it's their responsibility to educate their children."[27]

The explicit framing of public versus private in economic terms—the argument that market forces of supply and demand outperform government as a route to efficient and effective policies—can be dated to the middle of the last century. That's when the conservative economist Milton Friedman crafted the influential argument that a voucher-based system combining public funding with private provision would force schools to compete for students, leading to gains in social efficiency, responsiveness to family needs, and academic performance.[28] The pro-market formulation embedded a number of interlocking claims: free interactions between suppliers and informed consumers are the most effective way to match services to desires; competition among providers produces efficiencies, innovations, and responsiveness; and government monopolies, because they can use taxing power to coerce payments even from dissatisfied customers, are more insidious than private monopolies.

Though frequently chattered about before then, these ideas did not really gain leverage in policy circles until the mid-1980s. This was partly because the market theories seemed academic and abstract to many, but also because most Americans were proud and protective of their public schools, believing them to reflect local values and assuming them to be among the best in the world. Two things happened in the 1980s that prepared the ground for a more vibrant and politically viable privatization movement in education. First, the combination of domestic economic difficulties, the growing visibility of Japan and other nations as global competitors, and the negative portrait of American educational performance that was crystallized in the *Nation at Risk* report began to erode popular smugness about the superiority of America's schools.

Second, the Reagan administration, by linking market framing to magnet schools and other existing public school choice arrangements, made the case that what previously had seemed abstract, academic, and risky not only was realistic but was already operating to good effect. If small doses of choice were associated with innovative programs, satisfied families, and integrated schools, Reagan argued, imagine the benefits that might accrue if choice could be more fully unleashed as an antidote to the inertia and sameness associated with the bureaucracy and public monopoly typical of the standard school district.[29]

Americans were still wary about radical visions of privatized education, as witnessed by the rejection of school voucher programs when they were put to public vote.[30] But charter schools emerged as a gentler form of privatization, introducing parental choices, greater competition among schools, private management at the school level, and substantial deregulation of curriculum and teaching while maintaining enough public oversight to assuage many of the concerns about equity, stratification, racial resegregation, and commingling of church and state that had plagued more Friedmanesque models. At the same time that charters were proliferating, a much broader private education sector began to expand, comprising not only for-profit and nonprofit charter management organizations, but also providers of supplementary education, testing, professional development, curriculum, and other supporting groups with both market and political strength.[31]

General-Purpose Versus Single-Purpose Governance: The Least-Understood Fault Line

Considerable attention has been focused on the institutional battles around federalism and privatization. Less has been paid to the third axis of institutional change: the gradual reassertion of general-purpose government and politics in education, a realm that had previously been dominated by single-purpose institutions focused on education alone.

The attention to federalism and privatization is warranted. Each is linked directly to deep-seated ideological battles over states' rights versus national leadership, governmental growth and regulation versus individual freedom and dynamic markets. The choice between general- and single-purpose governance has not carried the same ideological and partisan freight. Indeed, the original impetus to separate education from the governance of other local functions was primarily as an antidote to partisanship, and for many decades the anomalous treatment of public education was accepted by those on all sides of the political spectrum as an unobjectionable *fait accompli.* Yet the decision whether or not to assign education to general-purpose government and politics is closely related to both centralization and privatization. And its ultimate implications, while less understood, might be just as consequential.

The United States is a crazy quilt of governments. In addition to the national government and the fifty states, there are roughly 89,500 other units of government with different powers, functions, and geographic focus. The national and state governments are known as general-purpose governments. That is to say, they take responsibility for a broad range of functions—for example, health, human services, transportation, parks, housing, education, criminal justice, and the like. General-purpose governments typically create specialized agencies to carry out their policies, but they retain for themselves the critical policy making responsibilities. They make decisions about how to allocate public attention and budgetary commitments across a range of problems and opportunities.[32]

The picture is more complicated at the substate level, where, despite the greater attention given to the White House by media and commentators, much of the real story of school reform continues to unfold. States have created a panoply of substate governments, including some that have general-purpose decision-making responsibility and some that have been narrowly tailored to focus on a single function.[33] Substate general-purpose governments—counties, municipalities, towns, and townships—control more money and are generally more visible, but there are actually more single-purpose than general-purpose governments overall. School districts are the most important of these, but others are focused on functions such as air pollution, conservation, drainage, transportation, economic development, fire protection, housing, hospitals, and mosquito abatement. What makes these "governments," rather than simply agencies or departments, is the higher degree of authority and independence that the states delegate to them.

As of 2007, there were 89,476 governments operating at the substate level, roughly 44 percent of which were general purpose and 56 percent were single purpose (see table 1.1).[34] Just under 39 percent of the single-purpose governments are school systems, but they account for what is by far the largest number of employees.

Table 1.2 presents the full-time employment and payroll data for school-focused and nonschool single-purpose governments. Between them, elementary and secondary districts and special governments focusing on higher education employed almost 5.2 million full-time workers, more than eight and one-half times the number for all other single-purpose districts combined. Among the other types of single-purpose governments, the largest focus on health and hospitals, transit, and housing and community development.[35]

Overall, general-purpose governments at the state and local level account for more employees and capacity than single-purpose government. But elementary and secondary education school districts, by

TABLE 1.1

Number of local general- and single-purpose governments by type

General purpose	
Total GP	39,044
County	3,033
Municipal	19,492
Town or township	16,519
Single purpose	
Total SP	50,432
Non-school	37,381
School	14,561
Total	**89,476**

Source: U.S. Census Bureau, 2007 Census of Governments.

TABLE 1.2

Employment and payroll data for special governments

U.S. total employment and payroll data by state and government function

	Full-time employees	Total pay
School-focused		
Elementary and secondary education	4,971,674	$19,765,530,812
Higher education	183,566	$1,128,074,298
Nonschool single-purpose		
Hospitals	179,034	$818,051,722
Transit	114,819	$495,600,005
Housing and community development	50,737	$168,154,881
Water supply	37,879	$168,117,646
Health	31,105	$104,130,099
Fire protection	27,630	$154,702,554
Sewerage	24,759	$113,526,511
Electric power	23,986	$143,251,560
Libraries	22,774	$97,417,755
Parks and recreation	17,839	$89,724,041
Natural resources	17,267	$64,893,765
Air transportation	12,381	$58,910,162
Solid waste management	5,260	$19,876,110
Highways	5,001	$21,673,194
Water transport and terminals	4,159	$19,884,095
Public welfare	3,576	$8,652,762
Gas supply	2,166	$7,307,778
Corrections	1,500	$4,246,822
Police protection	167	$911,402
All other and unallocable	16,851	$92,334,405
All state and local general-purpose	8,925,156	$40,599,817,030

Source: This data was generated by the author from the U.S. Census Bureau's Build-a-Table tool with data from the Census of Government Employment, March 2007. For information about the data's sampling error, nonsampling error, and definitions, see http://www.census.gov/govs/apes/cog_employment_methodology.html.

Note: Data is in whole numbers.

themselves, account for about one in three public sector employees at the state and local level. That this substantial treasure trove of jobs and resources is largely outside the direct control of governors, state legislatures, mayors, and city councils has been an anomaly, one that I argue is under pressure and beginning to fray.

As is the case with all substate governments, the origin and details for single-purpose governments are established by the states, which have the discretion to set the rules and to restructure or eliminate the government should they opt to do so.[36] On average, there are .85 general-purpose governments for every single-purpose government, but there is considerable variation in the extent to which states have turned to single-purpose governments as a tool. Of the fifty states, California is the most prone to establish single-purpose units of governance; it has more than seven such governments (including school districts) to every one of its general-purpose counties, municipalities, and townships. Minnesota is at the other extreme, with over 3.4 general-purpose governments to every single-purpose one.

A GENERAL PERSPECTIVE ON SINGLE-PURPOSE VERSUS GENERAL-PURPOSE GOVERNANCE

Finding the "best" form of governance is an important aspiration. Good institutions do not promise good behavior or good results, but they increase the probabilities in their favor.[37] Intellectual wrestling about what features of governance institutions are desirable typically hinges on competing political philosophies and empirical evidence about whether certain features are associated with better outcomes in economic performance, social well-being, or the quality of civic life. In this section I review some of the broad rationales both for and against single-purpose governance structures. One caveat: the fact that it's possible to deliberate about the pros and cons of different governance institutions doesn't mean that lofty, rational assessments account for the institutions we have inherited or are likely to produce in the future. Happenstance, incrementalism, and political maneuvering for advantage may also play a role, an observation to which I will soon return.

The Rationale for Single-Purpose Government

Why did states create single-purpose governments in the first place? Some approach this as a question of administration and efficiency.[38] They argue that single-purpose governments can be more efficient and effective because the key decision makers have more focused knowledge and expertise. Proponents of single-purpose governments suggest that they are better equipped to buffer decisions from partisan and interest group politics, since the formal decision makers often are appointed based on their expertise and are only occasionally professional politicians, and thus can decide issues based on their merits and the best available evidence. In the particular case of education, the argument for bolstering school-specific institutions of governance has been closely intertwined with the belief that "politics should be kept out" of education.

From a management standpoint, it can be easier, too, to "fit" single-purpose governments to the geographic scope of some problems that spill over the geographic boundaries of counties, cities, and states.[39] An example is regional transit infrastructure systems like the Port Authority of New York and New Jersey, which oversees LaGuardia and Newark airports, marine terminals and ports, the PATH rail transit system, six tunnels and bridges between New York and New Jersey, the Port Authority Bus Terminal in Manhattan, and the World Trade Center.[40] Another example is the Metropolitan Water District of Southern California, which has a 5,200-square-mile service area including twenty-six cities and smaller water districts and has revenues of over $1 billion.[41]

Single-purpose governments also can increase democratic accountability by making it clearer where citizens should go—and whom they should hold responsible—for dealing with a particular type of problem. In general-purpose governments, legislative and regulatory priorities are often shaped as part of multi-issue bargaining and logrolling that obscures the origin and rationale for particular components of policy and practice. Even when citizens believe they know which elected officials are accountable, the ballot box is an inadequate tool for expressing their satisfaction or dissatisfaction. Joe-the-average-voter might be incensed that the city took so long to plow his street last winter and might want to hold the mayor accountable for that. Yet at the same time, he might be pleased about crime protection or downtown renewal. Should he vote to oust the mayor because of his concern about snow removal, or vote to reelect the mayor because of his satisfaction on other fronts? This presents a dilemma for Joe, but it also defines a dilemma for democracy. No matter which way people like Joe vote, the vote itself will send a fuzzy signal about issues and priorities. Since other voters might also like some things and dislike some other things about the mayor's policies, a general-purpose election provides imprecise feedback about the public's values and concerns.

This kind of relationship between democratic responsibility and reliance on general- versus single-purpose government has come to the fore in some cities as they have debated or implemented mayoral control of schools—the most visible face of the end of education exceptionalism. New York City, as I'll discuss later in fuller detail, is perhaps the most sharply defined instance of mayoral control in the country. In 2002, early in Mayor Michael Bloomberg's first term in office, the New York state legislature granted Bloomberg's request to be given control of the school system, with the provision that this arrangement be reviewed and either ended or extended in the spring of 2009. In November 2009, after a year of broad and heated debate that culminated in the extension of mayoral control, Bloomberg won reelection to a third term by a margin of 51 to 46 percent. The mayor and the school chancellor he had selected, Joel Klein, publicly interpreted this as a supportive mandate for their education program, but exit polls found that only 16 percent of voters indicated that education was the issue that mattered most in influencing their vote (versus 40 percent who prioritized the economy and jobs) and the mayor won only 43 percent of the votes of public school parents compared to 55 percent for his Democratic competitor.[42]

The electoral process played out differently for the champion of mayoral control in Washington, DC, but the lesson about blurred accountability seems the same. There, incumbent Mayor Adrian Fenty, who had asked for and received control of the school system early in his first term as well, lost his 2010 bid to win nomination for a second term. While some blamed this loss on the controversies surrounding his hand-picked and high-profile school chancellor, Michelle Rhee, others argued that the election should be read less as a referendum on Fenty's school reform policies than a reflection of tactical miscalculations and the public's disillusionment with his general governance style.[43] In each of these instances, at least, incorporating education within the general-purpose municipal government made it less clear what voting for the incumbent meant as far as education policy than it would have in a more traditional arrangement in which school policy is set by an issue-specific board of education.

The Rationale for General-Purpose Government

While single-purpose governments might simplify policy administration and democratic accountability in at least some ways, general-purpose government also has some advantages. Complex social problems like education don't exist in single-issue silos. Because their causes and consequences overflow the boundaries of single-purpose agencies and governments, mounting effective policies to address them might require mobilizing and coordinating resources and knowledge across a broader range of government. At the same time that specialization makes possible the mobilization of advanced technical expertise, it can make government incoherent and uncoordinated, a danger that political scientist Theodore Lowi warned about more than four decades ago. Bureaucracies, or what Lowi called the "new machines," have made cities "well run but ungoverned" by allowing neglect "of those activities around which bureaucracies are not organized, or those that fall between or among agencies' jurisdictions."[44]

In the particular case of education, issue-specific governance silos can reinforce a dysfunctional political stand-off between those who favor school-based versus society-based approaches to improving the educational achievement of children from low-income households and high-poverty neighborhoods. General-purpose governance institutions, precisely because they encompass the various agencies and tools that would be needed to launch a more coordinated effort, might hold out better prospects for outflanking this either-or formulation. This rationale has not played as prominent a role in contemporary education reform debates as have claims that general-purpose governance leads to better management prospects, but it might be the most important opportunity posed by the end of exceptionalism in American education.

In addition to coordination, general-purpose government may also be necessary in order to establish priorities when issue-specific initiatives clash or when resource constraints demand that some worthwhile efforts be put to one side. Government cannot do everything that the majority of citizens would like it to do. In idealized visions of rational and comprehensive policy making, choices among competing initiatives are oriented around a unified vision of the collective good and a relative ranking of collective values. In heterogeneous societies such as ours, it's difficult to imagine broad agreement on the overall goals of government and even more difficult to imagine agreement on a hierarchy of societal values. Even if we could craft such an agreement, changing conditions, new information, and shifting attitudes would make it instantaneously obsolete.

While idealized visions of democracy envision a deliberative, open-minded resolution of competing values and interest, in practice general-purpose governments are as often steered by partisan, ideological, and interest group politics, in a clash that metaphorically looks more like war than a New England town meeting. The bargaining, logrolling, and contingent compromises that result are often messy; they do not so much *resolve* competing priorities as they *accommodate* them in ways that allow collective action despite continuing disagreements. Messy though it may be, this might represent a more realistic, adaptable, and democratic process of sorting through competing priorities than is the case when functions are artificially meted out to single-purpose governments that operate rationally within their focused spheres. The constraining aspects of single-purpose governments are especially apparent when they are granted their own dedicated revenue streams, as is frequently the case with schools. Such earmarked dedication of taxes to a particular use constrains government's ability to respond to changing conditions, knowledge, and public values.

General-purpose government may have an additional advantage, best understood as a lower vulnerability to a particular kind of political distortion. The same things that make single-purpose government attractive as a tool for rational governance—its focus and clear lines of accountability—can also make it attractive to narrow interest groups as a way to lock in and defend advantages. Political scientists have highlighted the potential danger to democratic control when programs and agencies are captured by the small but highly attentive and mobilized interests that are their intended targets.[45] Writing generally about single-purpose governments, both Nancy Burns and Kathryn Foster emphasized that their lower political visibility and the legitimacy they give to technical expertise tend to constrain participation and work to the advantage of particular private interests.[46] Writing specifically about education policy, Terry Moe emphasized the ways in which low turnout in school district elections allows teacher unions to exercise disproportionate influence that they would be hard-pressed to match within the bigger arenas of general-purpose elections.[47] While less common than the capture of programs or agencies, because more costly and difficult to pull off, the creation or capture of single-purpose governments can be a powerful political strategy. General-purpose government is not invulnerable to domination by privileged interests, but its broader scope, visibility, and pluralistic complexity make it relatively less likely that any single interest could prevail and hold its advantage over time.[48]

AN INTEGRATED PERSPECTIVE

Shifts along the fault lines of centralization, privatization, and the distinction between single- and general-purpose governance interact in ways that influence receptivity to different political interests and policy ideas. Figure 1.1 illustrates this in schematic form. The vertical dimension represents the trend toward centralization as states and the national government become more actively involved in shaping education policy. The relative scope of authority exercised by education-specific units and the extent to which they are buffered from general-purpose government has differed, historically, at each of level of government.[49] The scope of involvement is represented by the relative size of general-purpose versus education-specific cells.

The sway of education exceptionalism has been strongest at the local level, where school districts have dominated, and weakest at the

FIGURE 1.1

The shift from education-specific to general-purpose arenas: schematic overview

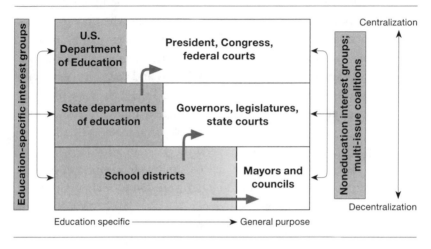

national level, where education was upgraded to a cabinet-level department only in 1979. Centralization, accordingly, has contributed to the reabsorption of education decisions into general-purpose politics simply by virtue of shifting more, and more important, policy decisions to levels of government where education-specific units are weaker, both in formal power and in terms of having their own political constituency.

At each governmental level, moreover, a shift is occurring toward broader scope and more direct involvement by general-purpose units. I describe the growing role of mayors, governors, and presidents in greater detail in chapter 2. In chapter 3, I discuss the growing role of courts and legislatures, describing how federal and state courts, despite institutionalized reticence, were drawn more deeply into involvement with matters like staffing and curriculum that lie closer to the core of teaching and learning.

The lines separating general- and single-purpose governance represent the potential for actors within one venue to influence the other. Figure 1.1 portrays the boundaries as progressively more permeable as one moves up the levels and, as I will argue, they are becoming more so over time. That these *are* permeable reflects the fact that the separation of general-purpose from education-specific governments in actuality is a question of degree.

The lines between single- and general-purpose governance of education are permeable even at the local level, where elected school boards and school superintendents historically have dominated education decision making. Mayoral control, at its extreme, eliminates school boards, but there are formal distinctions even among districts where school boards are still in place. Roughly one out of ten school systems is formally "dependent" on general-purpose government, receiving its budget from the general-purpose legislatures (municipalities, counties, or, in some instances, states). Such dependent districts are something of a hybrid between a pure single-purpose school district and an agency of a general-purpose government. The prevalence of dependent school districts varies cross-sectionally and over time. Excluding DC and Hawaii (both special cases), there are four states that have *exclusively* dependent school systems (Alaska, Maryland, North Carolina, and Virginia), five with *predominantly* dependent districts (Connecticut, Maine, Massachusetts, Rhode Island, and Tennessee), and ten with *at least one* dependent district.[50] Between 1992 and 2007, the number of dependent school systems increased by 6.9 percent, while the number of school districts decreased by 9.5 percent. And even in localities where formally independent school districts remain prominent, mayors often use informal powers to insert themselves in education policy debates.[51]

At the same time, higher up the ladder of federalism, the thinner buffer protecting education-specific departments and agencies from governors and presidents leaves room for variation in their de facto autonomy across states and over time. At the national level, where the president has the power to appoint and remove the secretary of education, and at the state level, where a growing number of governors have authority to appoint the state board of education and chief state school officer, bureaucracies have the motivation and political wherewithal to deflect efforts to steer them by elected executives, legislatures, and courts. Political scientists refer to this potential for bureaucracies to elevate their own agendas as a "principal-agent dilemma," a "democracy-bureaucracy problem," or a "challenge of political control of bureaucracy."[52] Issue-specific agencies' technical expertise and relative monopoly on information are their biggest weapons in frustrating elected officials' efforts to hold them to account.

There are countermoves open to legislators, so in the normal course of events this principal-agent relationship is one of push and pull rather than a complete untethering of agency action from legislative intent.[53] But agencies can sometimes develop powerful political constituencies of their own, usually comprising those who are the beneficiaries of the services they provide or the putative target of the regulations they enforce—constituencies that elected legislators and chief executives might find difficult to rein in. Even if they have the power to do so, they might find reining them in sufficiently costly politically that they are reluctant to pay the price. Sometimes the agencies are the ones that call the shots, deciding when to mobilize their constituencies and on what terms, but in other cases it can be the client groups that are in control. In either case, the result can be a single-issue arena that operates relatively autonomously from the general-purpose institutions and multi-issue and multi-interest political dynamics, creating a situation that mimics single-purpose governance to at least some degree.

Figure 1.1 also illustrates how the governance changes can interact with interest group politics to alter the policy agenda. Interest groups that traditionally have specialized in education—such as teacher unions, parent organizations, groups focusing on the rights of student subpopulations such as special education and English learners, or professional associations representing educators and those concerned about the teaching of particular subjects like science or math—have developed reciprocal relationships and patterns of access that make it easier for them to exert influence within school districts and education departments than in general-purpose governments, where they must compete with a wider array of interest groups. Traditional education interests do not always get their way in education-specific venues, and they do not always come out losers when they compete in general-purpose arenas. But their odds of winning and the amount of effort they must exercise to present their cases differ in the two types of governance institutions, which explains why there is a political dimension to institutional politics that abstract discussions of "what are the best institutional arrangements?" fail to take into account.

What Determines the Mix of General-Purpose Versus Single-Purpose Governance?

In myth and aspiration, the design of our political institutions is entrusted to sagacious founding fathers, modified by social learning to adapt to changing needs and by evidence about what best works to maximize the public good. Importantly, though, the decisions that shape our governance arrangements along all three institutional fault lines are not dictated by competing political philosophies or evidence of best practices alone. Recognizing that other factors come into play does not mean that we have to cynically discount the fact that clear thought and informed judgment also can play a role.

One rival explanation puts greater stock in happenstance and habit. Sometimes seemingly small decisions, made without full attention, set sharp and consequential directions. Social scientists who study political institutions and public policy refer to this as *path dependency*.[54] Metaphorically, we can understand this in terms of a traveler, not unlike Robert Frost's protagonist in the famous "The Road Not Taken" poem. At the key decision point, the path divides, and the differences between the options at the fork may be very uncertain. It is possible the two roads will end up running parallel, with multiple cross-paths for moving back and forth between them. But it is also possible that the initial choice will be compounded over time, with the paths diverging more and more and no obvious way to undo the initial decision without turning back completely. According to this perspective, the origin of exceptionalism in American education does not matter much; it was the result of decisions made in a much earlier era when both attention and stakes were low. Once in place, habit, tradition, and momentum maintained the divergence between school districts and general-purpose governance. Path dependency played a role in the creation of school-specific governance in the U.S., and it is part of the story of the end of exceptionalism unfolding today.

But much of the story of governance creation, maintenance, and change can best be understood from a third perspective, one that rests on politics and power rather than reason, evidence, happenstance, or tradition. The setting, changing, and defending of institutional arrangements are deeply political, which interest groups of various stripes recognize as having implications for their own power and agendas.

Normal Politics Versus Institutional Politics

On a day-to-day basis, most policy decisions are made within institutional boundaries that are reasonably stable and defined. As a result, they and the influences they exert can fade into the background unnoticed. Much more at the forefront are interest group and electoral politics. We can refer to this pattern as *normal politics*, where the day-to-day drama of politics occurs.[55] A local union leader calls a press conference to complain about teacher layoffs. A candidate for governor denounces the incumbent for failing to insist on higher standards and announces that, if she is elected, her focus on schooling will lead her to become known as the "education governor." A national school reform organization demands that Congress require districts receiving federal funding to facilitate the approval of charter schools.

In this sense, interest group and electoral politics are to institutional politics as weather is to climate. Climate is the broad patterns of the things that create weather—pressure, temperature, and various atmospheric conditions. Weather is the day-to-day instantiation of climate—rain, snow, etc. Climate tells you what weather to expect, and puts general (but not hard) limitations on what the weather will be. Climate is what makes it very unlikely, for instance, that it will snow in North Carolina in June. It's not impossible, in a freak weather occurrence, but the climate makes it very unlikely.[56]

The ups and downs of the weather are what occupy our attention: will there be thunderstorms when I have to be out on Tuesday? Is this the hottest day ever? Will the snow be likely to melt? Television newscasts dedicate huge chunks of costly airtime to these issues, while questions about global warming get dealt with in an occasional documentary. Yet it is climate that sets the broad parameters that, while taken for granted, more emphatically affect the conditions within which we live our daily lives.

The fault lines discussed in this chapter identify sites of institutional change along the boundaries of a set of reasonably discrete decision-making venues. I refer to these as *fault lines* because the boundaries between the venues they encapsulate, usually relatively stable over extended periods, are experiencing tremors and signs of incipient change. There are three sets of competing venues that are experiencing flux. One set, relating to privatization, distinguishes government from the private sector, and within the private sector marks off markets versus civil society. The second and third relate to competing decision-making venues within the public sector. The centralization-decentralization fault line exists among local versus state versus national government. The third fault line—and the special focus of this book—involves the distinction between general-purpose and single-purpose institutions.

We can think of these, in the abstract, as distinct decision-making venues, each serving different functions for which it is suited and each differing in terms of its primary actors, norms, and decision rules. Indeed, that is how they most often are discussed. Markets, for example, function to allocate goods and services that are material and divisible; they involve suppliers and consumers who freely trade and arrive at deals when both actors in the transaction stand to gain. Civil society comprises families, associations, and nonprofit groups of various sorts; it's believed to be driven less by self-interest and profit maximization than by a sense of social purpose. Government is a formal realm for making and enforcing authoritative decisions that affect public goods— things that affect broad swaths of individuals and groups and for which the application of some degree of legal coercion (e.g., taxation) might be required in order to avoid free-riders, maintain order, and reduce inequities. In deliberations about how best to structure governance, the framing tends to assume that the public interest is known, and that the issues at stake are ones of assigning delivery responsibilities across venues so as to best maximize social well-being.

But these institutional venues mark more than just competing modes of service delivery; they are also decision-making arenas through which competing private interests are mediated and competing visions of the collective interest are negotiated and resolved. Institutional choices, such as the creation of single-purpose or general-purpose governments, matter a great deal. As Nancy Burns has written, "they define the limits of particular arrangements of political power, particular kinds of service provision, certain characteristics of political participation and political accountability, and certain arrangements for funding." In doing so, "they provide boundaries that define citizenship and embody values ranging from antitax sentiments to racial exclusion."[57] Accordingly, such assignment decisions are political in their consequences: some groups win and others lose.

Figure 1.2 illustrates some ways in which the institutional choices associated with the three major fault lines define distinct decision-making venues that differ in their motivating incentives, key resources, primary actors, and core values.

Political interests compete to shape policy outcomes within these various venues, with some interest groups operating within all venues and others strategically targeting those in which they believe they have a greater chance to succeed. Whether an interest group emerges victorious in any particular battle depends on many things, including the legitimacy of its cause, the power of its arguments, and the sheer amount of resources it can bring to bear in pursuing its cause. But the fit between venue and group matters as well.[58] Groups with deep pockets might have an advantage in a venue that is more market-oriented; for example, a national publisher might have the economic leverage to push aside smaller, more localized competitors to win a contract to provide materials and training oriented to the Common Core curriculum, using its greater scale to underbid, at least initially, as a way to gain a critical toehold in the local market. Other interests—for example, those that can field large numbers of voters—might have an edge in the public sector, where their potential to mobilize pressure would carry weight with elected officials. In decentralized venues, groups that are geographically mobile can use exit, or the threat of it, to increase their bargaining power, and groups that are concentrated and locked in place can cultivate access to local politicians; in a centralized national arena, an edge might go to groups that can mobilize even bare majorities in a large number of congressional districts.

FIGURE 1.2

Institutional choices along the three fault lines

	PUBLIC SECTOR VERSUS PRIVATE SECTOR			CENTRALIZATION VERSUS DECENTRALIZATION		SINGLE-PURPOSE VERSUS GENERAL-PURPOSE GOVERNANCE	
	Government	Market	Voluntary/ nonprofit	Centralized	Decentralized	Specialized	General-purpose
Motivations/ incentives	Public good; influence; power	Material benefits; profit-motive; self-interest	Purposive; altruistic	The one best system	Laboratories of democracy	Internal coherence	Integration with other policy domains
Key resources	Power	Money	Inspiration	Majorities; mobilization; dispersion; money	Concentration (cultivated access); mobility (venue shopping); social capital	Expertise; intensity	Broad appeal among mobilized electorate; coalitional support
Central actors	Voters; parties; interest groups; politicians; bureaucracy	Consumers; firms; investors	Donors; foundations; nonprofit service delivery organizations; "clients"	Education executives (mayors, governors, presidents); state and national political entrepreneurs; political parties; nonmembership organizations; mobile business (financial community); national foundations	School boards; superintendents; local school bureaucracies; parents; civic leaders; downtown business associations; teachers and teacher unions; local foundations; spatially concentrated minorities	Educators including teacher unions; school boards; superintendents; mobilized parents; private education service providers (new); local employers	Education executives (mayors, governors, presidents); legislative entrepreneurs; multi-issue groups; mobile capital and national and international business
Central values (dominant norms)	Consistency; universality; equity; constitutionalism	Efficiency; responsiveness; mobility; flexibility; "the customer is always right"	Helping; voluntarism	Generalizable models; scale	Local experience and context; "dividing the pie"	Expertise; professionalism	Majoritarianism; responsiveness; efficiency

The last two columns in figure 1.2 zero in on the institutional fault line that is most central to the thesis of this book—that distinguishing specialized versus general-purpose government. In a single-purpose government setting, intensity of interest and claims to technical expertise might carry more weight; this is one reason that teacher unions have held disproportionate power in school reform debates.[59] In more general-purpose arenas, groups with an integrated comprehensive vision of how their interest aligns with those of others and those willing to join multi-issue coalitions might have the advantage. General-purpose arenas are likely to be comparatively more accessible to groups with a less intense stake in public schools—older citizens, singles, those more concerned about tax burdens than service quality. The end of exceptionalism in American education would mean a growing pressure to align education proposals with approaches in other domains of domestic policy, less deference to teachers' claims of special expertise, more competition between education advocates and other political actors, and more need to frame appeals to win allies who might not have school-age children and who might be quicker to ask "how much will this cost?" and "how do I know this will really work as claimed?"

When decision-making venues are sharply distinct, with spheres of responsibility that do not overlap, political interests have little recourse but to engage in normal politics: either to slug it out within the established rules of the game or to accept whatever outcomes are handed to them. If all personnel decisions are delegated to the school level, a parent unhappy about a child's teacher might have no option but to plead the case to the principal. If all school funding decisions are restricted to the local district, nonparents who think school funding is bloated might have no option but to try to unseat current school board members. If all decisions about curriculum are left to the state, families that favor teaching intelligent design would have no option but to lobby the state legislature.

In practice, however, boundaries are often vague and spheres of responsibility overlap, and during particular time periods their lines of demarcation can become more unstable. Central-office delegations of authority to school principals are subject to revocation when fiscal conditions change, district leaders reconsider, or powerful people complain. State legislatures or statewide referenda can constrain local funding decisions, as occurred in California in 1978 with Proposition 13.[60] Federalism, as Morton Grodzins explained, is not a layer cake in which responsibilities are neatly divided, without ambiguity, across levels of government; rather, it is a marble cake of swirling and blended governmental responsibilities and powers.[61]

Because competing interests are aware of what's at stake, because the assignment of responsibilities across institutional venues is not fixed or predetermined, and because the decisions made are shaped by the assertion of power and not just by rational analysis, collective decisions about institutional responsibilities are political in function and focus and need to be considered in those terms. Normal politics, which takes place when institutional parameters are stable and well defined, tends to be incremental and routine; groups with an advantage in their institutional niche can maintain their elite status and fend off most challenges unless unusual events conspire to unseat them. This style of politics is like the standard professional sporting event. The ground rules are known, competition takes place within those ground rules, and those with more of the conventional skills will win more often than not.

But when boundaries overlap, are porous, or are in flux, three additional kinds of politics come into play. Each can be considered a form of institutional politics. *Venue defense* is a strategic option for interests that benefit from the existing governance structure. Political scientists use the term *iron triangles* to refer to the mutually supportive relationships that often develop among sponsoring legislators, administering agencies, and beneficiary interest groups that share a stake in maintaining and expanding a particular program or institutional arrangement.[62]

For groups that feel disadvantaged by the rules of the game, *venue shopping* for a more hospitable decision-making arena can be smart politics, as "alternative venues give policy makers and advocacy groups who are on the losing side of policy an opportunity to go over the heads of, or around, a policy elite intent on maintaining the status quo."[63] Venue shopping does not change the basic institutional parameters, but it allows some flexible and highly resourced groups to tactically shift their battles into more congenial intuitional niches. Business interests, unhappy with the school board, might look to a state legislature to give power to a mayor more attentive to business priorities. In a similar fashion, minority groups that feel excluded by the local school board might venue shop by bringing a lawsuit, thereby getting courts and judges into the foreground and shifting to an arena in which civil rights, rather than raw political power, might triumph.

Institutional change is the final and least common alternative. Institutions are hard and costly to change, so when groups can win through defense of established channels or venue shopping, they most often will settle for these. The up-front costs might take institutional change off the table for some groups altogether. But institutional change—including the creation of new institutions or the broad reassignment of responsibilities across existing ones—has potential to lock in power. If carried out successfully, it can lead to long-term and accumulated benefits. Even in cases where it only modestly shifts the probabilities of winning particular battles, institutional change has the potential to accrue over time—like compounded interest in bank accounts (when bank accounts still provided interest!).[64]

Acknowledging the potential role of institutional politics has two implications for how we should think about the end of education exceptionalism. It means attending to how the shift away from school-specific arenas might alter the access and influence of competing stakeholder groups, such as teacher unions, parents, downtown business communities, for-profit providers of education services, taxpayers, and various racial and ethnic groups. And it means attending to the possibility that some groups will specifically engage in efforts to gain advantage by creating new institutional parameters, defending the old ones, or tactically shopping around among venues to find those more likely to generate the outcomes they prefer.

OUTLINE OF THE BOOK

The various scraps and threads that signal the end of education exceptionalism will be familiar to many readers. The challenge I undertake in this book is to pull those together into a tapestry that adds coherence and goes to the core of the more systemic changes that are slowly redefining the ground rules under which education politics and policy are being shaped.

Chapter 2 starts off with the rise of the education executives. Popular accounts highlight the stories of this or that "education governor," this or that "education president," and this or that mayor who has wrestled away from school boards the levers for controlling local education. These accounts are often highly personalized, deeply rooted in geographical and temporal context, and they lack crisp distinctions between changes in formal authority and personal aggressiveness in utilizing powers already at hand. I will review the emergence of the new education executives and identify patterns in timing, place, and political dynamics. I will show that this is a broader phenomenon than conventionally portrayed, one that extends beyond tinkering with formal governance structures to include a range of informal political factors relating to power and shifting agendas. Its origins and consequences are intertwined with the structural shifts in federalism and privatization.

The high profile of mayors, governors, and presidents makes it easy to treat their growing involvement in education as deriving from the executive branch's greater sensitivity to the need for school reform, and its special capability to steer reform from conceptualization through implementation. In chapter 3, however, I argue that courts and legislatures are also deeply implicated in the institutional changes under way. Courts have historically played a catalytic role. Their relative insensitivity to certain political challenges allowed them to take on challenges related to race and class that made public schools a political hot potato, one that directly elected executives and legislatures were reticent to handle. While courts started the ball rolling, and executives often took the higher-profile role, legislatures—at the national, state, and local levels—inevitably were drawn deeper into the details of education delivery. The resulting pull and tug among the three branches—a checks-and-balances process that simultaneously provides openings to more voices and risks stalemate and incoherence—is common in the American political process. But it came later to the sheltered world of education than it had to other areas of domestic policy.

As important as institutions are for shaping decisions, they do not make policy themselves. Their influence is felt via the differential access they provide to competing ideas and interests. In chapter 4, I will discuss the role that general-purpose institutions played in the emergence of new policy ideas—such as greater emphasis on academic excellence versus equity and on market-like approaches such as charter schools—and the emergence of new political dynamics, as educators and parents find themselves competing with a new set of organized stakeholders and squeezed more to the periphery of power and influence.

Will the end of education exceptionalism make a substantial difference in the kinds of policies we get, and if so, is that something to welcome or to dread? These are the questions I address in chapter 5. There will be changes. They will make a difference. But as is typical in the complex and fragmented landscape of American policy and politics, the results will almost certainly fall short of the dramatic realignment of education that many hope for; reformers who see school-specific institutions as the root cause of policy incoherence and incrementalism will be disappointed if they believe that expanding the role of general-purpose governance will save the day. In the emerging institutional landscape, the ideas that come into play will be new, but not necessarily better. The range of voices heard will be broader, but not necessarily more equitable or democratic. Whether the new educational landscape will generate more collective learning and more effective social intervention will not be dictated by the institutions to which we assign decision-making authority, but rather will depend on whether we use the existing institutions wisely and well. While it presents some risks, and while it will not deliver solutions on its own, the end of education exceptionalism does present important opportunities, and it is on those hopeful notes that I will conclude.

CHAPTER TWO

THE NEW EDUCATION EXECUTIVES

In the olden days, we had a board that was answerable to nobody. And the Legislature said it was just not working, and they gave the mayor control. Mayoral control means mayoral control, thank you very much.

—New York City Mayor Michael Bloomberg[1]

It's like a one-way vector force, where there's continual force for governors to gain control of education policy . . . The governors are on the offense, and the people supporting traditional arrangements where education should be separately governed . . . are on the defense.

—Michael Kirst, education scholar and
California state board of education president[2]

I want to be the education president.

—George H. W. Bush[3]

I N AN ARRAY of settings and at all levels of our federal system, elected executives are increasing their formal power and political engagement with issues relating to education and school reform. In some cases they are leading the demand for a stronger role; in other cases they are responding to such a demand voiced by others.

On the contemporary scene, it is mayoral control of schools that has received the most attention, with proponents arguing that it catalyzes reform and opponents complaining that it marginalizes parent and community groups. But the shift of formal power from school boards to mayors needs to be understood in conjunction with similar expansions of executive involvement at the state and national levels. Indeed, the emergence of so-called education governors and education presidents predated the movement toward mayoral control.

Attention to the general phenomenon of education governors, presidents, and mayors has been remarkably ad hoc and narrowly focused.[4] Journalistic accounts often exhibit a "great man" perspective that heavily emphasizes the political vision and skills of the particular elected executives who spotted or created opportunities overlooked by their predecessors. This perspective understates the importance of the broader political institutional landscape, and the ways in which shifts in the views and power of other powerful interests helped to determine whether and when executive muscle could be effectively exercised. Scholarly portrayals more often give due weight to the institutional and political contexts within which leaders operate, but even these have tended to focus separately on either governors *or* presidents *or* mayors, treating the three movements as distinct, each accounted for by elements specific to the level of government, the political venues in which they are located, and the nature of the pressures and opportunities presented by conditions at the time.[5]

An important exception to this criticism is the body of scholarly analysis focusing on the so-called "excellence" movement that emerged in the 1980s and leading up to the enactment of the No Child Left Behind Act in 2001 (NCLB). Growing concern about American competitiveness in a global economy set the stage for a reconsideration of the nation's pride in the presumed superiority of its public school system. What had been a focus on inputs and equity—on improving education by adding more resources to a proven model and by ratcheting up expenditures in communities where resources historically had been constrained—began to shift to a focus on outputs, on holding schools, teachers, and students accountable for meeting measurable standards of academic achievement. Accounts of this reform era tell a tale about changes in federalism; about coalitions among business interests, governors, and the White House; about the weakening grip of the traditional education lobby.⁶ Their sophisticated attention to the interactions among governance institutions, electoral and interest group politics, and competing educational visions make these accounts worth emulating, and I draw upon them and their approach in this book and in this chapter especially. Yet they, too, miss an important part of the story. By focusing intently on changes in authority among localities, states, and the national government, they fail to take due account of the shifting of authority and influence, within each level, from single-purpose, education-specific arenas to general-purpose government and politics.

This chapter reviews the emergence of the new education executives with several objectives in mind. The first objective is to establish that there is indeed something real and important going on: rather than an episodic flexing of muscles by the occasional strong leader, the expanding role of mayors, governors, and presidents in shaping the education policy agenda represents a shift in governance arrangements that is occurring at all levels of our federal system and that has been occurring over a sustained period of time. The second objective is to identify patterns in timing and place that provide clues to the underlying mechanisms and causes of this shift: these suggest that this is a broader phenomenon than conventionally portrayed, and that it extends beyond tinkering with formal governance structures to include a range of informal political factors connecting to relationships of power and elected leaders' efforts to claim responsibility but also avoid blame. Solving the riddle of the recent expansion of executive involvement requires attending also to the question of why it did not happen sooner. Part of the answer, I'll suggest, may have to do with the volatile history of race and public education, and the high-intensity nature of education politics that made it, for many years, a political hot potato that politicians were not eager to grasp. The final objective is to underscore that this shift of authority toward elected executives is intertwined with the expanding role of states and the national government, but also a distinct phenomenon with push and pull elements—and long-term implications for politics and policy—all its own.

Compared to policy makers within education-specific governments and agencies, elected leaders in general-purpose governments bring to bear different experiences, perspectives, and policy tool bags. Even when their goals for education are similar, the political contexts in which they operate provide a different set of opportunities and cross-pressures that induce them to pursue those goals in different ways. Understanding the new education executives as a key element in the end of exceptionalism, accordingly, sheds light on the changes in the landscape of American school politics beyond those provided by political histories centering on individual leaders, the weakening role of localism, or the standards movement alone.

THE RISE OF THE EDUCATION GOVERNORS

First out of the gate were the so-called education governors. During the 1970s a handful of mostly southern governors began to take a more proactive stance in engaging with K–12 public education, framing school improvement as a critical component in their efforts to attract and hold jobs. Among the standouts, as identified by education historian Maris Vinovskis, were Lamar Alexander (R-TN; took office in 1979), Bill Clinton (D-AR; 1979), Bob Graham (D-FL; 1979), James Hunt (D-NC; 1977), Thomas Kean (R-NJ; 1982), Richard Riley (D-SC; 1979), and William Winter (D-MS; 1980).[7] Several would later carry their interest and experience in education to important positions at the national level.[8]

Throughout American history, one central fact has remained constant: constitutional authority for public education has been vested in the states. While some of the nation's founding fathers cared deeply about education, responsibility to establish a public education system is neither a specifically enumerated power of the national government within the U.S. Constitution nor is it credibly even an implied one.[9] When it comes to states versus local districts, it is also unambiguously clear that states hold the cards where formal authority is concerned. School districts— like all other substate units of government, such as counties, municipalities, townships, and special districts of one kind or another—strictly speaking are creations of the state. The classic statement is known as Dillon's Rule, after Judge John Forrest Dillon, Chief Justice of the Iowa Supreme Court, who declared, in an 1868 case: "Municipal corporations owe their origin to, and derive their powers and rights wholly from, the legislature. It breathes into them the breath of life, without which they cannot exist. As it creates, so may it destroy. If it may destroy, it may abridge and control."[10] While holding the formal reins of authority, state governments until relatively recently left those reins slack, leaving most of the key decisions about public schooling—particularly K–12—to local government. Against this backdrop, the emergence of the education governors appears anomalous and calls out for explanation.

To the extent that there is a standard explanation of the expanding role of governors, it focuses on the catalytic role played by these early governors acting in the role of policy entrepreneurs. The concept of policy entrepreneurship in the public sector builds on the image of the private-market entrepreneur, who spots a latent demand, mobilizes investment to create the product to fill that demand, and realizes profit in return for acumen and the assumption of risk. Policy entrepreneurs, analogously, detect an unmet societal need, unrepresented constituency, or untried policy and carry it onto the policy agenda, reaping political support and influence as the primary reward.[11] Even before *A Nation at Risk* famously galvanized attention to the need to improve America's schools, some governors were drawing a direct link between education and the challenge of attracting and holding employers and jobs. Economic pressures associated with global competition had been accumulating for years, but the recession, which "forced thirty-seven states to adopt austerity budgets in fiscal 1982," was the catalyst that drew that connection into sharper relief.[12] "Governors of both political parties from Mississippi to Maine began to champion school reform as part of an effort to bolster their states' failing economies," Thomas Toch observed. "'Education is the keystone to economic prosperity,' Texas governor Mark White told the National Conference of State Legislators in 1983, and Governor Rudy Perpich of Minnesota warned his state that year that 'knowledge will be the steel of this post-industrial society.'"[13]

Left somewhat ambiguous in the standard accounts is whether these early "education governors" were unusually astute—spotting needs and possibilities their predecessors had overlooked—or whether they were responding to changing conditions that made education either more important to the states' well-being or more politically appealing to ambitious politicians. Several factors lend weight to the latter interpretation. First, the near-simultaneity of the emergence of this cohort of education governors across a range of states suggests that something beyond individual perspicacity was involved. Second, this initial wave of governors acting individually very quickly evolved into a more collective phenomenon. In the 1980s and 1990s, the National Governors Association (NGA) became a prominent voice in reformers' efforts to push education higher on the national agenda and place greater emphasis on standards and accountability.[14] Finally, as discussed in the following section, the expanding role of governors was not simply a case of aggressive leaders pushing the envelope of powers that had been long present, but latent, in the office. The assertion of leadership on the education issue often was accompanied by formal changes in governors' authority over education.

Structural Change: Shifts in Formal Power

While the popular lore about education governors focuses on the personalities and strategies of individual leaders, scholars who study governors more typically zero in on how state laws either do or do not give governors the formal power to make and shape policies. Political scientists who study governors measure their power by looking at formal authority along several dimensions, the most commonly included ones being: tenure potential (length of terms, term limits), appointment power (ability to appoint heads of key agencies and degree to which this requires approval by other bodies), budgetary power (exclusive or shared with others), and veto power (line-item veto power and how hard it is for a legislature to override).[15] Measured this way, the states with the strongest governors are West Virginia, New York, Maryland, Massachusetts, North Dakota, and Washington; those with the weakest are New Hampshire, Vermont, Indiana, Rhode Island, North Carolina, and Maine. Reviewing the empirical literature on changes in gubernatorial authority, Charles Barrilleaux and Michael Berkman concluded that "overall, state governors are stronger than ever before."[16]

But a governor's overall power may or may not translate into the realm of public education. The standard way to measure the role of governors specifically in education policy is by examining their formal role in selecting chief state school officers (CSSOs) and state boards of education. Giving governors more power to appoint CSSOs and state boards of education expands the reach of general-purpose governance and politics by narrowing the range of discretion within which education specialists in the state government are free to operate.

If CSSOs are either directly elected or appointed by elected state boards of education, executive oversight of education is divided, with governors less able to act authoritatively, dependent for implementing their policies on agencies whose loyalties may lie elsewhere, and facing rivals who can use the reality and reputation for having greater educational expertise as tools for developing their own bases of support. When Washington Governor Christine Gregoire floated the idea of creating a cabinet-level department of education, headed by a secretary that she would appoint, for example, the state's elected superintendent of public instruction made it clear that he considered himself to have his own constituency. "I answer to the people, not to a secretary of education," he declared. "Are you going to try to subvert and limit an elected official's power?"[17] If state boards of education are elected, governors must pitch and pursue their educational agendas in competition with board members who have their own priorities, political ambitions, constituencies, and claims to electoral mandates.

Tracing the changing status of governors' formal power over education shows two things. First, states began granting stronger education power to governors even before the 1980s and the blossoming of attention to the American education crisis as declared by *A Nation at Risk*; in that sense, there is at least some evidence that formal power may have been a catalyst that enabled governors to step up more aggressively. Second, that expanding role, and in particular the authority to appoint the CSSO, accelerated through the 1980s' period of standards-based education; as states began more assertively involving themselves in details of education policy that were previously left in the hands of education specialists and local districts, they began to give governors more tools with which to take a leadership role.

Part A of figure 2.1 shows two broad shifts in the way states have selected their CSSOs.[18]

Beginning sometime in the late 1940s, there was a steady shift away from direct election of the CSSO to selection by the state board of

FIGURE 2.1

Selection of chief state school officers and state boards of education

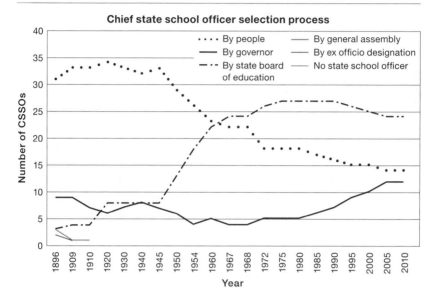

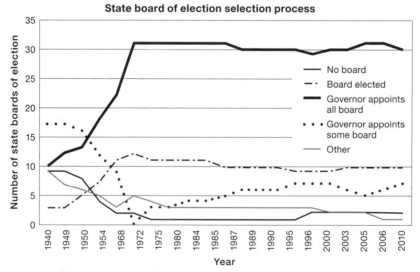

Source: Historical data compiled from (Beach & Will, 1955; Deffenbaugh & Keesecker, 1940; Fuller & Pearson, 1969; Keesecker, 1950; McCarthy, Langdon, & Olson, 1993). For 1975–2010, I relied on data generously shared by Paul Manna, Department of Political Science, College of William & Mary.

education. From 1945 to 1967 the number of states electing the CSSO dropped from thirty-three to twenty-two, while the number giving the state board authority to appoint the CSSO increased from eight to twenty-four. Direct appointment by governors was rare and declined slowly throughout the first two-thirds of the twentieth century; at the turn of that century nine governors had that power, and in 1967 only four did. But the second shift, unfolding over the last forty years, has seen a substantial increase in the governor's appointment power. The sharpest period of change was between 1980 and 2005, with the number of states allowing governors to appoint CSSOs increasing from five to fourteen.

Even when they do not directly appoint the CSSO, governors can exercise formal power through their role in selecting the members of the state boards of education. New York, in 1784, was the first state to establish a state board of education; by 1850 there were twenty-four such states; and, by 1950, forty states had formed state boards of education.[19] These boards were created under the beliefs that a board is more representative of the state's population than an individual, that a board is able to protect education from partisan politics, that a board allows for continuity in educational policy, and that a board is a defense against abuse of power. Governors have long played a role in state boards of education; in 1940, governors were ex officio members of state boards of education in fifteen states and actually chaired the board in two of these. The number of states with elected boards has been relatively stable for over fifty years. Between 1950 and 1972, there was a sharp increase in the number of states empowering governors to select all, instead of just some, of the board members; for the most part, this strengthening of the governors' formal role came as a result of the reduction in the number of state board members who served ex officio (figure 2.1, part B).[20] As of 2010, governors had total appointment power (thirty states) or partial appointment power (seven states) in three-quarters of the states, with direct election of the board in ten states.[21] Two states, Wisconsin and Minnesota, do not have state boards.

Battles to extend the governors' formal power over education governance continue. In March 2011, Hawaii Governor Neal Abercrombie exercised his newly granted power to name the nine members of the state school board.[22] In June 2011, Nevada Governor Brian Sandoval was granted the power to hire and fire the CSSO, who previously served at the pleasure of the state board of education; at the same time, the elected board was replaced by an appointed one, with the governor selecting three of the seven members.[23] Only six months into her first term as governor, in June 2011, South Carolina's Nikki Haley was battling with the state legislature in the hopes of gaining authority to appoint the state superintendent of education.[24] Midway through 2011, legislation had "emerged in at least 14 states this year to change or strip the power" of state boards of education.[25]

In states where governors cannot directly select CSSOs, some have sought to extend their power by shifting responsibility to newly created offices that they *do* control. In Massachusetts, in 2008, Governor Deval Patrick won approval for a plan to restructure the state's education governance system, creating a new position—secretary of education—over which he had appointment power, and giving the holder of that position some of the powers that previously had been exercised by the state board.[26] In Oregon, in June 2011, Democratic Governor John Kitzhaber won the creation of an education investment board that was given broad powers over education policy, with the governor chairing the group and appointing its members.[27] At that same time, the legislature provided that the separate position of elected state superintendent would be eliminated when the incumbent finished her term; when she stepped down one year later, Governor Kitzhaber simply assumed the additional job of Superintendent of Public Instruction.[28] And even when legislatures or the courts have blocked changes in the governance structures, some governors have been able to convert their efforts to garner formal authority into increased informal leverage. Governor Ted Strickland failed to get the Ohio state legislature to approve an arrangement similar to the one instituted in Massachusetts—creating a new and powerful position of state education director that he would name—but "his efforts were widely seen as leading Susan Tave Zelman, who was appointed Ohio's superintendent by the state education board in 1999, to step down," and the legislature subsequently worked cooperatively with the governor in naming a new state superintendent and initiating key elements of his school reform agenda.[29] In the spring of 2012, Vermont legislators gave preliminary approval to a bill to replace the state's board-appointed commissioner of education to a cabinet-level secretary of education appointed by the governor.[30]

Beyond Formal Power

Formal power is like a shovel in the woodshed. Its availability makes it more likely that a hole will be dug, but for that to happen someone has to pick it up and have the will and skill to use it. The empirical literature investigating governors' influence on policy outcomes makes it clear that other variables also are important: whether the governor's party controls the legislature, how strong the governor is within his or her own party, the professionalism of the legislature, the existence and mobilization of supporting interest groups, and the ambition of the governor's objectives, to name a few. Even governors who lack formal appointment power can use the bully pulpit—their ability to get public and media attention—to focus attention and shape the agenda, and many of the so-called education governors of the 1970s and 1980s made their mark despite weak formal powers.[31] When formal and informal powers converge, the potency of gubernatorial influence increases, and the likelihood that gubernatorial expansion of involvement will prove to be ephemeral declines.

Some governors are crossing swords with state school chiefs and local school boards whether or not they have new or substantial constitutional authority. New Jersey Governor Chris Christie, for example, sought to hit leaders of education-specific governance units where it hurts: in the pocketbook. In 2010, Christie insisted on pay cuts for roughly two-thirds of local superintendents and moved to force the Parsippany–Troy Hills school board "to rescind the contract of superintendent Lee Seitz, whom the governor [had] called a "poster boy" for overpaid school chiefs."[32] Oklahoma's Republican governor, Mary Fallin, managed to strip the state board of education of many of its formal powers, but rather than switch those to the governor, the governance change assigned them to the state's independently elected CSSO. Since the latter was also a Republican with whom Fallin was expected to work with amicably, however, the result was seen as a substantial increase in Fallin's informal power to get things done.[33]

Whether or not they have strong formal powers, it is clear that governors pay consistent attention to education. Or, to be more precise, they at least *talk* about it a lot. Daniel DiLeo and James Lech coded the presence or absence of various topics in governors' state-of-the-state speeches for forty states.[34] To avoid including empty rhetoric, they coded only mentions that were tied to explicit calls for policy action. Based on their analysis of 320 governors' speeches between 1991 and 1998, they found that education is what Eric Herzik labeled a *perennial* issue: one that gets steady attention year after year.[35] Across the eight-year period, almost every governor (95 percent on average) called for action regarding some aspect of education, by far the most—and most consistently—mentioned topic. Comparable figures for other perennial issues ranged from health care (mentioned in an average year in 78 percent of the speeches) and welfare (63 percent) to highways (30 percent) and election laws (18 percent).

But what impels governors to pick up the education policy shovel? As general-purpose officials, governors have a wide range of issues to attend to. And as politicians who must win office in general-purpose elections, they have many constituencies they could choose to appeal to. What convinces a governor who has strong appointment power in the education arena to focus on education rather than jobs, or crime, or keeping taxes low? What can convince a governor lacking strong formal power in education to spend political capital trying to make up for that weakness? Why, especially, would one do so when norm and traditions have reinforced so strongly the notion that the responsibility for education lies elsewhere—in local communities as the true source of democratic legitimacy and in single-issue institutions as the true source of educational expertise?

The data compiled by DiLeo and Lech is illuminating; it belies the notion that gubernatorial attention to education, at least in the contemporary era, is dependent on strong formal powers or occasional policy entrepreneurs. It has at least two important limitations as a window for analyzing gubernatorial emphasis on education, however. First, it encompasses only forty states. Second, the time frame is stunted at both the front and back ends. To get at the kinds of tectonic shifts that are the focus of this book, it would be incredibly valuable to have an indicator of gubernatorial involvement in education that goes beyond formal powers (which may or may not be wielded), includes all states, and can provide a sense of changes that may be incremental and unfold over many decades.

To develop a rough measure of gubernatorial leadership on education issues across all fifty states and throughout their political history as states, I turned to an online database of over 2,300 governor biographies compiled by the National Governors Association.[36] To identify education governors, my research assistant and I first searched the NGA database for all governors whose biographies included the keyword *education, school,* or *schools.* We then skimmed each of these selected biographies and determined whether the biography included a substantive reference to K–12 education policy. Those that did were coded 1 for "education governor."[37] These education sentences often make broad statements about a governor's interest in education. For example, Governor Bob Riley's education sentence reads, "Riley has improved education, put Alabama's economy on the right track, and fostered honesty in the Governor's Office." Other education governor biographies include general references to education changes, often in the passive voice, which makes it difficult to ascertain how active a role the governor played in the education reform. For example, Governor George Smith Houston's education sentence reads, "During Houston's two terms, the 1875 Alabama Constitution was ratified, the public school system was reorganized, and the Alabama State Board of Health was established."

Since these biographies are designed to be overviews, they do not provide definitive information as to which governors prioritized education. The advantages of having near-universal coverage of governors from all states throughout their history makes even this imperfect source valuable, however, as a window into the phenomenon of governors' involvement with education. There's an additional advantage as well. Studies of education leaders suggest the need to distinguish between rhetoric and symbolic action, on the one hand, and substantive involvement on the other.[38] The advantage of historical perspective combined with the discipline imposed by the process of distilling a governor's accomplishments into a short biographical blurb increases the probability that this operationalization of gubernatorial involvement will capture genuine commitment and not simply posturing.

Figure 2.2 summarizes the percentage of governors, over time, that qualify as education governors based on the indication that they made K–12 education a prominent element in their agenda.[39]

The time spans represented by the pre-1950 bars simply mark off intervals of roughly fifty years. The last three bars roughly mark off the period when school desegregation began dominating school policy and politics (1950–1982), the state-led standards reform movement following *A Nation at Risk* (1983–1994), and the most contemporary period, encompassing national reform initiatives from the Clinton into the Obama years (1995–2009). Not too much attention should be paid to the specific cut-offs; what is interesting is the broad trend. As with governors' formal appointment power, this measure of governors' informal involvement with education shows a growing role, especially over the last fifteen years. This does not appear to be an artifact of growing media coverage, so the increase reflects a greater relative attention to education.[40] While the overall length of the NGA biographies increased

FIGURE 2.2

Education governors, 1775–2009

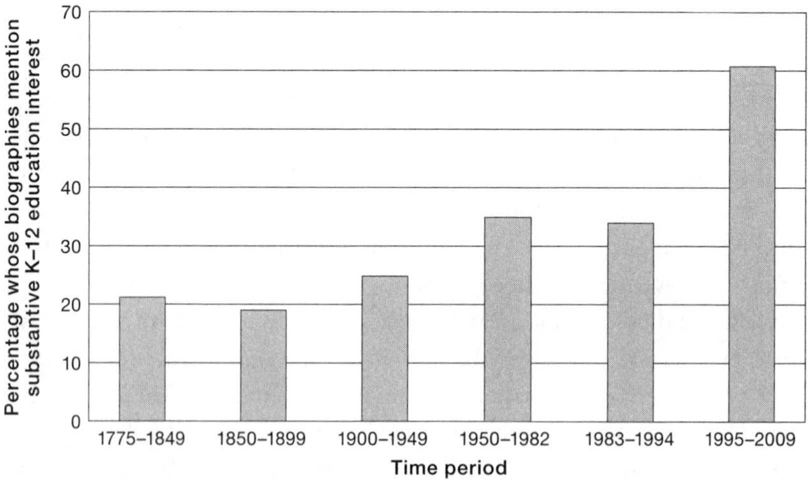

Source: Author's coding of data downloaded from http://www.nga.org/cms/home/governors/past-governors-bios.html.

slightly over time, bios mentioning education post-1983 were no longer than those in earlier years. Education governors were no more or less likely to come from large, or urban, or older states, but their prevalence was higher in southern states (37 percent) than in the rest of the country (22 percent).[41] Reinforcing the fact that formal power does not automatically translate into action, there is no correlation between this measure and the extent to which governors are legally empowered to appoint state boards and superintendents. North Carolina, whose four-term governor James Hunt is often cited as the prototype education governor, also has had the highest percentage of governors who earn the label "education governor" on this index, yet measured on a scale of formal gubernatorial appointment power it is among the weaker states.

How Are Formal and Informal Power Related?

We have seen that the formal power of governors is increasing, that education is a perennial issue in contemporary governors' state-of-the-state speeches, and that governors of the modern era are more likely to qualify as education governors based on our analysis of the NGA compilation of governors' biographies. But what is the relationship between formal power and proactive involvement in the education sphere? Do governors who have more formal education power actually use that to elevate education on the policy agenda? Does granting a governor stronger appointment power over CSSOs and state boards of education lead to greater gubernatorial activity on education, or is the governor's involvement dependent on idiosyncratic personal proclivities, situational politics, or the political, economic, and cultural character of his or her state?

One way to probe these questions is to look at states that change the formal education power of the governor to see if that leads to higher levels of involvement. Since 1975, sixteen states have changed the formal education appointment powers of the governor. Fourteen of the states made changes that strengthened the governor's role in appointing either or both the CSSO and state board of education. Three states made changes in the opposite direction.[42] Table 2.1 lists each of these states and provides information on the extent to which they had education

TABLE 2.1

Traditions of "education governors" in states that changed governors' formal education power in the contemporary reform era (post-1975)

State	Year of increase in formal power to appoint CSSO	Year of increase in formal power to appoint state board of education	Year of decrease in formal power to appoint state board of education	Percentage of "education governors" prior to 1975
New Mexico	2004	1987	2004	0.0
Washington		2006		7.1
New Hampshire	2005			9.6
Rhode Island		2005		14.5
South Dakota	1991			16.7
Indiana			2010	19.5
Ohio		1996		19.6
Minnesota	1983	2000[a]		21.9
Mississippi	1984	1984		25.0
Texas	1991			25.6
Delaware	1997			27.3
Florida	2003			28.6
Iowa	1987			30.6
Pennsylvania			1989	31.1
Louisiana	1988			39.6
Kentucky	1991			53.1
Summary				
States where governors' power strengthened (N=14)				22.8
States where governors' power weakened (N=2)[b]				25.3
States where governors' power remained the same (N=34)				20.2

Note: States are ordered based on their pre-1975 tradition of having active education governors, from low to high (last column).

[a] Minnesota's change in 2000 was to eliminate the state board of education altogether.

[b] New Mexico is not classified as "weakened" in the summary section because its 2004 reversion to an elected board coincided with a strengthening of the governor's authority to appoint the CSSO.

governors (as measured by our NGA-based index) historically (percent of all governors prior to 1975).

States that increased formal gubernatorial power were slightly more likely to have prior histories of active governor involvement, but so were the states that weakened the governor's formal power. Multivariate analysis indicates that states that gave governors appointment power over the CSSO were historically more likely to have had active governors, but there was no relationship between past governors' involvement and moves to strengthen or weaken appointment power over the state board of education.[43]

The case of Mississippi illustrates the complexity of the relationship between formal and informal gubernatorial power. One-quarter (eleven out of forty-four) of Mississippi governors prior to 1975 placed sufficient emphasis on K–12 education to warrant attention in the short NGA biographies and therefore qualify as education governors by the operationalization we are relying on here. This percentage increased slightly in the post-1975 period before 1984 (to 33 percent; one out of three), when the state increased the governor's power to appoint both the state board of education and the CSSO, and has been much higher since that formal change. While the pattern suggests that formal power increases informal involvement, that narrative may be too simple. The Mississippi governor in office immediately preceding the 1984 change was William Forrest Winter, one of those whom historian Maris Vinovskis identified as an especially notable educational leader, thus raising the possibility that it was experience with a more active education governor that helped set the stage for the formal change in authority.

It is possible to weave interesting and speculative stories about what might account for the patterns for particular states, but the overall pattern suggests that the relationship between formal power and active involvement in education at best is attenuated and indirect. Across the states that changed formal powers, the history of gubernatorial activism was decidedly mixed. Some, like Kentucky and Louisiana, had long histories of gubernatorial involvement, but in others, like New Mexico, Washington, Rhode Island, and South Dakota, education governors had been rare. The two states that ran against the tide by reducing their governors' formal power in education looked no different in their pre-1975 patterns than those that went the other direction. In the period from 1975 until they instituted a change, the states that did augment the formal power had more active governors on average than they had had prior to 1975 (38.3 percent versus 22.8 percent), but so did the two states that reduced their governor's power (50 percent versus 25.3 percent) and the thirty-four states that did not alter the structures at all (44.1 percent versus 20.2 percent).

Did the formal changes in power ramp up involvement? Our ability to answer this question statistically is limited by the relatively short time period since the formal changes; in several of the states there have only been one or two governors in office subsequent to the change. But the pattern fails to offer much support to the notion that formal change leads to a major boost in involvement. Ten of the fourteen states that increased formal power had more education governors afterward than their historical average, but this for the most part reflects the broad trend toward increased gubernatorial involvement evident even in states that have not had formal change in authority. And in three of the cases (South Dakota, Texas, and Delaware) the increase in the governor's involvement in education was very evident in the years immediately preceding the formal change. Three states (Kentucky, Florida, and Rhode Island) have had lower percentages of education governors since increasing formal power than they had had historically.[44]

Formal power is important, but its relationship to broader political dynamics is too intricate and complex to allow for easy generalizations about its impact. Governors who can appoint the key leaders in the education-specific sectors of state government have a tool for influence that others may lack. This does not appear to be a case of the "law of the instrument": the dictum that if you give a child a hammer everything begins to look like a nail. Governors with strong formal powers over education often have formal powers in other areas of domestic policy as well, and the incentive to act in those areas can outweigh those of getting involved in education, especially if there are political risks of doing so or the chances of demonstrable success are low. Governors who lack those formal powers have other ways to assert their influence, when they are inclined to try to do so. Whether or not particular governors do grasp the levers of influence seems to depend less on whether those levers are placed right before them, and more on either broad factors affecting states regardless of their formal governance arrangements or idiosyncratic factors that may be operating in specific states.

HERE COME THE EDUCATION PRESIDENTS

The emergence of the so-called education presidents followed that of the education governors by about two decades. Dating such matters is tricky, of course. Presidents had sporadically turned their attention to education earlier, but sustained and deep commitment to the issue was nonexistent before the very end of the twentieth century. Maurice Berube labels Thomas Jefferson the nation's "first education president," but admits that Jefferson's claim to such a title depends mostly on his writing and actions "outside the presidential office," and characterizes the role of presidents in education policy as "periodic" prior to Lyndon Johnson.[45] Lawrence McAndrews, in *The Era of Education*, labels Johnson the "first self-proclaimed" education president.[46] In calling for Congress to rename the U.S. Department of Education building after Lyndon Johnson, Democratic Congressman Gene Green, in March 2007, said, "Lyndon Johnson's first priority in life was education, and he was the first education president." Backing up that claim was the fact that Johnson had signed more than sixty education bills during his presidency, including the path-breaking Elementary and Secondary Education Act (ESEA), the Higher Education Act, and the creation of Head Start, marking him as a key leader at all levels of the education enterprise.[47]

Earlier presidents, of course, occasionally took prominent actions that related to education. In 1957, for example, Dwight Eisenhower issued an executive order calling for National Guard troops under his authority to ensure the safe and orderly integration of Central High School in Little Rock, Arkansas. While a signature moment in his administration, this involved access to schools and not what went on within them, came reluctantly, and was intended to be temporary. As he took pains to note, "Nor are the troops there for the purpose of taking over the responsibility of the School Board and the other responsible local officials in running Central High School. The running of our school system and the maintenance of peace and order in each of our States are strictly local affairs and the Federal Government does not interfere except in a very few special cases and when requested by one of the several States."[48] Similarly, John F. Kennedy was drawn into the whirlpool of school desegregation, federalizing the National Guard in 1962 in support of James Meredith's effort to enroll in the University of Mississippi and then again in 1963 when Governor George Wallace threatened to block black students attempting to integrate the University of Alabama. Compared to Eisenhower, Kennedy may have seen a stronger affirmative role for the presidency in promoting education, but for the most part his efforts were subordinated to the broader battle to promote civil rights.

Although federal spending on education increased substantially during his administration, Richard Nixon would hardly lay stake to being an education president. Much of the funding increases were driven by Congress and against his will. Part of his resistance was premised on emerging research, such as that associated with the famous Coleman Report, which challenged the simple notion that more money translates directly into better educational outcomes. But Nixon's skepticism seemed more emotional and deeply rooted than that of some of his advisors, like Daniel Patrick Moynihan and Chester Finn, who were genuinely interested in building a more research-based education policy. "I've never assumed that education is the sacred cow some believe it is," Nixon told his Council for Urban Affairs when reacting to a House vote to add money to his budget request for education funding. "It is so goddamn ridiculous to assume everyone should go to college."[49]

Based on one signature accomplishment, it might be tempting to label Jimmy Carter as something of an education president. It was during his administration that the U.S. Department of Education was accorded status as an independent cabinet-level agency. During his presidential campaign, Carter had indicated support for the idea—promoted by the National Education Association (NEA)—of pulling education out of the Department of Health, Education, and Welfare (HEW), where it was somewhat overshadowed, and creating a separate education department that also would consolidate education-related responsibilities that were fragmented throughout the federal bureaucracy. If this were just a matter of a newly elected Democratic president paying back a favor to an important part of his electoral constituency, it would not be much to comment upon, but Carter stuck to this promise despite opposition within his administration (for example, from HEW secretary Joseph Califano) and despite the fact that even the education community was divided (the American Federation of Teachers, for example, opposed the move).[50] There is a difference, though, between a president undertaking some proeducation initiatives and one who makes public education a central priority, and Carter did not fall into the latter camp. On the domestic policy front, he is better known for his efforts regarding energy policy and urban policy. Rather than indicating deep commitment to a stronger federal role in public education, accounts by Beryl Radin and Willis Hawley and by Paul Manna suggest that the creation of the Department of Education was more about rationalizing bureaucratic organization than advancing substantive goals.[51] Some go so far as to suggest that Carter supported creating the department precisely to avoid making more costly commitments to higher levels of education funding.[52]

Despite the ambiguity in timing, the transition from Ronald Reagan to George H. W. Bush provides something like a continental divide. Reagan came into office in some ways as the antithesis of an educational entrepreneur. He conceived of education as properly the province of states and localities, and his primary objectives at the national level were to dismantle the U.S. Department of Education that had been created under Jimmy Carter and to institute education vouchers as a way to reduce the government role more generally in favor of an education marketplace driven by supply and demand. Despite his inclination to disengage the White House from education policy, Reagan ended up having considerable influence. The timing of *A Nation at Risk*, which was released during his first term, and the fact that the report was produced by a "National Commission" (on Education and Excellence), is often mistakenly taken as an indication that this high-profile call for national action was Reagan's idea. In truth, Reagan was reluctant, and the real responsibility for bringing it about is attributable to his secretary of education, Terrel Bell.[53] Chester Finn, who goes so far as to call him the "original education president," did not miss the irony that "Reagan's legacy includes a larger role for the federal government itself in education than he could have imagined, perhaps larger than he would have liked."[54]

If Reagan was a reluctant education president, George H. W. Bush was eager to take that mantle. Eight years after the 1980 election, while still in office as Reagan's vice president, he made a national leadership role in education reform a central defining characteristic of his presidential campaign. In office, Bush combined high-visibility pronouncements on education with a generally lackluster legislative record in terms of actually getting things done. In September 1989, Bush assembled a group of governors in Charlottesville, Virginia, for an "education summit." By working directly with the nation's governors, he was able to combine a cheerleader role with traditional Republican deference to states' rights. As Manna explains, Bush wanted to show that he was following through on his commitment to be the education president, but his actual agenda for the summit was a limited one: "to share education success stories and exchange ideas." The governors had had enough of talking and pressed for more, leading to a joint commitment to accomplish a list of specific national education goals.[55]

Bush was not the pro-market ideologue that Reagan had been, and his vision of education policy included a role for federal standards, not simply letting parents decide. Bush, nonetheless, was being criticized in some quarters for having failed to generate any real momentum on education reform, and as the next presidential election began to loom on the agenda, he began talking more about education, and at the same time began adopting more of the pro-voucher, market-oriented language that he had previously downplayed. In January 1992, less than one month before the New Hampshire primary, Bush announced a planned "GI bill for children." Labeled "Federal Grants for State and Local 'GI' Bills for Children," the proposal sought simultaneously to conjure a major governmental initiative and maintain rhetorical allegiance to the notion that the national government would be confined to the role of helping states. The legislation would have provided grants to states and localities that offered thousand-dollar "scholarships" to low- and middle-income families; these scholarships could be used to pay for supplementary educational services (such as afterschool programs) or applied toward tuition at private secular or religious schools.

In emphasizing education, George H. W. Bush was responding to a changing set of public expectations for presidential leadership in this area. From the 1960 election that pitted Kennedy against Nixon, through the 1984 election between Mondale and Reagan, education had never ranked among the top ten issues named as "most important" to the American public. When Bush ran against Dukakis in 1988, education issues ranked eighth out of twenty-six in the months leading up to the election; in 1992, when Bush ran against Clinton, they ranked fifth.[56]

Figure 2.3 shows the relative emphasis presidents have put on education in their State of the Union speeches since 1948. With the exception of that for President Obama, the data are drawn from the Policy

FIGURE 2.3

Education emphasis in State of Union addresses

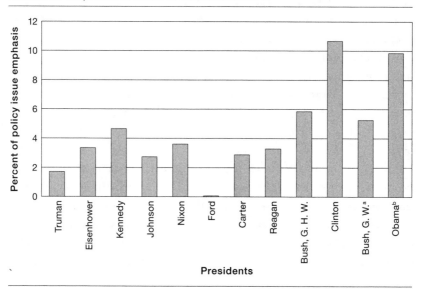

Source: Original analysis of data downloaded from the Policy Agendas Project, www.policyagendas.org.

[a] Through 2005.

[b] Obama's data is drawn from the Smart Politics blog, http://blog.lib.umn.edu/cspg/smartpolitics/2011/01/a_content_analysis_of_barack_o.php.

Agendas Project and summarizes the percent of the speeches that deal with education as opposed to other policy areas.[57]

George H. W. Bush gave about 75 percent more emphasis to education than did Reagan; Bill Clinton was by far the overall leader, with more than one in ten of his policy references being to education. Gerald Ford gave only one brief address in which he did not mention education. Overall, the three presidents who were first elected after *A Nation at Risk* (George H. W. Bush, Clinton, and George W. Bush) gave more than two and one-half times the relative emphasis to education than did the seven that preceded them.

Although the Policy Agendas Project data runs only though 2005, *Smart Politics*, a political analysis blog hosted by the University of Minnesota's Humphrey School of Public Affairs, did a similar content analysis of President Obama's annual addresses to Congress for the years 2009–2011.[58] Because the coding schemes and procedures are not identical, the comparison in the bar graph is inexact, but it provides further evidence to support the notion that education is a major focus of attention for contemporary presidents. In a 2009 address to Congress, Obama cited education behind only the banking system and budget issues relating to deficit, debt, and spending. Education dropped sharply in attention during his 2010 State of the Union address, when the economy, jobs, and budget issues dominated, but rebounded to take up a greater part of his 2011 State of the Union address than any other of over twenty-six issues mentioned.

Just as important as the increased volume of messages about education is the degree to which presidential involvement in education has shifted from marginal and deferential to assertive and core. As president, George W. Bush did not talk about education as much as Bill Clinton had, but No Child Left Behind was, by almost anyone's calibration, a major escalation in the national government's reach into the day-to-day practices of schools.[59] Clinton's pursuit of national standards and accountability was moderated by Republicans' suspicions of a White House–led encroachment on states' rights, but because Bush was a Republican—one of them—in a classic twist on the "Nixon goes to China" phenomenon, he was able to push the federal role further than any of his Democratic predecessors.

Barack Obama emphasized the economy and health care more than education in his 2008 campaign, but once in office he continued the leveraging up of the federal government's role. Obama and his aggressive secretary of education, Arne Duncan, pledged to keep up the pressure begun under NCLB. But what really ratcheted up the visibility and muscle of the president's impact was Race to the Top (RTTT). RTTT began somewhat as a ride-along on the American Recovery and Reinvestment Act (ARRA), the administration's effort to stimulate the economy after the huge financial collapse it confronted in its first months in office. ARRA provided $100 billion in education funds. Of that amount, $4.35 billion was set aside for state incentive grants in education, which became RTTT.[60] RTTT took the form of a competitive grant. Since the passage of ESEA in 1965, the bulk of federal support to K–12 education had been formula grants. Congress can attach various policy conditions to formula grants, and NCLB, as noted, marked a ratcheting up of the prescriptive components, but formula grants in general tend to be less narrowly directive than competitive grants.[61] By attaching strong conditions and a weighting system that penalized applications that failed to include program elements it favored, the U.S. Department of Education was able to entice many states to make commitments (e.g., raising caps on the number of charter schools) that they were not otherwise inclined to make. Largely because of this policy leverage, Frederick Hess concluded that RTTT had "arguably become the most visible and celebrated school reform effort in American history."[62]

Presidents "see scant political reward for spending time on education," Chester Finn wrote in 1977.[63] Some thirty-five years later, it appears that this observation has been turned on its head. Although much of the first two years of the Obama administration was spent wrestling with the economy and health care, those issues had the White House often playing defense, while RTTT was a source for broad praise and considerable bipartisan support. In his State of the Union address leading into last half of his first term in office, President Obama sought to build on that foundation; symbolically calling forth education as a unifying rallying point, he pulled out the old trope of global competitiveness. Speaking of education, he framed the issue as "our generation's *Sputnik* moment."

The growing role of presidents in education policy is of interest in its own right, but also sheds light on the phenomenon of education governors. Unlike at the state level, understanding the growing role of executive leaders at the national level presents no need to disentangle informal from formal political changes. In many states, as we've seen, governors have been granted stronger powers to appoint state superintendents and school board members, but presidents after Reagan have no stronger constitutional authority over education than did their predecessors, and to the extent that NCLB or competitive grant programs such as RTTT offer more programmatic and policy levers for them to pull, these seem better understood as being the *results* of their greater activism than the *causes* of such.

That presidents neither required nor received additional formal power as a prerequisite to expanding their involvement in education lends credence to the hypothesis that informal political, economic, and social factors have been critical at both the state and national levels. In the era of global competition, business, media, and the voting public have been quicker to blame economic hard times (such as the national recessions that ran from July 1981 through November 1982, July 1990 through March 1991, March 2001 through November 2001, and December 2007 through June 2009) on an education system that was once seen as above criticism. The sense of education crisis and the framing of education reform as tied to economic performance helped set the stage for greater executive involvement—while governors and presidents have not always been expected to know or do much about education, fixing economic problems has long been a part of their job description. And, once in for a dime, they have often found themselves in for a dollar; since obtaining demonstrable results is not easy or assured, they have had to mobilize a wide range of their resources—formal and informal—to bring to bear, lest they be charged with failing to meet the challenge.

MAYORAL CONTROL

The erosion of traditional education-specific policy institutions has been more evident at the local level than in the White House or governors' mansions. That is not because the local level is where the role of general-purpose government and politics is most prevalent—to the contrary—but because it is at the local level that education-specific institutions historically have held sway. It is the sharpness of the shift, from long-dominant school boards to newly mobilized mayors, that has made mayoral control the most talked-about manifestation of the end of education exceptionalism.[64]

Led by Boston, a series of large urban school systems have formally strengthened the mayor's role, by giving them greater power in selecting superintendents, selecting school boards, authorizing charter schools, determining the budget, or all of the above. Mayoral control of schools in itself is nothing new. Indeed, before the Progressive Era reforms in the early twentieth century, public education in large cities most often was housed in an agency reporting to a mayor, much as would be the case with law enforcement or public works. What *is* new is its reemergence as a favored reform after decades in which a rival vision held sway.

During the Progressive Era, many communities removed oversight of schools from the mayor's responsibility in the belief that this would lead to a more professional approach and one less responsive to partisan politics and the temptation to use school jobs and school building contracts as forms of patronage. The strategy for depoliticizing education was to place school governance in the hands of an independently elected school board, often elected off-cycle from general elections and often with a dedicated revenue stream. Some urban districts—such as Chicago; New Haven, Connecticut; and Jackson, Mississippi—never took schools out of the mayor's portfolio of control, but of the large districts currently under mayoral control, many gave their mayors stronger formal roles during the past fifteen years after decades of strong school board governance.

Table 2.2 lists the major examples of mayoral control, distinguishing those that have historically retained strong mayoral roles versus those that adopted mayoral control more recently. It also provides details about the forms that mayoral control can take.[65]

While the rate at which large districts are adopting the model seems to have slowed for the moment, the possibility of moving in that direction remains under discussion in a number of other places, including

TABLE 2.2

Specific features of mayoral governance of school districts

City	Start date	Important changes	Specific features
Baltimore	Historical (1899)	Augmented in 1997 to include state involvement.	Mayor and governor jointly appoint board and superintendent (from a short list generated by the state superintendent).
Boston	1992	Voters reaffirmed mayoral control in 1996.	Mayor appoints all of board (from citizens' panel choices), which appoints superintendent.
Chicago	1995 (historical aspects present prior to this date)		Mayor appoints all of board (and top five administrators), which appoints superintendent. Each school has a council (six parents, two teachers, two community members, the principal, and, at high schools, a student) responsible for hiring and evaluating principals, developing academic goals, and approving school budgets.
Cleveland	1998	Reaffirmed by referendum in 2002.	Eleven-member nominating committee, including three members appointed by the mayor, reviews board applications and whittles the candidate list to an agreed-upon number. The mayor then appoints board members from the shortened list. The board appoints a superintendent (mayor had the appointment power at first, but the initial legislation provided for this to revert to the appointed board after thirty months).
Detroit	1999	Mayoral control ended in 2004; reassertion currently being actively discussed and promoted by Mayor Dave Bing.	While in place, the mayor appointed six of seven board members (governor appointed the seventh and had veto power), which appointed the superintendent.
Harrisburg, Pennsylvania	2000		Mayor appoints a seven-member board of control and selects the superintendent.

(continued)

TABLE 2.2 *(continued)*

Specific features of mayoral governance of school districts

City	Start date	Important changes	Specific features
Hartford, Connecticut	2005	Instituted following a state takeover of the schools. The first mayor with control named himself to the board.	Mayor appoints majority of board (five of nine), which then selects superintendent.
Jackson, Mississippi	Historical		Mayor appoints board, which is confirmed by city council.
New Haven, Connecticut	Historical		Mayor appoints board.
New York City	2002	Initial legislation required reauthorization by 2009. After some controversy, this was extended, with some moderate changes, into 2015.	Mayor appoints majority of board (and can fire at will) with others appointed by borough presidents. Mayor appoints the superintendent/chancellor. Schools have leadership teams, which are mostly advisory.
Oakland, California	2000	Fiscal problems led to state intervention in 2003, and the creation of a mixed elected and mayoral appointed board. In 2009, the state restored control to a fully elected board.	Mayor appoints two members and governor appoints three to the school reform committee. State senate confirms all.
Philadelphia	Historical	2001, state converted to partnership arrangement.	Mayor appoints two members and governor appoints three to the school reform committee. State senate confirms all.
Prince George's County, Maryland	2002	State replaced elected board in 2002. Reverted to locally elected board in 2006.	While in place, governor and county executive (a position comparable to a mayor's) appointed board, which in turn appointed superintendent.
Providence	2003 (historical aspects present prior to this date)		Mayor appoints all of board, which appoints superintendent.

(continued)

TABLE 2.2 *(continued)*

Specific features of mayoral governance of school districts

City	Start date	Important changes	Specific features
Trenton, New Jersey	Historical (1978)		Mayor appoints board, which hires superintendent.
Washington, DC	2000 (partial)	2007, augmented to full mayoral control.	Mayor appoints chancellor; former local board now functions as a state board.
Yonkers, New York	Historical		Mayor appoints board, which appoints superintendent.

Source: Data is compiled from various sources, including (Chambers, 2006; Moore, 2007; Wong et al., 2007); and individual city websites.

Note: This is an updated version of a table that appeared in J. Henig and E. Thurston Fraser, "Correlates of Mayoral Takeovers in City School Systems" in *Urban and Regional Policy and Its Effects: Volume 2*, eds. Nancy Pindus, Howard Wial, and Harold Wolman (Washington DC: Brookings Institution Press, 2009).

Indianapolis, Milwaukee, Newark, Los Angeles, Sacramento, Rochester, and Rockford, Illinois. "Whomever is sitting in the Mayor's Office of the City of Rockford should be legally required to be involved in our schools and held accountable for the success or failure of our schools," Mayor Larry Morrissey declared in his 2011 "state of the city" address.[66] Detroit, which had mayoral control from 1999 to 2004, is talking about it once again.[67] "Schools aren't under my command; they are run by a school board that is dominated by teachers unions," announced Detroit Mayor Dave Bing. "One of my goals is to have mayoral control of the school system."[68]

As with governors, giving formal authority to mayors—to appoint school boards, to hire superintendents, to set school budgets—does not ensure they will take up the cause of school reform with wisdom or even energy. In Baltimore, for example—where the mayors long held power to appoint the school board and, through their power on the city's board of estimates, to tightly control spending—even a strong and dynamic mayor like William Donald Schaeffer preferred to focus his attention on other issues, like downtown development, where successes were more likely and more visible.[69] This is the case in Chicago as well, where during the years from 1947 to 1980, while the mayor formally controlled both the board and budget, "most mayors avoided public school debates and disavowed any responsibility for their problems."[70]

Nor does lack of formal authority preclude strong mayoral leadership in the education arena. Michael Kirst and Fritz Edelstein highlight Long Beach, California, as a "prime example of how mayoral involvement in education need not rely on formal changes to governance." There, Mayor Beverly O'Neill has worked closely with the superintendent's office in a partnership that appears to have provided much of the multiagency coordination and public support that proponents of mayoral control talk about. Long Beach won the Broad Prize in Urban Education in 2003.[71] Francis Shlay, mayor of St. Louis, made up for a lack of appointment power by backing a slate of reform-oriented school board candidates and helping them all get elected. Kenneth Wong et al. cite Douglas Wilder, mayor of Richmond, Virginia, as an example of a politically skillful mayor who has used his informal power and authority to hold the superintendent accountable to him even when there was no formal line of authority to call upon.[72]

Probably the strongest formal version of mayoral control is the one instituted in New York City beginning in 2002. Previously, New York City school governance had comprised thirty-two separate school districts that dealt mainly with elementary through middle schools, with a citywide board of education that hired the chancellor and ran high schools. At the request of newly elected Mayor Michael Bloomberg, in June 2002 the state legislature greatly strengthened the mayor's authority. Among the formal changes were empowering the mayor to appoint the chancellor (i.e., superintendent) of the system and eight of the thirteen members of the city's board of education (which Bloomberg renamed the Panel for Educational Policy). Some grants of formal appointment authority are more checked and limited than others. Consider the U.S. president's authority to appoint a Supreme Court justice, which is limited at the front end by the requirement for the Senate to provide its "advice and consent," and at the back end by the fact that the appointment, once made, cannot be rescinded. In the New York City case, Mayor Bloomberg was given the power to select an appointee without the need for subsequent approval and with the unchecked power to revoke such appointment should the mayor so choose.[73]

While the legislation was strong, what made the New York City form of mayoral control extreme had as much to do with the aggressive use of the delegated authority and mobilization of informal power by Bloomberg and his first chancellor, Joel Klein. For example, a mayor's formal power to appoint school board members can in practice be a mild form of control or a strong one. The formal power is mild if the mayor relies heavily on the judgment of others in identifying candidates, heavily weighs the views of education experts, seeks consensus candidates, avoids second-guessing and challenging appointees once they are in office, and accommodates decisions by the board even when they might differ from the mayor's preferences. The same formal power can be strong if the mayor aggressively manages the process of identifying and selecting nominees, puts allegiance to the mayor's agenda and priorities above educational expertise as a selection criterion, and uses the formal power to remove members to enforce loyalty to that agenda and priorities after the board member is in office.

Midway through Michael Bloomberg's first term in office, when a few members of the Panel for Educational Policy expressed doubts about approving the chancellor's plan to end social promotion for the city's third graders, Bloomberg, as reported in the *New York Times*, simply "fired them, had three new members appointed and rammed his policy home—in one workday."[74] The mayor had no compunctions about using his formal authority to the fullest; pressed on the issue, he asserted: "Mayoral control means mayoral control, thank you very much. They are my representatives, and they are going to vote for things that I believe in."[75] Less visibly and directly, Bloomberg and Klein worked to marginalize the thirty-two community districts, which the legislature quite deliberately had refused to eliminate.[76]

The New York City case provides a useful illustration of an additional aspect of mayoral control more generally. Although the movement from elected school boards toward more active mayors takes place at the local level, its unfolding often involves states and sometimes even national actors, an example of how the broad institutional shifts discussed in chapter 1 can overlap and feed one another. Initiating mayoral control in all states requires at minimum the consent of the state legislature, and sometimes the impetus has come largely from the state level, when governors or legislatures became frustrated by what they considered to be recalcitrant districts.[77] In New York City, the legislature was something of a reluctant partner. Rudolph Giuliani, Bloomberg's predecessor, had tried and failed to get such power while he was mayor. And in extending the power to the mayor in 2002, the legislature included a sunset provision so the arrangement would expire at the end of June 2009 unless affirmatively renewed before that time.[78]

The role of the national government in reinforcing mayoral control for the most part has been more indirect. Arguably, the accountability pressures exerted by NCLB have added to the sense of dissatisfaction with school boards and districts, making the soil more fertile for proposals for governance reform. However, during the debate surrounding the extension of mayoral control in New York City, the Obama administration took an even more forceful stand. At the height of the debate, and despite criticisms by some parents' groups that were concerned that mayoral control, New York style, had resulted in a far too centralized regime, U.S. Education Secretary Arne Duncan told a local newspaper: "I absolutely, fundamentally believe that mayoral control is extraordinarily important. I'm absolutely a proponent."[79] "At the end of my tenure, if only seven mayors are in control, I think I will have failed," Duncan told a group of mayors and education leaders in April 2009.[80] "I'll come to your cities," Duncan said. "I'll meet with your editorial boards. I'll talk with your business communities. I will be there."[81] White House support for mayoral control also became a central focus of controversy in Milwaukee, where the governor and other supporters of an effort to institute mayoral control openly argued that failure to do so would put the state's effort to win a federal Race to the Top grant in jeopardy.[82]

MOVING BEYOND PERSONALITIES AND LEVEL-SPECIFIC EXPLANATIONS

Discussions about education governors, presidents, and mayors tend to be personality based and level specific. By *personality based*, I mean that discussions often focus on individual leaders and the traits, motives, and tactics they bring to bear. Popular accounts emphasize the political vision and skills of the particular elected executives who spotted or created opportunities overlooked by their predecessors. It's Lyndon Johnson's War on Poverty; Martin Luther King's civil rights movement; Ronald Reagan's victory as the wall tumbles down between East and West Germany. *Waiting for Superman*, the controversial documentary about education reform, addresses this "great man perspective" in two ways, only one of which is intentional. By intention, the movie is meant to criticize the idea of waiting for a superhero to fly down and solve tough social problems; the call is for people to take responsibility to do so themselves, both individually and collectively. At the same time, the heavy emphasis on strong personalities to represent competing ideas and social movements—Geoffrey Canada as the knight of charter schools and reform; Randi Weingarten as the queen of union resistance—unintentionally reinforces the premise that strong leaders drive history.

Attributing special abilities and causal influence to strong personalities simplifies any narrative. Often events are attributable to multiple and interacting causes, but communicating this is a complicated challenge. Sometimes events are random or probabilistic in their origin, but a story built around happenstance lacks much that is compelling. It is easy to see how tales about this or that strong leader take root; contemporaneous accounts focus on a prominent actor and then get picked up by those from a distance (time or place) who lack deep knowledge of the ambiguities and complexities.

By *level specific*, I mean that the literature on the national-, state-, and local-level governance changes has comprised three separate streams with little cross-fertilization. When applied to governors, this level-specific perspective has led commentators to emphasize entrepreneurial southern governors responding to the opportunity to attract business and investment at a particular era in which changing technologies (e.g., air conditioning), transportation infrastructures (national highway system; fully developed commercial and passenger air travel system), and improved communication made it more possible for businesses to shift their operations from the North and to take advantage of the lower taxes and weaker unions that previously had been insufficient inducements. When applied to presidents, the level-specific frame of reference encouraged explanations rooted in national partisan politics, such as the realization on the part of the Republican Party that it needed a more affirmative educational platform than to simply evoke states' rights and local control, or the even more general bipartisan history of executive aggrandizement as presidents, frustrated by congressional stalemates and under pressure to get things done, have maxed out their claims of executive authority across policy issues from foreign to domestic policy.[83] When applied to mayors, it has meant focusing on the specific failure of urban school boards or on the conjured image of a "new-style" mayor, more pragmatic and attuned to business interests than the old-style mayors who saw schools as a patronage pool.[84] This tendency to engage in level-specific analysis reflects lines of organization within political commentary, the media, and political science that mimic the layer effect of our federal system, and sometimes miss or obscure the multiple ways in which phenomena at one layer of our federal system may mimic, model, or instigate changes at the other levels.[85]

But an uncritical adoption of strong-leader and level-specific perspectives as a way to understand education presidents, governors, and mayors understates the importance of the broader political institutional landscape and ignores the ways in which actions by other powerful interests help determine whether and when executive muscle can be effectively exercised. As this chapter has shown, the expanding role of the "education executives" involves changes in formal power and not simply shifting personal ambitions. The breadth of the phenomenon—that gubernatorial assertion takes several different forms and extends across so many states and years; that presidential activism now spans both parties; that mayors are becoming more involved in education politics even when they lack a formal governance role—suggests that the emergence of the education executives draws on broader political dynamics.

Some preliminary observations are in order. The drive toward greater executive branch leadership in education politics and policy involves both push and pull factors.[86] *Push* factors have to do with general dissatisfaction with the status quo in American education, a dissatisfaction that extends to the issue-specific structures that have historically characterized school governance. *Pull* factors account for the appeal of general-purpose leadership to interests outside the traditional education sector looking for a reliable partner in pursuit of their vision of school reform. In addition to push and pull factors that may be propelling the change, part of the story of the new education executives involves a relaxation of a countervailing pressure that for decades had made presidents, governors, and mayors quite content to leave potentially explosive decisions to be resolved in school-specific arenas.

Push Factors: Antipathy Toward School Boards and Education Bureaucracies

To some extent, the movement toward executive leadership is simply the latest in a series of reform impulses broadly characterized as "anything's got to be better than what we have now." Although much of the reform impulse has been attached to specific programmatic or curricular ideas, some have argued that the basic governance structure characterizing U.S. education is the real source of the problem. Elected school boards, particularly those elected at the ward level rather than citywide, have been criticized for a range of sins, including petty politics, micromanagement, amateurishness, lack of imagination, kowtowing to the teacher unions, corruption, and waste. The tenor of the discussion is captured by the titles of an edited volume of scholarly analyses of school boards and local school governance—*Besieged*—and a more journalistic assessment that appeared in the *Atlantic Monthly*, "First, Kill All the School Boards."[87] In a symbolic underscoring of the deteriorating image of elected school boards, New Jersey passed legislation in 2010 requiring that all local board members undergo criminal background checks, complete with fingerprinting.[88]

The push away from education bureaucracies is a little different from the antipathy toward school boards. Some critics of schools boards see them as examples of amateurism gone wild. School board members sometimes lack credentials of professional expertise; they are supposed to bring to bear common sense and close ties to the people who elected them, but to critics this translates into naïveté, overfascination with educational fads, and a short time horizon. Education bureaucracies, on the other hand, are attacked as the home of careerists who use their claim to special expertise as a political weapon that allows them to pursue their own agenda without regard for what the public wants. The one is a case of too much democracy; the other of too little. But in both cases, it is school-specific arenas that are found to be wanting.

This animus toward school boards and education bureaucracies has played a role in fueling the other two major institutional shifts in the educational landscape. Dissatisfaction with school boards weakened the historical power of appeals to local control, making the growing state and national government role more politically feasible, and discredited public institutions generally in a way that helped open opportunities for privatization in education. Although the school-specific decision-making venues at the state and national levels were never so sharply differentiated as those locally, state boards of education, chief state school officers, and the U.S. Department of Education have also been tarnished by the broader reversal of American sentiment about education professionalism; where specialization and professionalism were once celebrated as the guarantors of neutral competence and scientific expertise, they are now as likely to be disparaged as the sheep's clothing behind which lurks bureaucratic self-interest and the elevation of the needs of adults over those of the children.[89]

Pull Factors: Reliable Partners

To suggest that the existing governance arrangements need to be changed is one thing. That accounts for the push part of the equation, but it does not account for the pull toward governors, presidents, and mayors as the mechanisms of control. There are plenty of other notions about what it would take to improve public schools, each with enthusiastic boosters. Vouchers, charter schools, small classrooms, test-based accountability, alternative certification for teachers, educational technologies—take your pick. To reformers impatient with the slow pace of progress under existing governance institutions, these hot new reform ideas can seem newer, fresher, and less incremental than a simple call to give more authority to familiar actors like mayors, governors, and presidents.

Part of the pull factor is an instrumental one: the new educational executives are seen as more likely than school boards and bureaucracies to give a fair hearing to these various reform ideas by virtue of being less invested in the status quo. Contemporary mayors, governors, and even presidents are seen as a pragmatic bunch, more problem solvers than ideologues. Many of the reform ideas, moreover, have been incubated in the corporate sector, which often has good access to elected executives, and some are based on models of contracting out and private provision of services that are familiar to public-sector decision makers in other areas of domestic policy.

Another part of the pull factor may have to do with the general appeal of a "muscular executive" as organizational leader in complex and challenging environments. As government grows—in personnel; in professionalism; in scope of responsibility; in regulatory reach, management, and administration—the challenging task of riding herd on the governmental apparatus becomes more important in actuality and in people's minds. That, arguably, creates an environment in which the executive branch stands to gain in stature relative to the legislature and judiciary. Not just in the United States, but also throughout the Western world, analysts have commented on the rise of the *regulatory state*, a governance regime in which rules, oversight, and public contracting to some extent displace direct government provision, legislation, taxing, and spending as the mechanisms through which governments operate.[90] New data systems that give agencies informational advantages also may add to the musculature of the executive branch.

Some of these changes speak more to the potency of the executive branch than to the chief executive per se. Indeed, in some ways the forces at play may make it more difficult for presidents, governors, or mayors, as principals, to steer the bureaucracy as their putative agents. Relative to the other branches, though, the executive gains extra clout. And although analysts of the regulatory state argue that the emphasis on rules can also give increased power to the judiciary, recent battles in the United States over executive privilege and its role in responding to terrorism suggest that a strong executive may still be able to stonewall a probing judiciary. The growing importance of the media in simplifying issues for the public also gives a president, governor, or mayor opportunities to gain leverage, through a greater ability to commandeer the bully pulpit, over faceless bureaucracies and multiheaded legislatures.

While it is tempting to attribute evidence of growing executive branch influence to evolutionary advantage—as if secular trends bound up in the very nature of modernity and progress determine that executive functions will expand—there is another, more political, explanation to consider as well. The conception of a powerful Chief Executive Officer (CEO), who plays the primary management and leadership role in the organization, is familiar and appealing within the corporate world, and business interests may be playing a role in grafting the model onto the public sector. In education, specifically, the corporate metaphor has been a contributing factor driving organizational changes. Some large urban school districts in recent years have been renaming existing positions or generating new ones with labels that are rooted more in the boardroom than in the traditions of school administration. Increasingly, they are boasting titles like Chief Executive Officer, Chief Operating Officer, Director of Portfolio Management, and Chief Talent Officer in place of position titles more closely aligned with curriculum, instruction, and human resources. Business is not a new actor in education policy and politics—and I've argued elsewhere that its commitment and staying power are sometimes overstated—but in the new landscape of urban education, private sector actors from the for-profit, nonprofit, and foundation communities are increasingly prominent.[91] The corporate, CEO-style framing may flow in part from the fact that these interests are more important—either as a direct source of the metaphor, reflecting their own terms of understanding, or because others employ the metaphor as a strategy for winning their support.

Beyond being more likely to give new reform ideas a fair hearing and beyond their appeal as managers able to ride herd on policy implementation, education executives can be attractive partners because of the political sensitivities, skills, and connections they bring to the table. An increasingly important factor pulling in the direction of executive leadership is the realization that the other reform notions being promoted as panaceas all are prone to failure absent healthy politics and governance capacity. It has been roughly thirty years since the launch of the standards-based reform movement; almost twenty-five since *Fortune* magazine pronounced that computers had come of age in the classroom; and more than two decades since the initiation of the nation's first serious voucher experiment in Milwaukee and the first charter school legislation in Minnesota.[92] Each new panacea has been shown to work in some places at some times, and each has been shown to disappoint in many others. To the extent that sufficient funding support, attention to the details of implementation, dexterity to learn and adjust, coordination across various agencies, and a supportive political constituency are what separates the successes from the failures, it makes sense to look to governors, presidents, and mayors as the ones who control the levers that matter.

Facilitating Factors: Decoupling Education from the Politics of Race and Class

The various push and pull arguments tell us something about why *others* may have preferred elected executives to wrest away power from education-specific institutions that had come to be seen as obstacles to school reform. The general presumption in political science is that elected officials are motivated primarily by the desire to stay in office or move to higher office.[93] Under normal conditions, this has been supposed to induce them to seek and claim greater power since power allows them to deliver goodies to their constituents in the form of roads and highways, police and fire protection, intergovernmental grants, and the jobs and contracts that go along with all of these. When it is not possible to deliver tangible benefits to their constituents, the political science literature suggests that elected officials will look for broadly popular causes and seek to align themselves with those through symbolic and ritualistic behavior.[94]

On its face, public education represents a huge pool of distributable benefits. Local, state, and federal governments collected over $590 billion in revenues for elementary and secondary public education in 2008–2009.[95] And despite the general sense that American education is falling behind, the public continues to strongly support the idea of public education. The loyalty Americans show to the ideals of the traditional system is sufficiently strong that Terry Moe has referred to this as the "public school ideology."[96] That elected executives for many years did not seek to maximize their role in public education seems paradoxical from this perspective.

It's possible that the explanation for the expanding role of mayors, governors, and presidents has to do with changes that have simply made education too important to ignore. Globalization, competition for investment, and the importance of human capital as sources of labor productivity and innovation arguably have changed the way both citizens and leaders think about the centrality of public schools. The reframing of education as an economic development issue, which appears to have been important in the emergence of the southern education governors, also appears relevant to understanding the growing willingness and ability of mayors and presidents to get involved. Paul Peterson argues that the pursuit of development is the primary interest that drives a city's behavior; to the extent that public schooling represents a way to attract and hold residents and businesses that pay more in taxes relative to what they use in services, he would predict that cities would be drawn to invest in schools and that mayors, responsible for the fiscal health of the city overall, would be more attuned to this developmental dimension of education than single-purpose institutions like school boards.[97]

The incentive for presidents to respond to this economic argument for advancing education requires a bit more explanation, since public education is not an enumerated constitutional power of the national government and federal expenditures on K–12 schooling are modest compared to the rest of the federal budget as well as to states and localities. Until the 1980s, neither voters nor powerful interest groups were likely see the quality of education as a primary factor in presidential campaigns, so presidents had only limited incentive to divert their attention from the range of other issues more likely to determine their success. *A Nation at Risk*, however, dramatically characterized the country's educational crisis in terms of international competitiveness. This was the tack established by its very first sentences: "Our Nation is at risk. Our once unchallenged preeminence in commerce, industry, science, and technological innovation is being overtaken by competitors throughout the world . . . We report to the American people that while we can take justifiable pride in what our schools and colleges have historically accomplished and contributed to the United States and the well-being of its people, the educational foundations of our society are presently being eroded by a rising tide of mediocrity that threatens our very future as a Nation and a people."[98]

This framing of the issue has several consequences, only some of which have been noted by others. On the positive side, it created a rationale for national governmental action. Reagan, who was opposed to national intrusion on states' rights, was wary of the commission that produced the *Nation at Risk* report for just this reason. After the fact, his administration realized that this air of crisis and mandate for White House involvement could be used to advantage in promoting its agenda, including challenging large urban education bureaucracies and promoting a more market-oriented agenda of school choice and educational privatization. More immediately apparent, though, was the positive role this framing played in appealing to elements within the corporate sector that were genuinely concerned about global competitiveness and frustrated about the slow and piecemeal pattern of state-led reform.

Just as important as the reframing was in providing a positive rationale for executive leadership was the role it played in helping to decouple education politics from two contentious and politically divisive issues—race and class—that led earlier generations of governors, mayors, and presidents to see it as a political hot potato. *Brown v. Board of Education* and the subsequent efforts to enforce it meant that the southern governors who played the strongest public role were those, like Orval Faubus (Arkansas) and George Wallace (Alabama), who were blocking the schoolhouse door. That may have provided them with local constituencies, but also precluded southern governors from being credible advocates for quality public education on the national stage. It may be no mere coincidence then, that the emergence of an early cohort of education governors came after the South dropped its massive resistance, after real progress had begun to be made in dismantling dual education systems, after the federal courts had begun to shift their attention to segregation in the North, and after the political backlash against busing had begun to temper the nation's enthusiasm to push onward from racial opportunity to more demanding levels of equity.

At the national level, the civil rights movement had created a legal and moral imperative for presidential leadership, but for Eisenhower,

Kennedy, and Johnson, filling that role was replete with political risks. History regards Johnson as heroic in his strong stance in championing education and civil rights, but even in his administration the notion that education was politically too hot to handle meant the president often was kept a step removed. "To involve the President, without legal necessity, in so controversial an arena as school desegregation has seemed to us administratively and politically unwise," one member of the administration admitted. 'We feel that the President should remain above the battle . . . and that the Commissioner rather than the President should defend school desegregation policies.'"[99] With race and judicial intervention dominating the framing, even if they wanted to presidents could not venture into the school quality issue without it being interpreted within the polarizing context of race, desegregation, and states' rights. Lawrence McAndrews describes a May 26, 1976, news conference in Columbus, Ohio: "Ford found himself having to respond to a reporter's implication that 'quality education' were code words for 'segregation.'"[100]

At the local level, race also complicated the political currents around schooling in ways that may have deterred mayors from becoming more involved. Compared to the national and state level, racial politics at the local level was less about ideas and principles and more about direct control over public institutions. African Americans would never by themselves constitute electoral majorities at the state or national level, but beginning in the 1960s and 1970s the numbers and power in large cities began to shift from white to black. In places like Washington, DC, Detroit, Baltimore, Cleveland, and Atlanta, blacks began to make political inroads, capturing jobs and then leadership positions in public school systems before other agencies, and before they had the muscle to win at-large elections for general-purpose government offices like at-large city council seats or the mayoralty.[101] In some cities, predominantly white civic and political elites made deliberate decisions to cede control of schools to African Americans as a strategy to defuse pressure for even broader forms of regime change.[102]

When African Americans did begin to launch viable campaigns for the mayor's office, they were typically forced to deemphasize issues that carried strong racial overtones, running "deracialized" campaigns that featured their pragmatic problem-solving skills over appeals to civil rights and cross-racial brokering over their ability to mobilize a constituency around themes of redistribution or racial justice.[103] As at the state and national levels, the volatility of school politics decreased as racial conflict became a less prominent accompaniment. Redistributive politics, according to Peterson, is the death knell to cities and their elected leaders because any effort to systematically shift the balance of taxation and expenditures to benefit less affluent members of the community will spark out-migration by above-average taxpayers, leaving the city in a spiral of fiscal decline. Schooling might be characterized as a developmental policy in the homogenous suburbs, and therefore be seen as an expand-the-pie issue that garners broad political support, but at least during the 1960s and 1970s urban school politics had a Robin Hood character that made it the focus of intense intergroup competition. By this measure, too, it might be argued that race and schools had to have been somewhat decoupled before general-purpose politicians would find it safe and even politically profitable to take a leadership role.

In addition to push and pull factors, then, there may be a "bramble-clearing" component to the explanation of what had to happen before the divergent paths that separated education from general-purpose government could be rejoined. The natural inclination of general-purpose elected officials to seek greater influence over the big bucks of education spending were moderated for decades by the perceived high risks of getting involved with the highly volatile value-laden issues that school politics brought to the fore. Redefining education as a tool of economic development took some of the rough edges off the issue. Still, as discussed in the next chapter, it may also have taken the courts—the least politically attuned of the branches of government—to make it safe for the education executives to grab hold.

––––––

This chapter has expanded our focus beyond separate layers of the federal system and beyond indicators of formal power to consider a wider field of political dynamics. Mayors, governors, and presidents have broader issue portfolios and political constituencies than do leaders in school-specific arenas such as school districts, state boards of education, or the U.S. Department of Education. That they have other matters to worry about helps account for the fact that they were often willing to stand back, especially when general satisfaction with American education reduced the imperative to get involved and when the risk of getting embroiled in the hot politics of race increased the disincentives to do so. But their broader portfolios also exposed them to different ways of thinking about education (for instance, as a tool for economic development) and to different ways of implementing governmental power (for instance, within output-oriented systems of performance accountability). And their broader constituencies meant that they were both subject to stronger pressures from interest groups for whom school spending was not necessarily the highest priority and less constrained by the need to satisfy teachers and parents. General movement toward centralization, a shifting focus from equity to excellence, and greater interest in market-based approaches for meeting public goals were important parts of the story of this era, but these were closely entwined in complicated and reciprocal causal relationships with the expanding role of education executives whose operating milieu was general-purpose governance and politics.

But the story in this chapter has retained a narrow span of vision in at least two ways. First, it has attended to the educational arena without acknowledging the possibility that what is occurring may parallel and reflect changes in other arenas for social policy. Having more long-term implications than an explanation based on ad hoc opportunities or simple diffusion and imitation would be the hypothesis that the growing prominence of presidents, governors, and mayors represents a strengthening of the executive branch across most policy issues. Second, this chapter has discussed emerging executives as if the other branches of government were passive bystanders. Chapter 3 expands the terms of the end of education exceptionalism by taking this wider compass into account.

CHAPTER THREE

AN EXPANDED ROLE FOR
LEGISLATURES AND THE COURTS

I N THE late spring of 2011, the New York City Council delivered a
message. Mayor Michael Bloomberg had announced a plan to eliminate 4,100 teaching jobs through layoffs, and about 2,000 through attri-
tion. This would represent "the first significant layoffs of teachers since
the fiscal crisis of the 1970s."[1] Council members were offended—not
just on the substance of the issue, but also by what they took to be the
cavalier way it was announced, with the mayor delegating the shorter-
than-usual presentation to his budget director. "His attitude was like,
'gotta go,'" one council member told journalists. "It reflects the mayor's
disdain, his disrespect and his lack of coalition-building with the City
Council."[2] Three weeks later, the council fired back. Christine Quinn,
the council speaker and normally a close ally of the mayor, announced
that the council had other plans. She presented the council's own set
of budget changes designed to minimize layoffs, sending "a clear signal that big differences remain between the City Council and City Hall
when it comes to bridging the city's multibillion-dollar budget gap."[3]
Faced with this pushback, the administration reconsidered. An agreement was negotiated that averted all teacher layoffs other than by attri-
tion. The mayor put a positive face on the agreement, but at least some
speculated that the deal threatened to "undermine his credibility, given
that he has declared for two consecutive years that layoffs were inevitable, only to see them averted in a budget deal."[4]

New York City under Mayor Bloomberg presents the nation's starkest example of strong mayoral control of public schools. The mayor's formal authority to appoint—and remove at will—the majority of the city's school board (the Panel for Educational Policy) led that body to consistently acquiesce to the decisions of the mayor and the chancellor he appointed. Add Bloomberg's informal political power to the mix—supercharged by his personal wealth, philanthropic activity, and the support of a local business community that saw him as one of their own—and the Big Apple stands as the apotheosis of the end of exceptionalism: public schools as one among other agencies reporting to an elected executive with a multi-issue portfolio and constituency.

Strong as he was in this extreme case, Mayor Bloomberg could not inscribe his vision of public education into practice without risk of being challenged, however. The school board may have functioned as a rubber stamp as critics charged, but checks and balances within the governing system remained. Significantly, these checks and balances lie within other corners of general-purpose governance and politics. Besides the local city council, another point of friction lay within the state legislature, which granted and then extended mayoral control, but both times as a time-limited commitment rather than a permanent change. While the state legislature also has a multi-issue portfolio, its constituency and priorities are its own. Elements within the legislature, particularly in the city's delegation and among the black caucus, were responsive to complaints by parent activists who felt that mayor control was shutting them out. The legislature blocked the administration's early effort to dismantle community school districts and, in extending mayoral control in 2009, added requirements for impact statements and public hearings before the city's department of education could close schools. The courts represented a rival decision point as well. A state supreme court judge, for example, ruled in March 2010 that the city had failed to fully comply with the state legislature's mandated procedures and accordingly blocked the department's plan to close nineteen schools. On July 1, after the city appealed, a state appeals court unanimously upheld the decision, forcing the city to keep the schools open for the next academic year.

The previous chapter reviewed the growing role of mayors, governors, and presidents in setting education policies, a shift that needs to be understood in terms of broad institutional and political changes and not simply as the compelling story of strong leaders. Some leaders *are* special, of course, and the epistemological stance that individuals at times may alter paths of history is one that must be taken seriously. Among political scientists who study institutional development, considerable attention has been paid to political entrepreneurs, defined by Adam Sheingate as "individuals whose creative acts have transformative effects on politics, policies, or institutions."[5] In John Kingdon's classic formulation, it is entrepreneurs who exploit opportunities, and sometimes create them, to bring together perceived problems and conducive political contexts in order to springboard onto the agenda new policies that would otherwise be ignored.[6] "Weaving together facts, norms, and rhetoric," Jesse Rhodes observes, political entrepreneurs "provide cause for abandoning existing institutional commitments and establishing new ones."[7] But, as Rhodes argues, entrepreneurship is itself "institutionally bounded."[8] Strong leaders under unusual circumstances can catalyze institutional change, but ingrained institutions on a day-to-day basis define the range of the possible, probable, and costly waste of time.

Shifting from a great man perspective to an institutional perspective also invites consideration of executive leadership *relative* to other institutions, and it is here that this chapter moves the argument about the end of education exceptionalism a few steps beyond the observation that mayors, governors, and presidents are talking and doing more about education. Courts and legislatures are also general-purpose governance institutions, and they have not been passive bystanders as presidents, governors, and mayors maneuvered onto center stage. Courts, precisely because they are somewhat buffered from normal politics, played a leading role in unsettling some of the institutional parameters that had been protecting the local government single-purpose arena, playing a catalyzing role that opened the ground for broader change. And legislatures played important but underappreciated roles, sometimes leading the executive branch in their attention to public education and often getting further pulled into the currents as supporters or checks on executive authority once it had been asserted.

This is a distinction in perspective that could make a large difference. Proponents of stronger executive leadership hold out the prospect that this could lead to more coherent policies, tighter linkage between policy and implementation, and less of the kind of policy "churn" that substitutes shallow and ephemeral change for sustained change in core educational functions.[9] If general-purpose institutions more broadly are being activated, however, such high hopes might prove naïve. Courts and legislatures might pursue agendas that differ from those of executives; the checks and balances they provide might generate a new form of education policy gridlock. Critics of strong mayors, governors, and presidents, on the other hand, have fretted about an overcentralization of authority that they see as promoting a narrowness of vision and coming at the expense of traditional mechanisms for asserting democratic control. If general-purpose institutions more broadly are being activated, there may be prospects for a more pluralist approach to agenda setting, one in which courts and legislatures bring to the fore rights, values, and contrasting ideas that currently are marginalized.

THE COURTS LOOSEN THE GROUND

Like the executive and legislative branches, courts are general-purpose governance institutions. Education is but one part of the judiciary's issue portfolio. Judges, for the most part, lack deep expertise in the details of schooling. In evaluating cases that involve education, they are not free to treat them as sui generis; the precedents and underlying rationales they apply to education decisions must be compatible with those that evolved from and shape their actions across the full panoply of cases. There may at times be elements of an education-related case that distinguish it in important ways, but if the court decides to treat education as a thing apart it must first hurdle a high bar to justify that course of action. Because courts themselves are general-purpose governance institutions, evidence that they are intruding upon the autonomy of local school districts constitutes direct support for the end of exceptionalism thesis.

But courts differ from the other branches of government in important ways as well. Chapter 1 discussed how institutions mark off distinct decision-making venues, each serving different functions and each differing in terms of its primary actors, norms, and decision rules. There our attention was on distinctions among the levels of our federal system, between government and markets, and between general-and single-purpose governments. But courts, legislatures, and executives present different venues also, with characteristics that affect the agendas they set for themselves, their favored modes of resolving conflicts, and the tools they employ in pursuing their objectives.

Although the judiciary itself is a general-purpose structure, one would not normally consider the courts to be the leading edge of a broadscale institutional shift such as the erosion of school-specific governance structures. Compared to the executive and legislative branches, courts are designed to be somewhat out of step with—and typically a step behind—contemporary politics. At the national level, the Supreme Court famously is buffered by lifetime appointments that protect judges from losing office simply for making decisions that are out of the political mainstream. The selection and retention process for state courts varies. Some elect their judges in partisan elections, some nonpartisan elections, and some have various mechanisms meant to lead to appointment based on merit; terms of office vary widely, from one year to lifetime.[10] Even when state judges are elected, norms of nonpartisanship, low turnout, and a strong bias in favor of incumbents means that most state courts turn over slowly and judges only rarely have to appeal directly to the public in order to stay in office.[11]

Other features also make courts less limber and responsive in the issues they take on. Unlike a governor who can give a speech or propose a law at any time on any issue, or legislatures that can more or less do the same, courts need to wait until questions are brought to them by individuals with standing, meaning those who can show they have been injured in some way, not simply that they anticipate injury or worry that others are or will be ill-served. And even at that point, due to their limited time in any given session, higher-level courts often turn down many more cases than they hear. That limited agenda space can make it hard for issues to break through.[12] Adding to the tendency for courts to trail, rather than lead, substantial reform is the fact that deference to legal precedent is such a powerful norm within the judiciary, raising the bar that a case must pass over in order to warrant a decision that breaks new ground. On most issues, and most of the time, these attributes—the deliberate buffering from contemporary opinion, the long terms and slow turnover making the courts more reflective of a bygone political mood, the forced role as reactor rather than initiator of cases, and deference to precedent—work in sync to make courts a drag on change, creating deliberate friction against mobilizations of short-term enthusiasm.

But occasionally the internal logic of the courts puts them in position to be a catalyst for changes broader than those that the more politically attuned branches would make on their own initiative. "Given their insulation from the political process in a way that legislatures and agencies are not, the courts constitute a governmental institution that engages in a comparatively more 'evenhanded' type of decision making than these other institutions," writes Benjamin Superfine in summarizing some of the literature on court-driven reform of educational governance. "As such, the courts have been hailed as an institution more willing and able to overcome political inertia or resistance than federal or state legislatures to restructure the public school system to protect the rights of underrepresented student groups."[13] The U.S. Supreme Court's decision in *Brown v. Board of Education* is the classical case in point. There are those who argue that its singularity and impact have been overstated—that the decision was not the sharp break with dominant values, traditions, and politics that commonly is portrayed, and that its impact on public education was severely attenuated by the political backlash it set in motion—but the very fact and intensity of the subsequent resistance strongly supports the view that the court stepped outside and beyond the prevailing winds and helped to create a new political climate.[14] Immediately after the *Brown I* decision, more than 80 percent of southerners thought the decision was wrong; by 1994 that number had fallen to only 15 percent.[15]

In retrospect, the case can be made that the courts played a catalytic role in sparking the end of exceptionalism in American education. Although reluctantly and against the grain of their normal deference to precedent and wariness of proactive policy making, courts have featured prominently as catalysts for the emergence of stronger executive leadership. They did this by challenging and diminishing the traditional role of local school boards, by helping to push education decision making up the ladder of federalism to the state and national levels where school-specific institutions were never as strong as locally, and, somewhat paradoxically, by making the minefields of race and class politics somewhat less treacherous for risk-averse politicians.

In this section, I argue these points. First, compared to the legislative and executive branches, the buffered role of the courts enabled them to grapple more readily with political hot potatoes, sometimes making them the lead institution in encroaching on localized, school-specific institutions. Second, despite judicial deference to localism, legislatures, and professionalism—deference that made the courts' inroads tentative and often incomplete—the dynamics of enforcement frequently drew the courts deeper into more direct and prescriptive involvement with core education activities. Third, the courts' direct intervention in education is likely self-limiting, so its long-term influence may prove to be a time-specific and more indirect one of clearing the way for more and continued involvement by the other branches of general-purpose government. Fourth, in particular, by absorbing some of the political cost of tackling political hot-potato issues dealing with race and class, the courts helped clear the way for general-purpose elected officials to enter an arena that they had previously regarded warily despite the substantial resources potentially in play.

First In, with Deference

The Supreme Court's dramatic decisions in *Brown* (*I* and *II*) are widely known and thoroughly analyzed. So have been the repercussions as the federal courts gradually moved their attention from the stark segregation that had characterized southern states with dual school systems to the North, where the line between de jure and de facto segregations was less sharply etched.[16] By pulling a reluctant federal government deeper into the whirlpool of education policy, judicial grappling with school desegregation helped reshape the institutional boundaries of federalism. But less well considered is the role the courts thereby played in eroding school-specific arenas across all levels of government.

In taking on school segregation, the judiciary, a general-purpose institution, came head-to-head with school districts. Local responses varied—from tooth-and-nail resistance, through resigned accommodation, to constructive and willing embrace—but districts' legitimacy and power were dented overall.[17] In the extreme cases, the courts literally displaced the districts, directly issuing orders or appointing special masters to gather information, shape remedies, and oversee implementation.[18] Even when they did not get quite so directly involved themselves, the effect of the courts' efforts was to push decisions further up the ladder of federalism and into general-purpose arenas like state legislatures or Congress: "As courts assert their legal authority in this fashion to leverage desegregation, they centralize the power to make decisions about equal educational opportunity in institutions that are sometimes geographically and institutionally distant from local levels where this change is to occur."[19]

Americans famously find it difficult to talk openly about race, preferring, when possible, to shift the dialogue to things like personal attributes, or poverty, or generic diversity.[20] So, to counteract that, let me be direct: racial prejudice and racial inequality have been extremely potent forces in American political history; perhaps no other issues have sparked the intensity of conflict, rage, and resentment. While racial politics is not at all restricted to education policies, schools and school policy have been the focus of some of the most animated conflicts. Racial reformers have seen schools as critical tools for attacking stereotypes that stunt the developing psyches of both black and white children, poison social relationships, and perpetuate cycles of inequality. But the vulnerability and impressionable nature of children also engage fiercely protective instincts on the part of their parents. Resistance to efforts to foster integration or reallocate resources to reduce inequalities is often grounded in the straightforward protection of privilege, but parents' protective instinct to shield their children from uncertain outcomes gives that resistance a wider base and added energy. The intensity around race and schools makes for a volatile issue that elected politicians regard warily, and it is the backdrop against which the federal judiciary's intervention needs to be understood.

The sitting justices in 1954 knew they were stepping into roiling political waters. They understood that the courts had to respect boundaries that established the legislature as the institution properly responsible for making law and policy; this made them reluctant to specify precise remedial steps or even timing. They understood that the judiciary was dependent on the other branches for enforcement, and this encouraged them to find a framing on which they could issue a unanimous opinion lest others take a split decision as a sign of uncertainty and an invitation to resist in the hopes of subsequent reversal.

On fiscal equity and adequacy issues, the courts' encroachment on the turf of local school districts was less dramatic; there were no televised images of children being escorted into previously segregated school buildings by police or the National Guard. But when it comes to the relationship between general-purpose institutions and single-purpose ones, the story line was similar to that with race and segregation. When courts found their states' school funding systems violated state constitutions, they typically opted, at least at first, to defer to the legislatures to create and implement the remedies. This in and of itself pushed decision making up the ladder of federalism, both because it was in state constitutions—not local law—that the courts found the violations and because the fiscal capacity to remedy the situation demanded state leadership.[21] As with desegregation, though, iterative efforts to force compliance also drew the courts deeper into the weeds of education practice.

Richard Lehne's history of one of the earliest fiscal equity cases— New Jersey's *Robinson v. Cahill*—details the process by which deference can mutate into prescription. One line of the court's thinking represented a head-on collision with local districts. Noting social changes had made populations more mobile, the court wrote: "Problems which are in no sense local in origin have become the special burden of those who cannot find a haven elsewhere."[22] "The stunning implication," Lehne observed, "was that perhaps the whole structure of local government itself was unconstitutional."[23] As with *Brown*, the court backed away from such strong claims and divisive issues in order to build a unanimous decision. Its general strategy was to nudge and not dictate. As one justice noted: "The quality of judicial writing is one of encouraging the legislature, setting activities in motion which will have secondary consequences to lead the senators and assemblymen to act . . . We can encourage the legislature to pass laws or taxes without directing them to do that."[24]

When it came to enacting the legislation that would be needed—in particular, approving a state income tax that the governor argued would be the best approach for redressing the state's reliance on property taxes—the legislature balked. Politically ambitious legislators had little incentive to be helpful. "One of the most insightful students of the New Jersey senate argues that the best way to understand the senate's actions," Lehne writes, "is to recognize that, when each senator looks in the mirror each morning, the senator says, 'Good morning, Governor—I mean, Senator.'"[25] Supporting a sitting governor under some circumstances is advantageous for an ambitious legislator in the same party, but that's much less likely when doing so requires voting for new taxes that will be highly controversial among active voters in the legislator's own district. The legislature, from 1973 to 1976, "seized every conceivable justification to postpone action" to solve the funding issue. "Finally, the patience of the New Jersey Supreme Court ran out," and in May 1976 it decided (its seventh decision in the case) that unless the legislature acted, by July 1, in a way the court felt resolved the unconstitutional financing system still in place, it would bar any public officials at any level of state or local government from spending any funds for the support of public schools—threatening, effectively, to close the system down. The legislature blinked; after missing the deadline by a little over a week—and forcing the court to go through with its order—it finally enacted a financial reform bill that created a state income tax and took an initial step toward reducing spending disparities.[26]

What had begun with judicial deference in both racial and fiscal matters ended with direct showdowns in which judges became increasingly assertive and increasingly involved. These early decisions involved important issues about enrollment and funding, but still left the core aspects of the education enterprise largely in the hands of local districts where the requisite expertise and democratic roots were presumed to lie. Yet currents continued to draw courts deeper into the specifics.

Drawn Deeper into the Core

From the time Federal Judge W. Arthur Garrity Jr. ordered the Boston schools to desegregate 18 months ago, many of the city's whites—especially in South Boston—have been fighting a tenacious rear-guard action against the ruling. Last week, after hearing black students at South

Boston High School testify that they had been beaten by white students and ignored by white teachers, Garrity's patience was at an end. He stripped the all-white School Committee of its control over "Southie," the city's racial trouble spot, and placed the school in federal receivership. He also ordered Southie Headmaster William Reid, its other administrators and Coach Arthur Perdigao transferred to some other school. (*Time* magazine, December 22, 1975)[27]

Although personally cautious and apparently reluctant to get deeply involved in the specifics of remedies, in addressing what was initially seen as a matter of who attended which of Boston's public schools, Judge Garrity ultimately was forced to deal with issues like magnet schools, community schools, parent participation, school funding, school closings, in-school teacher planning time, and racial biases in teacher hiring and firing.[28]

Direct takeovers were the extreme weapon in the judiciary's arsenal for enforcing its remedies. But even when courts stopped short of this, they often found themselves pulled into issues closer to the core of the educational enterprise than they likely envisioned. While critics often portrayed this as a dynamic driven by power-hungry judges (Garrity, for example, was the subject of numerous death threats and at least two aborted attempts on his life), it was usually in response to plaintiffs' further requests or defendants' resistance that courts were induced to get further involved in the specifics.[29] Even analysts who are critical of what they see as judicial overreaching acknowledge that the expansion of the courts' involvement often was reluctant and in some senses forced upon them. In a book that focuses on judicial interventions generally—including but not limited to desegregation of the schools—Ross Sandler and David Schoebrod note a recurring tendency: "Ongoing resistance to compliance with the law forced federal judges to undertake the policy-making work of school boards and, later, prison wardens . . . Understandably, the judges wanted the institutions under them to become not only legal but *better*."[30] "It made little sense to integrate school buildings but then allow administrators to resegregate classrooms through their decisions on tracking," R. Shep Melnick observes.

Were too many minority students being assigned to special education classes? Were they receiving harsher punishments and more frequent suspensions? Were they being excluded from extracurricular activities? Were minority students who spoke languages other than English being left behind? Given the track record of southern schools and the growing evidence that school officials in the north, too, had engaged in systematic racial discrimination, there seemed little reason for judges to rely on the good faith of school officials.[31]

Similar dynamics have applied in school finance cases. Unlike in cases involving racial discrimination, cases involving economic inequality have been the province of state rather than federal courts. The U.S. Supreme Court, in 1973, held that education was not a fundamental interest protected by the U.S. Constitution: challenges to unequal or inadequate funding would have to be pursued at the state level.[32] Superfine, in reviewing the relevant literature, notes that while court rulings in school finance cases "have traditionally issued vague orders or guidelines to state legislatures," a handful have "issued sets of rather precise orders about how to restructure funding across local districts," and over the last two decades several courts have moved beyond issues of funding to consider "precise types of resources that additional funding can buy, such as qualified teachers and staff, school supplies, facilities repairs, and lower student-teacher ratios."[33] In some states, courts have "specifically ordered funds to be used for the implementation of standards-based accountability systems, class size reduction programs, whole school reforms, and free pre-school programs for 'at-risk' students."[34]

While some judges restrict themselves to doing nothing more than kicking the problem to legislatures, others often find they must work with legislatures and executives to specify the details of remedies. Such collaboration on policy specification evokes alarm from those who fear that the courts are stepping outside their proper role and beyond their level of competence. James Q. Wilson, for example, highlights the risks if courts substitute their judgment for agencies that not only have more technical knowledge but also, he suggests, more appreciation for the complexities of implementation involving multiple actors in differing contexts. Discussing judicial intervention in air quality, he observes:

"When the courts stepped into this extraordinarily complex, decentralized and changing enforcement environment, they did it with all the finesse and grace of a two-ton rhinoceros."[35]

The transition from cases framed around equity to those framed around adequacy brought first the court, and then legislatures and executives, even deeper into the educational core. The decision by plaintiffs' attorneys to shift to an adequacy framing was driven by legal strategy and wording in state constitutions.[36] When courts had ruled against states based on equity grounds, remedies naturally focused on the amount and distribution of funds and taxing burdens: shifting around money did not require the courts to look at all deeply into what local districts did with the money once it was in their hands. Decisions based on adequacy provisions, however, led almost inevitably to considerations of what *adequacy*—the provision of a "sound basic education" in the words of some state constitutions—implied. Putting flesh on this concept of adequate education is difficult without taking a stance on matters that traditionally were considered the province of education specialists: what competencies can and should schools provide to their students? What are children able to learn? What level of competency is realistic and sufficient?

Also important, but less frequently noted, is the growing tendency for courts to get drawn into the nitty-gritty process of political coalition building. When they deal with contentious issues like those of race and class, judges can find that they need to work not only with formal policy makers but also with allies in the nongovernmental sector if their remedies are to have a chance to take hold.[37] That courts get drawn into relationships with advocacy groups and other nongovernmental leaders strikes some as equally or more problematic than their involvement in shaping policy details. But others see the capacity of courts to straddle the worlds of abstract principle and pluralistic politics as a positive development. Michael Rebell and Arthur Block studied the way courts handled a range of constitutional issues in education, involving regulations of student speech, staff rights, handicapped students, curriculum, and school finance. They concluded that "courts operate in a fashion that is more political than the role contemplated under the traditional model of court adjudication, but less political and more 'rational' than the decision-making processes of legislative bodies." The result is that "courts have been able to employ the full panoply of resources available to the litigants themselves in fashioning and implementing policy reforms."[38]

SELF-LIMITED BUT CATALYTIC

The institutional characteristics that occasionally make judges the first branch of government to take on politically ticklish issues do not ensure that they will continue to play a leadership role. The priority given to precedent, norms of deference to elected leadership, and a politically policed pressure on courts not to stray too far into the realm of policy making all serve as countervailing forces that tend to pull the courts back from a sustained leadership role. In addition, the courts are simply less well suited than the other branches to handle the intricacies of implementing remedies that require technical know-how about teaching and learning, or to handle the construction of sustainable political constituencies needed to ensure that reforms do not backslide. This is the argument made by Neil Komesar, Rebell, and others who approach the question of what courts can and should do from the perspective of comparative institutional advantage. "Clearly, the courts' principled approach to issues and their long-term staying power are essential for providing continuing guidance on constitutional requirements and sustained commitment to meeting constitutional goals," writes Rebell. But other general-purpose institutions have an advantage when solutions require that competing interests engage in mutual adjustment, in fashioning specific policies though broad political compromise, and in constructing supportive coalitions. "Legislatures . . . are better equipped to develop specific reform policies, and executive agencies are most effective in undertaking the day-to-day implementation tasks of 'explaining what is required, why it is required and how it can be done well, and then checking that districts can and do carry out those requirements.'"[39]

In the long run—and precisely because its own involvement may be self-limiting—the more important consequence of the courts' role may be an indirect one related to its effects on legislatures and elected executives. When judicial action induces greater involvement by other general-purpose governance institutions, this too constitutes support for the end-of-exceptionalism thesis. By helping to cool down—if not necessarily solve—the inflammation around the thorn of race and integration, the courts cleared the way for general-purpose elected officials to enter an arena that they had regarded warily despite the substantial resources potentially in play. By handing down school finance decisions that increased state budgetary investment in education, the courts provided legislatures and governors more incentive to get involved, and by focusing attention on the concept of educational adequacy, may have drawn legislatures and governors deeper into the weeds of curriculum, instruction, and measurement.

Making It Safe for Elected General-Purpose Politicians to Swim in Strong Currents

General-purpose politicians had incentives to take positions on education long before the contemporary school reform era. Political scientist David Mayhew and others argue that elected officials typically seek to control jobs and money, because these are the goodies that they can distribute to constituents in ways that build support and increase their prospects for reelection.[40] Mayhew refers to this behavior of rational politicians as *credit claiming*, situating themselves so they can share in the glow when things are going well.[41] The K–12 education sector generates about $600 billion per year; the jobs and contracts represented there add up to quite a lot of credit to claim.[42] That general-purpose politicians would be content to leave this in the hands of single-purpose (i.e., school-specific) institutions presents a puzzle.

But Mayhew also identifies *blame avoidance*, the flip side of credit claiming, as a motivation for elected officials. And blame avoidance gives general-purpose legislators an incentive to steer clear of education issues that are politically explosive. When the business community and civic groups complain to general-purpose political leaders about the mediocre performance of American schools, there are two options open. They can roll up their sleeves and take charge, arguing that "if people are going to hold me accountable for schools, then I'd better make darn sure I know what is going on there and that I've got the institutional leverage to bring about needed change." Alternatively, they can shrug and say, "Hey, the schools are not my affair. Go talk to the school board" (or superintendent or state board of education). General-purpose politicians claim larger constituencies and generally stronger power and standing than do school boards, superintendents, or other education-specific administrators and agencies. Had they made aggressive efforts to wrest control of the money and patronage in the K–12 system, it seems likely that we would have seen earlier evidence of the erosion of school-specific institutions, or at the very least some high-profile and politically bloody battles in the efforts to do so. Rather than deference to tradition or reticence to cross swords with iron triangles protecting the status quo, the standard politicians' impulse to expand their range of control may have been checked by the equally powerful disincentive to take on the political hot potatoes of race, class, religion, and local control that often swirled around schools.

Such value-based arenas and the "culture wars" they episodically endure are threatening to sitting politicians because competing sides imbue their positions with a moral fervor that makes them resistant to compromise.[43] Nice as it may be for legislators to report to constituents that they have delivered the bacon (or political pork projects, as it were), there are some risks not worth the taking. Incumbents have substantial advantages in reelection battles. They are in greater danger of being challenged because they do something that sets off a trip wire of anger than because of what they fail to do out of caution.[44]

Race in particular was a deterrent. As discussed in the previous chapter, even when they wanted to, elected executives could not venture into school-quality issues without it being interpreted within the polarizing context of race, desegregation, and states' rights. But tackling class is no political picnic either. Governors interested in promoting funding equity would have to stare down powerful suburban interests and shrug off the lesson of New Jersey Governor James Florio. Florio attempted to get out ahead of the courts on the equity issue; while he succeeded in getting equity-oriented legislation into law, the political backlash almost unseated fellow Democrat and Senator Bill Bradley, led to the subsequent defeat of many legislators who supported him and helped turn the legislature over to Republican control, and in 1993 contributed substantially to his defeat at the hands of Christine Todd Whitman.

At the local level, Howell Baum, writing about Baltimore, details the cultural and ideological forces that led even liberal groups and leaders to shy away from talking about race. William Donald Schaefer, that city's longtime mayor, directly refused to deal with issues of school desegregation because, as he put it, "immediately the question of race comes in."[45] Although Baltimore mayors had strong formal power over education, predating the contemporary movement to return to mayoral control, Schaefer gave them little attention, preferring instead to build his regime around urban redevelopment.[46] Urban mayors who directly took on school issues often paid a political price. Early in 1968, New York City Mayor John Lindsay was widely popular and seen as a strong contender for national office; by the end of the year, after his involvement with efforts to promote community control of schools got wrapped up in divisive racial politics, his reputation and political future were badly bruised.[47] Schaefer, who, as noted, built his Baltimore regime around downtown urban development, served four terms as mayor and then went on to be elected governor of Maryland. Kurt Schmoke, who succeeded him, was an African American who made education reform a central theme of his campaigns and his administration. Despite Schmoke's many early successes, poor test score performance and controversies—including over his efforts to privatize the management of some public schools—culminated in intervention by the state, weakening his position and likely contributing to his decision to step out of public office in 1999.

Judicial intervention could hardly be said to have "solved" the tough issues of race and equity, but by bringing them out in the open and by absorbing some of the body blows associated with impinging on local school board control, they arguably made it safer for both elected executives and legislatures to venture into the waters of school reform. That elected politicians are venturing more confidently into the territory of education policy—executives as discussed previously and legislatures as discussed shortly—is not only because they have new reasons to do so, but also because the courts have eliminated some of the longstanding obstacles and provided a measure of "political cover" to their doing so.

LEGISLATURES ENGAGED: CONGRESS, STATE LEGISLATURES, AND CITY COUNCILS

Presidents, governors, and mayors can claim the bully pulpit, and compared to any single legislator typically have a much easier time driving the public agenda. If the changing landscape of American education constitutes a broad reassertion of general-purpose governance, as I am suggesting, that should be evidenced by increased activity by Congress, state legislatures, and city councils as well as by the men and women at the head of the executive branch or those who sit on the courts. As general-purpose institutions, legislatures share certain characteristics with executives and the courts that differentiate them from school-specific units like school boards. Like executives and courts, legislatures have a broad portfolio of responsibilities, so the agenda status of education is not ensured; like executives, they have more control than the courts in setting their agenda, and therefore have more discretion to duck education issues when they are controversial and more ways in which to symbolically posture as education supporters when the issues are consensual.

But legislatures have a distinct set of motives, operating procedures, and capacity that may also come to bear in education policy making. As a result, the policy agenda that emerges from the interplay among the branches will be shaped by more than one vision, and the education policies enacted and implemented will bear the fingerprints of more than one pair of hands.

One difference has to do with the spatial alignment of the electoral districts that define their constituencies. Legislators typically are elected from smaller geographical areas than are the chief executives at the level of government in which they operate. Congressional districts, state legislative districts, and city council districts frequently align closely with the boundaries of individual school districts. To the extent that spatial boundaries capture local demographics and values, general-purpose legislatures at the national and state levels might be pulled in directions that are more similar to those of local school boards than those of the president or governor. At the state and national levels, more narrowly defined geographical loyalties mean, too, that many legislators may be more attuned to suburban or rural constituencies than are governors and residents who count central city schools and communities as important groups toward whose interests they must attend.

At the local level, the story may be more complicated. City council members who run in at-large elections face a geographically defined constituency that is the same as that of mayors, while ward-based council members might be pulled toward constituencies that are more neighborhood-based and more likely to define their interests around a subset of local schools.[48] Accordingly, in some instances legislators might align with school boards against education presidents or education governors—on particular issues or conceivably in protecting their institutional authority.

The electoral coalitions that keep legislators in office may differ from those constructed by executives in other ways than by virtue of differences in the spatial configuration of their electoral base. Large, locally based, and well-resourced interests are unlikely to focus exclusively on one branch versus the other, but smaller ones and those that may have a narrower and shorter-term stake in a particular policy or contract may find it rational to specialize. And some sorts of interest groups may be more aligned with the outlook and priorities of education executives than with legislatures who tend to be more protective of longstanding local constituencies. At the local level, for example, national foundations and national providers of education and education services have found mayors to be more accessible, often, than either city council or school board members, who rely more on unions, local nonprofits, state and local parties, and community-based organizations when it comes time to generate campaign funds and get out their vote. Consider a case where a governor, hoping to position the state as a reform leader, challenges teacher unions by threatening to radically restructure their benefit plans; school boards, often firmly aligned with unions that have disproportionate power in their election, are a likely source of resistance, but they will have a greater chance of success if they have allies within state legislatures.

In addition to differences in orientation, legislatures may differ in capacity and expertise. While legislators collectively must be generalists, some individual legislators and committees have deep, issue-specific expertise and responsibility. The internal committee structure of legislatures may allow them to play a steadier role in the education policy process than executives, whose attention to education may be short-lived because of competing demands and the need to jump, at times, from issue to issue to put out unexpected fires.

The Education Congress

President Lyndon Johnson may have been the first to say that he wanted to be known as the "education president," but count him also among those who realized that the national government's ramped-up responsibility extended beyond the White House.[49] In praising Congress for passing the Higher Education Facilities Bill, Johnson labeled it the "Education Congress" on December 10, 1963.[50]

When it comes to national policy initiatives in education, two events stand out: the initial passage of the Elementary and Secondary Education Act (ESEA) in 1965 and its later reauthorization as the No Child Left Behind Act (NCLB) in 2001. The dominating narrative in both cases focuses on executive leadership, and clearly both Johnson and George W. Bush were important factors in publicly framing the issues, in giving them high priority, and in helping to leverage the necessary votes. In both cases, however, there is a counternarrative in which legislatures loom large.

Johnson and the White House made the passage of ESEA their highest priority following the 1964 election. White House strategists deliberately framed the education bill as an extension of the War on Poverty as a way to push into the background two controversial issues that had bedeviled federal education policy efforts previously: states' rights as tied to race and desegregation, and funding for schools as it intersected with the question of religion and separation of church and state.[51] And the president's legendary phone calls, featuring sweet talk and arm twisting, clearly were important. But also important was the fact that the 1964 election had given Johnson better than a two-thirds majority to work with in both the Senate and House. Nor did White House strategizing and arm twisting bowl over a passive and accommodating Congress; some of the specific components, including the shape of the allocation formula—which spread the funding broadly rather than concentrating it where the need was greatest—and the general lack of specificity about how the funding should be used were crafted precisely to win sectors of congressional support.

Congress was at least as critical to the crafting of NCLB. The original Bush proposal was not a fleshed-out bill, but rather a thirty-page blueprint that pulled together various proposals that had come before and were known to have some built-in support. The administration was anxious to garner broad bipartisan support, and in order to get that it relied on bargaining on the Hill to shape key provisions. To bring in Democrats like Senator Edward Kennedy, for example, it was necessary to raise the envisioned amount of federal spending and drop the initial plan for vouchers. Congress worked through issues—for example, by dropping the highly controversial plan to include vouchers that could be used to send children to private schools in exchange for the less unsettling provision requiring failing schools to offer students supplemental educational services that could be delivered by private providers. The provision that teachers be "highly qualified" is another example of the powerful role of Congress in putting flesh on the bare bones of the original White House proposal. The latter "said nothing about highly qualified teachers," Paul Manna observes. "These provisions became part of the law during the legislative process as administration officials negotiated with congressional leaders, especially Democratic representative George Miller."[52] Though NCLB came to be seen as a "Bush law . . . the reality is that the final bill's 681 finely printed pages were filled with a tangled assemblage of Bush administration proposals, New Democrat proposals drawn from reforms crafted during the Clinton administration, liberal ideas put forth by leading Democrats like Kennedy and Miller and proposals and cautions introduced by countless other constituencies."[53]

Nuanced differences among the Republicans in Congress were important as well. Republican Bill Goodling, who had chaired the House Education and Workforce Committee, retired and was replaced by the more conservative John Boehner. Goodling's history of working across the party aisle on the face of it might have made him more likely than Boehner to carry the water on the White House initiatives, especially as those had to be renegotiated to build bipartisan support. Boehner had been a strong supporter of school choice, including private school vouchers. Yet, as Elizabeth DeBray's account suggests, Goodling—who had been a teacher, principal, and superintendent and spent twenty years on the relevant House committee—had deeply held views of his own, while Boehner, "who had worked mostly on labor issues and workforce issues and had not been very involved in education issues on the committee," proved more willing than expected to adopt and push through the president's agenda.[54] Regardless of whether one thinks it diluted or strengthened the policy that emerged, there is little question that Congress had its fingerprints all over the final product.[55]

In the previous chapter, I presented evidence of growing presidential involvement based on the extent to which education was emphasized in State of the Union speeches. Figure 3.1 presents a comparable measure of congressional attention to education drawn from the same Policy Agendas Project data. From 1946 to 2008, the Agendas database has coded over 65,500 congressional hearings, of which 1,549 dealt with

FIGURE 3.1

Relative attention to education

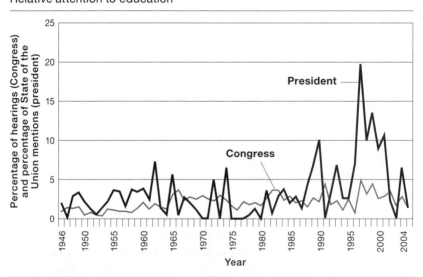

Source: Derived from the Policy Agendas Project, www.policyagendas.org.

some dimension of education as their major topic. The figure shows the relative attention paid to education by presidents (as percentages of quasi-sentences in State of the Union speeches) to the percentage of congressional hearings focused on education.

Several observations are warranted. First, as with the presidents, Congress shows increased attention to education as a percentage of its agenda. From 1946 through 1979, 1.64 percent of congressional hearings dealt with education; from 1980 through 2005, this number rose to 2.6 percent.

Second, Congress overall has been steadier and less erratic in its allocation of attention to education. Talk is cheap, so it is perhaps not surprising that presidential mentions of education can fluctuate more wildly and spike on occasion as they did in 1981 and in 1997 through 2001. A president who decides to emphasize an education issue can use a lot of sentences to do so, and some presidents accommodate this just by talking at greater length. Organizing a hearing is a more substantial undertaking, which makes it less likely that Congress will careen about from issue to issue. Also, and importantly, both the House and the Senate have committees for which education is a major part of their responsibility. Because these committees have other responsibilities besides public education, they are free to devote their time and attention elsewhere, but institutionally they represent what might be considered a more hospitable venue for educational enthusiasms to take root. Over 125 committees or special commissions are listed as having held hearings during this time period. Over the time period, 71.7 percent of the hearings dealing with education were held by either of the two primary education-focused committees: the House Committee on Education and the Workforce or the Senate Committee on Health, Education, Labor, and Pensions.[56] The other 28.3 percent were spread among forty-four committees. Chapter 4 will include a closer look at committees as decision-making venues and probe whether the two primary education committees are less hospitable to new interests and ideas than those that deal with education only occasionally.

Third, Congress is not just the tail on the dog. The late 1990s spike in presidential emphasis on education is probably the most prominent feature in the figure, but in many years Congress is devoting proportionally more attention to education than the president. There are three rather distinct periods in terms of the relative primacy put on education by the two institutions. Presidents gave greater emphasis to education in sixteen out of the seventeen years from 1946 to 1962. From 1963 to 1987, however, the relative emphasis shifted, with Congress giving a higher proportional emphasis to education in eighteen out of twenty-five years. After 1987, the scales tipped back to the president who placed a higher agenda priority on education in fourteen of those eighteen years. Congressional and presidential attention likely interact, feeding and responding directly to each other and also indirectly through the media, which may pick up and amplify their activities.

Education State Legislatures

When it comes to media and public attention, compared to other decision-making units within our federal system, state legislatures are something of a black hole. It's long been recognized that legislatures in general make less compelling focal points for media than do mayors, governors, or presidents. Narratives about individuals are easier to research and to relate than are stories about multiheaded complex institutions. But the structure of media contributes to making state legislatures even more mysterious than their counterparts at either the national or local level. In both television and print, the major media are institutionally focused around either a national or local orientation. States are less natural markets, state capitols are often less attractive for journalists to camp out in, and the issues state legislatures deal with often lack both the big drama of Congress and the immediacy of a city council decision that affects a particular neighborhood.[57]

But state legislatures have not been passive bystanders or simple rubber stamps of gubernatorial agendas any more than Congress has been so to the White House. Charter schools arguably are the most commented-upon change in the landscape of public education over the past two decades. While some governors were important early supporters, and while White House support from Clinton through Bush and Obama has added wind to the charter movement's sails, much of the entrepreneurial energy that led to the quick spread of charters was mobilized by state legislative champions.[58] Even when governors took the early lead, legislatures have been the focus of subsequent amendments that have reshaped the balance between decentralization and accountability as states have wrestled with the difference between abstract theories of market choice and the pragmatic realities and political crosscurrents once the programs begin to take root.

High-profile cases like charter schools are important and illuminating but capture only a narrow slice of the involvement of state legislatures in education. To get a broader sense of legislative activity regarding education, I compiled a data set of 12,443 laws dealing with prekindergarten through high schools and enacted from 1994 through 2009.[59] Population size is the strongest predictor of the amount of legislative activity, by itself accounting for about 24 percent of the cross-state variance. Some of the more active states are larger, urban ones like California and Illinois; some of the least active are small and rural (e.g., Alaska, Nebraska). But others are more active (e.g., Arkansas, Louisiana, Virginia) or less active (Pennsylvania, Massachusetts, New York) than would be predicted by their size alone.[60]

Figure 3.2 summarizes the proportional breakdown of these laws by fifteen issue types, further grouped into three broad and rough categories.

The largest category (42 percent overall) consists of what I label "school-focused reforms." These are levers for change that have been high on the agenda of the contemporary reform movement, including emphasis on standards and excellence, choice, and technology. The subcategories are identified on the figure by issue labels that are underlined, and include bills dealing with curriculum and teaching, accountability and standards, choice (including public school choice, magnets, charters, private schools, and homeschooling), the federal government (bills specifically responding to federal initiatives), and educational technology.[61] The second largest category (38 percent), with issue labels in bold text, comprises bills addressing basic "operational" elements of education systems, including a broad category for logistics/facilities/grade level, safety, finance, and governance. These matters have less to do with ideas about improving education than with the nitty-gritty aspects of keeping the system running and well organized. The third category (18 percent), with label text italicized, comprises legislation that identifies a

FIGURE 3.2

State Education-related Legislation, 1994–2009

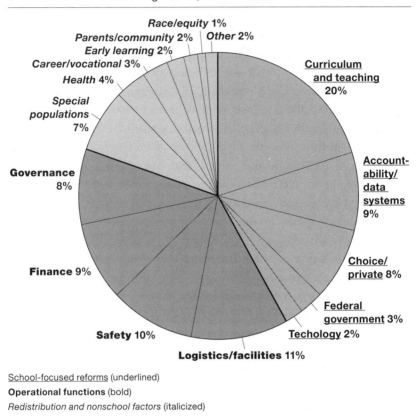

School-focused reforms (underlined)
Operational functions (bold)
Redistribution and nonschool factors (italicized)

specific target population (special populations, career/vocational, race/
equity) generally associated with redistributive efforts or those focusing
on nonschool factors (health, early childhood, parents and community).
This last set roughly identifies the bills that are potentially more reflective of the concerns of groups—such as the Broader Bolder Approach
to Education—that argue that narrowing educational achievement gaps
requires attention to nonschool factors including concentrated poverty,
segregation, school-readiness, public health, and parent and community
engagement.[62]

The substantial attention of state legislatures to school-focused reform issues and to core aspects of education such as curriculum and teaching reinforces the argument that general-purpose institutions are playing a significant role. There is a conventional image of state legislatures as relatively disengaged from education, content to delegate tough issues to the local level, hypersensitive about taking on core issues of instruction and ill-equipped to do so even if willing, and historically deferring on many issues to the seeming expertise of education professionals and, since *A Nation at Risk,* to strong governors. That image is overly generalized and part caricature, but to the extent that it captures what was once a common tendency it appears to be out-of-date. A familiar automobile commercial has the tag line "This is not your father's Cadillac." The legislatures seen here are not your father's legislatures.

Figure 3.3 presents the trend across the three broad types of issues from 1994 through 2009.

The sharp increase in school-focused reform bills from 1994 through 1997 was driven by two sets of issues, those dealing with curriculum

FIGURE 3.3

Types of state legislative activity, 1994–2009

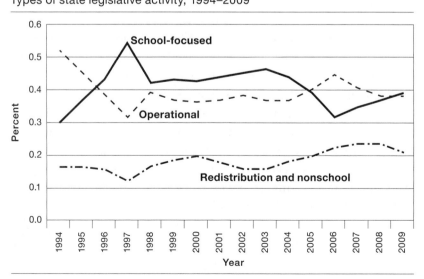

and those dealing with accountability, both of which increased sharply during this period.[63] Some analysts have been critical of the tendency for reform efforts to focus on symbolic or superficial activities that create the appearance that government is taking education seriously but leave the core elements—those that might have the most direct effect on learning—relatively untouched.[64] But curriculum and teaching was the second most common focus in 1994 and 1995 (following safety), and then the most common every year afterward and overall. Accountability and choice, two of the more controversial of the reform themes in this category, were consistently among the most common foci, although somewhat less so in recent years. There was a flurry of state legislation that attended to federal initiatives during the five years following the signing of No Child Left Behind; this is perhaps predictable, although the subsequent trailing off of attention to federal initiatives is a bit surprising. Although there has been a lot of attention in the media and among scholars to the potential for educational technology to revolutionize the delivery of instruction, state legislatures do not seem to have caught this particular bug to date.[65]

Much of the state legislative agenda focuses not on high-profile national debates, but rather on practical operational issues. Legislatures are more likely to spend time on nuts-and-bolts operational matters than executives who have—and take advantage of—the freedom to concentrate on higher-profile concerns. Logistics and facilities is the largest issue cluster within this category; it includes legislation focused on high school, attendance, scheduling and calendars, organization, logistics, sports and physical education, facilities, kindergarten, personnel, and grade configurations for middle school. The 1994–1997 decline in the relative attention to operational issues is accounted for almost entirely by a sharp decrease in the prominence of safety-related bills. In 1994 these safety concerns occupied 24 percent of all state legislative activity, falling steadily to 8 percent in 1998 and leveling out at about that degree of attention since. At times, school finance can be a high-profile, politically contentious issue, associated with more redistributive efforts to redress funding inequities across districts. For the most part, though, the bills in this grouping have to do with the kinds of steady, ever-present financing responsibilities that do not normally get much attention, and over the time period finance-related bills have accounted for fewer than 10 percent of the states' legislative agendas.

Strikingly less attended by state legislatures during these years are issues relating to high-need populations and nonschool factors. The most notable exception is special needs populations, which includes bills focused on at-risk students, special education, corrections education, alternative education, gifted and talented, migrant education, and military education. Overall, these account for just under 40 percent of the bills in this category and 7.3 percent of the states' legislative agenda overall. The higher levels of activity seen here may reflect the fact that some segments of the special needs population are represented by unusually well-organized and attentive interest groups, and that federal regulations and funding mandate or strongly incentivize states to attend to them. While attention to special populations makes up the largest set of bills within this category over the entire period, it has been becoming gradually a little less prominent, with health and career/vocational bills taking up a bit more attention. Race and parent and community engagement—issues that were prominent on the national agenda in the 1960s and 1970s and that remain as points of contestation at the local level—barely register as direct foci of state legislatures during this time period.

Although there are some ebbs and flows and some shifts in relative attention over time, state legislative attention across the fifteen issue areas and the three broader categories has been steady and consistent. As we saw in comparing Congress to the presidency, legislatures may be less disrupted by short-term and evanescent concerns—steadier workhorses compared to the higher-profile education governors. Simple activity, of course, is not necessarily an indicator of serious engagement; a single well-crafted, far-reaching piece of legislation could have more influence than a scattershot of minor bills. As at the national level, though, the extent and kind of legislative involvement is indicative of the fact that it is not just the executive branch that is actively involved. Legislative activity at the state level is associated with what is happening nationally; prior to NCLB (1994–2001) states averaged 10.2 bills per year, while afterward (2002–2008) that number almost doubled to 21.6.

Education City Councils

The education literature these days has lots to say about mayoral control of schools, but almost nothing to say about city councils. That would make sense if mayoral control were primarily an exercise of heroic leadership or if it were a manifestation of the growing importance of executive leadership. But city councils have not been idle spectators. As mayors have asserted themselves, in at least some cities and under some conditions city councils have found themselves further drawn into the education policy arena as well.

The momentum toward mayoral control, as we saw in the previous chapter, is partly driven by the push away from elected school boards. School boards are "an aberration," the Fordham Foundation's Chester Finn commented in discussing a school governance crisis in Pittsburgh. They are "an anachronism, an educational sinkhole."[66] But many of the arguments offered about the limitations of school boards could easily be read as veiled criticisms of legislatures generally. City councils share many characteristics with school boards. As with school boards, their members are often elected by ward, potentially leading them to put neighborhood concerns above those of the city as a whole. Also as with school boards, their election often depends on party support, potentially making council members hostile to proposals that impinge on the perceived interests of key groups within their party's core constituencies. Like school board members, city council members can be hypersensitive to the particularistic pleadings of groups or even individuals within their electoral district, inducing them to engage in micromanagement—to try to help a family move its child to a different school; to get involved with the design of new schools or additions—rather than restrict themselves to broad policy. And if some of the pull toward mayoral control is based on the advantages of having a single individual to hold accountable, city council involvement, like that of school boards, has the disadvantage of diffusing responsibility and thereby obscuring it so that dissatisfied citizens are left uncertain whom to blame.

At the same time, some of the characteristics of city councils might be welcomed as a moderating force on aspects of mayoral control that have been subjects of criticism. While both are general-purpose institutions, councils and mayors often differ in their electoral constituency, in ways similar to differences between state legislatures and governors. Most city councils elect at least some of their members by ward rather than citywide, and in large cities nearly half do so exclusively.[67] This puts council members into closer relationships with community-based organizations and less reliant on citywide institutions, like local media and business organizations, to mobilize their base. To the extent that mayoral control has been faulted for marginalizing community-based groups and putting parents into a generally passive role, city councils could become the counterbalance within general-purpose governance—the check on overly powerful mayors and the echo chamber for grassroots concerns that weakened school boards may no longer be able to provide.

A look at Washington, DC, and New York City, two of the highest-profile mayoral control cities, can provide some insights into the ways in which city councils are involved, either from the outset or in quick response. Because of their high profile, DC and New York City are not necessarily typical of all cities that have adopted mayoral control. Compared to places like Cleveland, Ohio, or Hartford, Connecticut, they draw tremendous attention from foundations and advocacy groups nationwide, and these outside actors contribute resources and can become significant actors in what might otherwise be political conflicts of purely local scope. To draw broad and generalizable lessons about the consequences of mayoral control, one would certainly want to study what happens in lower-visibility contexts as well, but the high-stakes maneuvering in places like DC and New York City (and other high-profile cases like Chicago and, to a somewhat lesser extent, Boston and Philadelphia) makes these critical case studies for understanding what happens when governance change intersects with the national impetus in education reform.

In both cases, mayors (Adrian Fenty in DC, and Michael Bloomberg in New York City) asked for and were granted a much stronger role, essentially marginalizing the previously responsible school boards and turning the public school system into the equivalent of other municipal agencies whose heads they appointed and who reported directly to them. In both cases, the mayors initially used their power to hire nontraditional superintendents (Michelle Rhee in DC, and Joel Klein in

New York City) who came in with big plans, no loyalties to the local bureaucracies, and no local constituencies of their own. In DC, mayoral control came in two steps; although outsiders paid little attention to the fact, the city council was involved from the beginning. In New York City, the council played no role in the institution of mayoral control and took some time to find its role and voice, but has become more vocal as a combination of missteps and lame duck status have made it politically safer to challenge the mayor.

Council involvement in the District of Columbia

On June 27, 2000, voters in the District of Columbia narrowly approved a referendum that converted what had been a thirteen-member school board, with eight members elected by ward and five at-large, to a mixed model in which five members would be elected citywide and four members appointed by the mayor.[68] The DC City Council had cleared the way four months earlier with a 7–6 vote approving the new structure pending the results of the referendum. Under the proposal, the council would have to confirm the members selected by the mayor.

Five years later, Adrian Fenty, a sitting council member, announced his candidacy for mayor. As a council member, in a March 2004 vote, Fenty had opposed sitting mayor Anthony Williams's attempt to expand even further his authority over the schools. "There is no direct correlation to the performance that comes out of the classrooms, when you look at who runs the school system, whether it's the mayor, an appointed board, or an elected board," Fenty said at the time. The problem "is probably not the governance structure. The problem probably is centered around the difficulty inherent in educating children that come up in urban environments in this country."[69] By the time of his election, in the fall of 2006, he had changed his tune. Just two weeks after his election, he announced his intention to convert the school board into an advisory panel and create a department of education; the school superintendent would report to the department head who, in turn, would report to the mayor.[70] On December 8, Fenty led a group of DC officials, including nine council members, on a fact-finding trip to New York City to meet with Mayor Bloomberg and school chancellor Joel Klein and to hear more about that city's experience with mayoral control.

As with the city's move to partial mayoral control in 2000, the city council was smack in the middle of the decision. The city council would need to approve the governance change (as would Congress because of the District of Columbia's special constitutional status as the nation's capital). Even more importantly, in the plan that Fenty ultimately offered, Fenty would propose the school budget, but the council would hold line-item veto power. Exquisitely attuned to the failures of their own institution and decision-making processes, some council members expressed concern. "What I'm still very concerned about is turning a lot of the role of the current school board over to the city council," one council member declared, apparently reflecting on the political pressures that made it hard for him and his colleagues to make tough calls such as trimming programs that had active and vocal beneficiaries. Another indicated that he did not want the schools to become "fodder in the deal making we sometimes do in the legislative process."[71] The council took its decision-making responsibility seriously, holding seven hearings comprising nearly sixty hours of testimony from local activists and politicians and well as national education leaders and academics. In April, the council approved the plan by a vote of 9–2.

It was not long at all after the council had voted to give the mayor the control he asked for that rifts began to develop between the two, however. Fenty and Michelle Rhee, the chancellor he appointed to directly oversee the District of Columbia Public Schools (DCPS), may have felt that it was their responsibility to set policy and act decisively, but council members were the targets of complaints from unhappy parents and teachers, and as the legislative body that had to approve city budgets they felt they had an institutional responsibility to be informed. The fact that Rhee often acted first and consulted later set in motion a dynamic in which the council began to assert its own authority. National and local media reports often portrayed Rhee's time in office as a story about her personal characteristics, whether told sympathetically as a profile of her indomitable commitment to bringing about needed change "for the children" or critically as a story about personal ambition and a tin ear for legitimate community and parent concerns. While personality no doubt played a role, also at play were the fundamental governance institutions that made the council, and in particular those members elected by wards, more in touch with and sensitive to grass-roots signals of discontent.

Seven months into Rhee's administration, for example, anger began to mount over her proposal to close over twenty schools and reassign the teachers. Rhee set up public hearings that she said were designed to solicit citizen input, but at the same time made statements that suggested she had already made up her mind. "I would be surprised if something comes up [at today's hearings] that I haven't already begun to make some plans around," Rhee told the *Washington Post*. "I cannot possibly take every single thing that a community member or a council member or someone says for me to do and actually enact that." To symbolize resentment against what were seen as insincere efforts on Rhee's part, two council members hosted their own "People's Meeting." With deeper roots in neighborhood-based politics, the council members were able to generate larger turnouts at their events than those at the official sessions that Rhee had declared.[72]

A month later, council members were expressing their frustration over the administration's lack of information about its budget performance and plans. "During four hours of grilling, the officials also were unable to say when they would submit an official fiscal 2008 budget or fully explain how an end-of-the-year surplus turned into a projected $100 million deficit." "We're five months into the fiscal year and there's no official budget. That makes us look bad," council member Marion Barry told the schools' chief financial officer. "That's no way to run a railroad." "We're just hard-pressed to know exactly where we are at this point," Council Chairman Vincent C. Gray (D) said.[73]

As we saw was the case with courts and legislatures, a little attention to schools led to even more need to be informed and deeply involved. The general-purpose councils found school-centered issues taking up more of their attention, affecting the resources they had to meet other demands, and becoming a frequent subject of discussion and complaint when they heard from constituents. While their role included a traditional checks-and-balances function that at times added transparency and improved democratic accountability, it also led to hands-on involvement in matters like school closings and hiring and firing, matters that some considered the rightful providence of the school administration.

In spring 2008, council members were drawn into controversy surrounding the Fenty/Rhee plans to fire nearly four hundred central-office workers. The council had explicitly granted Rhee authority to reclassify these positions, making the incumbents vulnerable to being fired, but council members expressed anger at the way the firings were carried out. Chairman Gray complained that he was informed about the firings after the fact. "Gray said Rhee visited him in his office about 90 minutes after he heard about the firings. He said she told him that the letters had to be reviewed and legal questions answered, leaving little time to inform the council. 'Her assertion was that this wasn't deliberate, and she apologized for it. It is where it is at this point,' he said."[74] A few years later, the council was even deeper in the weeds, taking a position on the administration's removal of a popular principal at the Hardy Middle School. "It is now, I think, firmly in my court," longtime Ward 2 council member Jack Evans announced in March 2011, "and it is an issue that continues to overshadow everything."[75]

In what might be seen as a culmination of the council's assertion of its own authority, its chairman, Vincent Gray, subsequently emerged as the primary challenger to Fenty's reelection, defeating him after his first term and assuming the mayoralty in January 2011.

Council involvement in New York City

The 2002 decision to give the mayor control of the system was made by the state legislature—a general-purpose institution—but the New York City Council did not have the formal role enjoyed by its counterpart in DC. Although the council went through the motion of holding its own hearings, it had neither the authority nor the political clout to alter the course of events.

Under Chancellor Joel Klein, the New York City Department of Education adopted a decision-making style that angered both parent activists and local legislators who were accustomed to having input. As in DC, electoral districts, as well as traditions of locally based political party organizations, kept both the local state legislative delegation and council members more in touch with and responsive to concerns about access in influence by community- and parent-based organizations. Klein and Bloomberg did their best to marginalize the community school districts that had provided a more decentralized governance structure for city schools for about four decades; the state legislature put a check on their efforts to eliminate them entirely, and the city council listened to the concerns from traditional school activists and often gave them a sounding board they no longer had on their own. One key council member, reflecting on the experience of the "hundreds and hundreds of parent leaders" serving on school leadership teams and community education councils, indicated that "those leaders have been shut out of the decision-making process or even true consultation," despite the fact that reigning state law seemed to give them a legitimate role. "In my opinion for the mayor and chancellor, consultation means we make the decision and we tell you later," he indicated. "We listen but the decision stays the same or we'll tweak it a bit after the fact."[76] This tension between officials responsible to the mayor and chancellor, on the one hand, and the council on the other was not just a by-product of clashing styles: it was grounded in fundamentally different visions of how education should be governed. Local legislators—council members and members of the New York City delegation to the state legislature—believed that it was their responsibility to act as a conduit between constituents and city bureaucracies. In the new department of education, they encountered an agency that took pride in ignoring their requests. "We have a rule there that we *never* give a job or assign a kid from a school based on a call from a politician," one top official said in an interview. "That drives [city council and state legislators] crazy." He characterized their expectations as being tied to the old way of doing business: "This is how it is supposed to be. 'My cousin put in her years, I think she'd make a great principal, I'd really like to have a building on this corner because . . .' That's about power. That doesn't work the same way when you have mayoral accountability, control, responsibility."[77]

During Mayor Bloomberg's first term, open clashes with the council were relatively rare and minor. The council made efforts to show it did not want to serve as a rubber stamp. In March 2004, for example, the *New York Times* reported that the council, in reply to the mayor's budget plan, was sending a message that it "is not simply adding more money for the public schools, which always get the single largest chunk of the fiscal pie." The mayor had made the end of social promotion a defining initiative; the council had other priorities. "By emphasizing smaller class sizes in the early grades, the Council is bellowing a message to the other side of City Hall, telling the mayor with all due respect that they think he is taking the wrong approach on the issue of social promotion and that they are going to put the city's money where they think his mouth ought to be."[78]

But momentum during this period remained with the administration. Partly this reflected the mayor's strong political position and brook-no-opposition governance style. Helping to smooth potential tensions, though, were the facts that the economy was growing and there was a perceived common enemy in the state. The local union, the United Federation of Teachers (UFT), was a powerful force, with the capacity to set the tenor of resistance, raising it tactically at times but also moderating it when there were openings for pragmatic deals that served members' interests. And despite Chancellor Klein's frequent chastisement of the unions, the UFT was able to negotiate quite favorable terms during most of the Bloomberg administration; salaries increased over 40 percent during his first two terms, although negotiations got tougher later.[79] The mayor joined with teachers and parents in condemning the state for inadequate educational funding for the city; their sense of being aggrieved had been legitimated by the state's highest court, which ruled in the Campaign for Fiscal Equity (CFE) case that the state had unconstitutionally underfunded the city's schools. The court eventually ruled that the state was required to spend at least $1.93 billion more per year on the city's schools, but the legislature's lassitude in responding gave all New York City residents a shared target of resentment.

A brief tussle between the council and mayor over school construction funds that the mayor initially cut from his budget was resolved in April 2005 with smiles all around. Two weeks after forty-nine council members signed a petition protesting the cuts, and two days after the council launched a grassroots campaign, the mayor relented. The mayor pointed the finger of blame at the state legislature; "Albany's failure to fulfill the obligations of the CFE lawsuit should not impact our schoolchildren," he declared in announcing his decision to restore the funds. City Councilman Robert Jackson, a frequent critic of the school system and also a lead plaintiff in the CFE case, was moved to declare their common ground: "When the executive branch and the legislative branch come together there is nothing we can't do," he said.[80] A year later, in delivering her budget address, City Council Speaker Christine Quinn took a positive tone: "As we look at neighborhoods and communities across New York, one cannot help but feel optimistic about how far we've come and where we are headed as a city. Crime is down to record lows. The unemployment rate is the lowest it's been since before 9/11 . . . We still have a long way to go, but our schools are getting better."[81]

During this period, the Bloomberg-Klein administration in some matters was able to bypass the council's budgetary oversight by relying on private funds to launch initiatives that might otherwise be controversial. They were aided in doing so by Bloomberg's own deep pockets, his close ties to the local business and philanthropic community, and the support of national education foundations that saw the city and the administration as ideal partners for implementing some of their own visions for school reform. A primary vehicle was the Fund for Public Schools, a 501(c)(3) nonprofit, which raised "more than $240 million for system-wide reforms and initiatives that support individual schools."[82] About $80 million of that amount went to support the New York City Leadership Academy, which the Bloomberg-Klein team promoted as a critical linchpin in the administration's plan to recruit and train a new cadre of principals focused on performance rather than compliance. The administration was able to use such private support as a form of venture capital, helping it to launch initiatives quickly without the normal political and bureaucratic checkpoints. Once established and marketed through extensive public relations as a success, the initiatives could be moved onto the public budget.[83]

Long-simmering council member resentments over the style of the Klein administration found a more substantive policy focus during the mayor's second term, however, and the administration's penchant for using private partners to bypass or attenuate normal budgetary oversight was one of the flashpoints. In November 2006, the council's Education Committee "grilled and berated top city education officials . . . about hundreds of millions of dollars in contracts awarded without the competitive bidding normally required of city agencies."[84] Despite the fact that the mayor generally treated the DOE as one among the many agencies reporting to him, under state law the school system retained its identity as a separate, state-authorized body, and the administration took the position that it was not subject to the rules on competitive bidding that characterized the rest of the municipal government. "There is virtually no oversight of the Department of Education's contracting practices," council member Jackson complained, "even though D.O.E. is the single largest purchaser of goods and services among city agencies."[85]

Several factors combined to bring council opposition to the mayor's school policies even more out in the open in 2008 and 2009. Two key decisions about the governance of the city and its schools stirred up a hornet's nest of discontent and weakened the perception that the mayor was too powerful to challenge; these, in turn, both increased pressure on council members to speak up and gave them confidence that if they did so there would be others protecting their backs. One was the mayor's decision to seek a third term in office. When Bloomberg first took office, an existing city statute limited him and other locally elected officials to two successive terms, but as the sand in the second-term hourglass began to run out, the mayor suddenly reversed his longstanding position in favor of term limits, calling on the city council to overturn the provisions and allow him to run for a third term.[86] He eventually won this battle, but it was a bruising one, and public opinion polls suggested that his image of being the antipolitician had been tarnished.

The second key decision involved the extension of mayoral control. Anticipating that the Bloomberg administration would be coming to a close in 2009, the state legislature had included a June 2009 sunset provision in its original legislation to create the mayoral control structures. With Bloomberg having subsequently won the right to run for a third term, the reauthorization battle took the shape of a referendum on Bloomberg's policies and style and proved to be a tougher fight than many had anticipated. Opponents focused less on eliminating mayoral control completely than on establishing checks and balances on mayoral power, forcing more transparency in decisions (including the awarding of contracts), and increasing responsiveness to parent and community organizations.

Here, too, the mayor and his allies ultimately prevailed, but at the cost of mobilizing and strengthening a range of challenging voices that opened the field for interest groups and political entrepreneurs with competing visions of how the system should be run. In December 2011, for example, the council voted 48–0 to override a Bloomberg veto of legislation it enacted to put greater controls on the administration's contracting.[87] Although perceived abuses of contracting by the New York City Department of Education played an important role, the bill had a broader scope—indicative of the body's general-purpose focus and emblematic of the ways in which the end of education exceptionalism can draw school policy into a broader, multi-issue realm.

––––––––

Presidents, governors, and mayors present the high-profile face of the end of education exceptionalism in the U.S. They command the airwaves and present a personal narrative that makes the underlying structural changes more visible and compelling. It is not the case, however, that their domination of the stage is *simply* a product of symbolism, simplification, and convenience of narrative line. When it comes to the politics of reshaping education policy, the education executives often are critical leaders who use their advantaged position to frame the issues and mobilize support. And when it comes to moving from policy to its implementation, executives as managers may play critical roles in harnessing and focusing the vast bureaucratic enterprise that oversees many of the particulars.

Yet framing the story solely in terms of executive leadership risks missing key dimensions, and can lead to misunderstandings about the likely course and consequences. I've argued in this chapter that courts and legislatures—the two other branches of general-purpose government—are substantially implicated in the end of education exceptionalism as well. This suggests that the emerging institutional landscape for decision making about school reform may be more complicated than presumed by those who portray muscular education executives as the harbingers of more rational and comprehensive education policies. It suggests a landscape in which there may be multiple access points for new ideas and multiple venues for interest groups to exploit.

CHAPTER FOUR

CHANGING ACTORS, ISSUES, AND POLICY IDEAS

O N JULY 18, 2011, President Obama hosted an education roundtable at the White House. Valerie Strauss, a regular blogger for the *Washington Post*, labeled the roundtable "unusual." "I'll give you one chance to guess who wasn't high on the guest list," she wrote. The guest list included former Secretary of State Colin Powell and his wife, a former governor, a couple of foundation presidents, and at least nine CEOs from the communications, technology, financial, and insurance worlds. Missing, Strauss was highlighting, were teachers, principals, representatives of the teacher unions, school superintendents, school board members, or universities.[1]

Governance change is not important for its own sake. It is important because it affects who has influence over what governments do and how they do it. As the walls have been breached between single-purpose education-specific and general-purpose venues, the mix of policy ideas and array of influential interest groups have shifted as well.

In the middle of the last century, education was still a largely self-contained and highly localized arena, dominated by decision makers and interest groups with intense and focused interest and expertise in public schooling. Education bureaucrats, teacher unions, elected school boards and, episodically, parent-based organizations were the featured actors. Outside of the education sector, in the meantime, the world of domestic policy was undergoing change. The 1960s through 1980s were times of substantial turmoil and reconfiguration in the way government approached a broad range of social policy issues. The old layer-cake form of federalism mutated into a marble cake as federal grants to states and localities expanded in amount and ambition.[2] Efforts to institute performance-based management at the federal level go back at least to the Nixon administration, with more systematic elements incorporated into 1980s job training programs, and with various state and local governments experimenting with performance budgeting and contracting for services across a wide range of service areas for many decades.[3] The traditional boundaries between government and civil society became blurrier as government grants to nonprofit organizations cemented them into mutual dependent partnership.[4] By the end of the period, more aggressive forms of privatization—including for-profit providers in contracting, franchising, or voucher-funded relationships—were gaining momentum.[5] What constituted rough waves of change in other social policy arenas, however, initially were felt as only minor ripples in education governance, buffered and apart as it was.

Some have attributed the relative impenetrability of the education sphere to the special power of teacher unions. After cataloguing some of the failures of American education, political scientist Terry Moe goes on to assert that the teachers "are at the heart of these problems." The National Education Association (NEA) and American Federation of Teachers (AFT) are "by far the most powerful groups in the American politics of education. No other groups are even in the same ballpark."[6] By the turn of the century, though, the teacher unions were being elbowed aside from their central role, along with other education-specific interest groups that had previously thrived. In her 2007 analysis of the changing politics of federal education policy, Elizabeth Debray-Pelot identified seven interest groups as "formerly influential" in setting federal education policy; each of them is education-specific in focus (American Association of School Administrators, AFT, Council of Chief State Officers, Council of Great City Schools, National Association of State Title 1 Directors, NEA, and the National School Boards Association). In contrast, five of the eight "newly influential" groups she identified are multi-issue organizations (Business Roundtable, EXPECT Coalition, Heritage Foundation, National Governors Association, and the

Progressive Policy Institute), and none of the newly influential education-focused groups (Education Trust, Education Leadership Council, and the Fordham Foundation) is a constituency-based group with members tied to the traditional education sector.[7] As a mark of the dynamism in the sector, new groups continue to emerge as important voices in national education policy debates. Paul Manna, writing at about the same time as Debray-Pelot, mentions education-focused groups such as Achieve, the Center on Education Policy, the 21st-Century Schools Project, the National Center on Education and the Economy, and the Center for Education Reform; others are multi-issue think tanks like the Center for American Progress, Economic Policy Institute, and the American Enterprise Institute.[8] And most recently, they include "a new generation of education advocacy groups . . . pushing for such policies as rigorous teacher evaluations based in part on evidence of student learning, increased access to high-quality charter schools, and higher academic standards for schools and students."[9] Stand for Children, StudentsFirst, and Democrats for Education Reform are three prominent examples of these latest comers, combining a school-specific focus with a self-conscious effort to build pressure in general-purpose elections behind reform ideas that traditional education stakeholder groups have regarded warily.

Shifting institutional boundaries change the landscape on which interest groups and ideas compete. As issue-specific arenas lose some of their monopoly over education decision making, groups that have an edge in general-purpose arenas are better able to exercise voice and influence. Issues and ideas that have been marginalized or ruled out within the traditional arenas dominated by education-focused organizations may gain credence more easily when raised within decision-making institutions that deal with a wider array of issues and are open to a wider array of interest groups.

This chapter reviews some evidence about the ways in which the end of education exceptionalism is intertwined with changes in where education battles are taking shape, which combatants have advantageous positions, and the kinds of priorities and policies that are more likely to get on the agenda as a result. The discussion draws on conceptions of venue defense, venue shopping, and institutional change, as introduced in chapter 1. The shifts occurring are slow and contested. New institutions do not displace the old ones so much as they add to and complicate the array of decision-making venues, and the links from institutions to interest groups, and from interest groups to issues and priorities, are neither direct nor definitive. Some things, nonetheless, are clear: once relatively buffered, the education policy arena is becoming much more porous, populated by new and energetic actors whose claims to expertise are grounded in different kinds of knowledge and experience, more susceptible to ideas and policy tools that have been tested elsewhere but are new and disruptive within education.

THE RISE OF THE "EXCELLENCE" AGENDA IN NATIONAL EDUCATION POLICY

One of the most dramatic changes in the way education issues have been framed in the U.S., particularly at the national level, is encapsulated in the relative shift from equal inputs to excellent outcomes as a guiding force. Equity and excellence are not necessarily incompatible goals, but in practice the two often push and pull in different directions. This has certainly been the case in education policy debates, where emphasis on excellence and emphasis on equity have often been seen as competitive values.[10] In historical context, the pursuit of educational equity was associated with an emphasis on access (racial desegregation, access for the disabled) and inputs (ensuring that schools attended by minorities and the poor received sufficient funds, comparable teachers, and adequate facilities).[11] The pursuit of excellence, in contrast, has emphasized higher standards and raising performance.

This perceived trade-off was etched particularly sharply during the Reagan administration, when some conservatives argued that a liberal tradition of focusing on the needs of the poor had eroded the nation's commitment to high standards. Blame for this perceived "leveling down" phenomenon was laid at the feet of a set of interest groups—teacher unions, legislative champions, and supporters within the public bureaucracy—that were portrayed as an *iron triangle* protecting institutions and policies that measured commitment to education by the amount of spending.

122

Using the Policy Agendas Project data that we drew on earlier, we can trace how the growing attention of presidents and Congress corresponded to shifts in the kinds of issues on the education agenda. The Policy Agendas Project applies the same issue-coding scheme to the State of the Union speeches and congressional hearings.

Table 4.1 compares the relative emphasis on different educational issues between the White House and Congress over time.[12]

The five time periods selected here are intended to capture five meaningful eras. Prior to the 1960s, the federal role in education was very limited. During the 1960s, civil rights legislation and the passage of the Elementary and Secondary Education Act (ESEA) marked an assertion of national government involvement around issues of equity and funding. The publication of *A Nation at Risk* in 1983 is generally credited for introducing a new focus on education outcomes and standards as a rival to the reigning emphasis on inputs and equity. The period from 1994 through 2001 is seen by many as a lead-in period to the No Child Left Behind Act (NCLB), marked by increased voter concern with educational issues in national elections, increased but still voluntary federal emphasis on standards, and aggressive leadership in accountability by some but not all states. Finally, the passage of NCLB in 2001 is seen by some as a "punctuation" in the historical equilibrium of education policy, a nonincremental and possibly irreversible shift into a new era of intense national government involvement.[13]

Several patterns in table 4.1 are worth noting. A sharp increase in attention to educational excellence is apparent, coincident with the publication of *A Nation at Risk*. Examples of what the Policy Agendas Project has coded as "educational excellence" include "promotion of excellence in education, promotion of science and math education, education standards and testing, improvement of science education facilities, [increased] foreign language competency in U.S. schools, programs to promote teacher excellence, grants for improving computer education in schools, [establishment of] centers for gifted and talented students, use of telecommunications to share teaching resources, grants for library construction, federal library program developments, public library facilities, [and] teacher certification standards for math and science teachers."[14] In this case, and as we have seen generally, the issue

TABLE 4.1

Presidential and congressional education agenda by issue (as percentage of education references)

	Educational excellence	Education of under-privileged	Elementary and secondary	General education	Higher education	Special education	Vocational education	Arts and humanities	Other education
Presidential State of the Union speeches									
1946–1960	9.0	0.8	16.4	66.4	4.9	0.0	0.0	2.5	0.0
1961–1982	4.7	8.1	6.1	37.8	24.3	0.0	1.4	17.6	0.0
1983–1994	42.1	9.1	5.8	29.8	10.7	0.0	2.5	0.0	0.0
1995–2000	43.9	4.0	20.9	7.1	20.6	0.0	0.0	2.4	1.2
2001–2005	25.9	6.9	58.6	1.7	6.9	0.0	0.0	0.0	0.0
Congressional hearings									
1946–1960	8.4	0.0	26.9	7.6	40.3	11.8	0.0	4.2	0.8
1961–1982	11.0	9.6	21.7	5.2	29.4	7.1	7.4	6.6	1.9
1983–1994	24.0	8.3	16.7	2.1	32.3	4.2	6.3	5.2	1.0
1995–2000	14.8	7.4	14.8	14.8	25.9	7.4	0.0	3.7	11.1
2001–2005	15.0	0.0	35.0	5.0	30.0	0.0	10.0	5.0	0.0

Source: Author's calculations are based on data coded and downloaded from the Policy Agendas Project, www.policyagendas.org.

agenda of the White House appears more excitable—that is, less constant over time—than that of Congress, which seems to keep a more even keel.

Compared to the White House, Congress has paid more and somewhat more consistent attention to higher education, special education, and vocational education. This might reflect the fact that Congress institutionally is specialized, with committees and subcommittees that emphasize key issues, or that some of its members are classic "policy entrepreneurs" who have strong personal interest or have built political reputations around areas of their special interest and expertise.[15] It also is possible that this is a reflection of the difference between holding hearings and State of the Union speeches, which, as rare and high-profile events, may naturally focus more narrowly on hot issues of the moment.

The rise in attention to excellence coincides with a less dramatic deemphasis on education for the underprivileged for both Congress and the president. The data understates the emphasis on the underprivileged to some extent, though, especially for Congress, since many of the hearings coded generally as "elementary and secondary education" deal with ESEA, which itself has a substantial orientation toward high-need populations. The popular perception that an expanded focus on excellence came at the expense of a focus on need gets some support, though, while at the same time it is important to recognize that the one did not *replace* the other.[16]

An examination of the year-by-year trends (not presented here) shows that the presidential emphasis on excellence spikes dramatically in 1983/1984, 1989/1990, and especially 1996–2000. Congress was not simply pulled in the wake of strong signals from the executive branch; its relative peaks of interest (albeit more moderated) came in 1980–1982, 1989–1992, and 1999–2000. More notably, Congress was much more consistent in its attention to issues of excellence. From 1946 to 2005, there were thirty-three years in which the State of the Union address failed to mention excellence issues, but only seven years in which Congress failed to hold a hearing on issues relating to an excellence agenda.

The emerging emphasis on educational excellence represents what Frank Baumgartner and Bryan Jones refer to as a *shift in problem definition*, an important precursor in their model to nonincremental policy change.[17] This framing of the issue was more consistent with the policies being promoted by the range of new interest groups that were beginning to challenge the traditional domination of the teacher unions and education-focused bureaucracies. Because interest groups that benefit from the status quo often can dominate traditional institutions, Baumgartner and Jones suggest that shifts in problem definition tend to find their initial expression through alternative decision-making venues. By looking more closely inside Congress, to the committee level, we can probe whether the new ideas and new interest groups showed up first in a different set of committees than those that normally shaped the congressional education policy agenda.

Alternative Committees as Avenues for New Actors and Issues

What accounts for the relative shift in problem definition at the national level from a dominant focus on inputs to a newer emphasis on outputs, from a dominant focus on funding to an increasing emphasis on test scores? While political science emphasizes the powerful forces of stasis in the American system—traditions, culture, iron triangles, and veto groups—periods of politically enforced equilibrium occasionally are punctuated by rapid and nonincremental change. Baumgartner and Jones suggest that sharp shifts in the agenda are made possible when an alternative problem definition is combined with a move to a new decision-making venue less controlled by the reigning elites and less invested in the reigning ideas.[18] Their ideas about the interaction among decision-making venues, new political actors, and new conceptualizations of policy problems have direct relevance to the thesis that a shift from single-purpose to general-purpose arenas will be marked by new groups and new policy approaches. In Congress, the Baumgartner and Jones formulation suggests that we look to see whether rival perspectives first emerge in committees that had not historically been the primary arena for dealing with K–12 education—in new committees less likely to have been captured by the dominant interest of the preceding era.

To probe this possibility, I take advantage of a subsample of the Policy Agendas Project congressional hearing data that has been recoded to provide more specific information on education issues and the witnesses that testified. Starting with the 792 hearings from 1970 to 2004 that originally were coded as relating to excellence, the underprivileged, or the more general category of elementary and secondary education, Ashley E. Jochim first narrowed these (based on hearing summaries on LexisNexis Congressional Universe) to those that could be recoded as dealing with any one of seven more specific policy foci: educational standards, testing, incentives, excellence, equitable funding, teachers and curriculum, and education of the disadvantaged.[19] She then selected from this universe a sample, stratified by year, of 167 hearings, and carried out a more detailed review to identify all witnesses who appeared.

Using this data, we can explore the relationship among venue, issue framing, and interest groups. Of the 167 hearings, 135 were held in the two core committees (the Senate Committee on Health, Education, Labor, and Pensions and the House Committee on Education and the Workforce); 32 were spread thinly among 13 other committees.[20] While the two main committees account for 80 percent of all the hearings in the sample, this dominance was markedly weaker during the period immediately following *A Nation at Risk* and running through 1994, the year in which President Clinton signed the Goals 2000 Act (see figure 4.1). This is the period in which some consider the standards

FIGURE 4.1

Percent of education hearings outside major education commitees

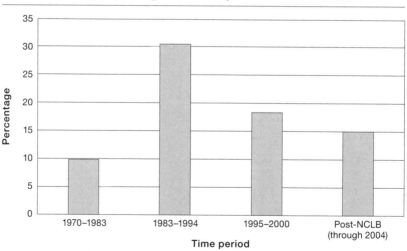

movement to have been born, a time in which both states and the national government rather dramatically expanded their role.

Also consistent with the Baumgartner and Jones thesis, the main education committees in Jochim's sample were more likely to have held hearings focused on the dominant issue framing of the prereform era. Since the passage of ESEA in 1965, federal education policy had heavily emphasized addressing the needs of low-income students, and figure 4.2 shows that the two main education committees maintained that emphasis.

The old problem definition did not die; rather, new formulations based on excellence and outcomes began to emerge in other corners of the institution that historically had not been major centers of education policy debate. From 1970 to 2004, more than one in four of their hearings focused on the underprivileged, roughly twice as many as emphasized education excellence (12.6 percent). For the other committees holding education-related hearings, the relative emphasis was the opposite. Over four out of ten of their hearings were coded as dealing with educational excellence, more than three times as many as dealt with underprivileged (12.5 percent).[21]

FIGURE 4.2

Issue emphasis by committee type

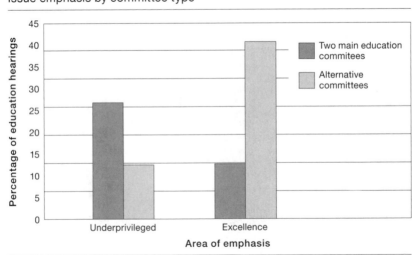

128

The rise in the education-related activity of nontraditional committees (especially in the critical 1983–1994 period) and their tendency to
place more emphasis on excellence and less on funding and disadvantaged groups are very much in line with Baumgartner and Jones's ideas
about the relationships among shifting venues, alternative problem definitions, and policy change. Baumgartner and Jones use the concept of
venue shopping to account for the dynamics behind such a pattern. Interest groups outside the reigning subsystem play a critical role by tactically steering decisions to fresh venues more likely to provide access to
them and to credit their rival issue framings. If that's right, we should
expect to see a different set of interest groups testifying in these nontraditional committees, while unions, local school boards, and constituent
groups of the traditional public education coalition presumably would
continue to dominate the main education committees within the Senate and House. But that is not quite what we find.

Figure 4.3 shows the percentage of witnesses in each type of committee who represented teacher unions and local districts.

During the critical years between the publication of *A Nation at
Risk* and the signing of NCLB, school districts and teacher unions

FIGURE 4.3

Teacher unions and local districts as witnesses, by committee type

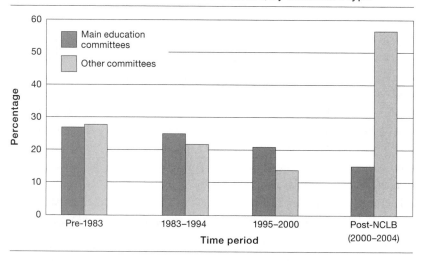

held somewhat more favorable access to the two main education committees, as anticipated, but the stronger finding is their relative loss of prominence across both types of committees.[22] This does not fit the picture of the kind of *venue capture* that Baumgartner and Jones predict, in which historically powerful interests tenaciously maintain advantages in traditional venues. Rather, it appears that something other than simple venue shopping within Congress is involved in the marginalization of the education-specific interest groups. Part of the explanation might be that the declining stature of the established education interest groups was powerful enough to infect even the institutional venues in which they historically had prevailed.[23] Part may be due to changes in the education delivery system in the U.S., leading to an expansion in the number and type of new interest groups with legitimate claims to educational expertise. Figure 4.3 also shows an unanticipated increase in the prominence of teacher unions and school districts in the post-NCLB period. This is a reminder that traditional interests can be resilient and responsive, and not necessarily consigned to marginalization in the changing governance landscape. Teacher unions, school districts, and other traditional school-specific organizations may not be able to reverse the reabsorption of education decision making into general-purpose arenas. If that is the case, they will be forced to compete in a game whose rules and regulations are less favorable than those to which they had grown accustomed. But that does not mean that they will not still be in the game.

VENUE SHOPPING IN THE STATES

From the vantage point of the 1960s and early 1970s, states seemed almost the last place to look for leadership in education reform. Part of the reason had to do with their general weakness. Christopher Jencks, in 1964, published one of the harshest critiques, in which he suggested it would not be such a bad thing if states essentially withered away. Candidates for state legislatures, he asserted, "tend to be local hacks" who, once in office, set salaries too low to attract talented bureaucrats: "A vicious circle is established in which mediocrity attracts mediocrity."[24] In

1971, the Citizens Conference on State Legislatures labeled states "the Sometime Governments," in a report that bemoaned the amateurishness and incapacity of states as governance bodies fit to deal with challenging social issues.[25] But the situation seemed especially dire when it came to education, where general feebleness combined with political paralysis. Deference to localism and skittishness over racial politics inclined legislatures and governors to adopt a generally passive stance. Coupled with the muscle of teacher organizations in many states, this created a constrained subsystem in which educators worked with sympathetic legislators (whom they had often helped to elect) and generally weak state chief state school officers and state boards of education to maintain an agenda that was simultaneously modest and attuned to the educators' desire for steady or increased funding and maximal professional discretion.[26]

Yet, by the mid- to late-1990s, states had become the primary entry point for new policy ideas that challenged the education establishment that had seemed so entrenched. While state involvement became energized across a range of education issues, two thrusts stand out. One, which began to take shape in the latter half of the 1980s, focused on excellence, standards, and accountability. States—and in particular, entrepreneurial governors and the National Governors Association (NGA)—played a role in launching the standards movement, as we have seen, providing a more amenable venue while the national government gradually shook off enough of its hang-ups about states' rights and local control to get more fully involved.

The other thrust of new ideas centered on school choice, and particularly charter schools. The charter school phenomenon was born in the 1990s, and although it came a step behind the push for standards and excellence, it in some ways represented a more dramatic challenge to the education policy status quo. While framed simply as a way to make schools and districts more responsive to families and students, the charter school movement was closely entwined with the shift toward general-purpose governance. Charter school proponents drew upon—and arguably contributed to—growing mistrust of traditional school districts. They had their greatest policy successes by targeting

131

state legislatures. And they pushed for charter authorization and oversight mechanisms outside the control of traditional school districts, delivering a serious blow to their authority and prestige.

Jeanne Allen and the Center for Education Reform (CER) provide an illuminating case study of this mistrust of the traditional governance among proponents of charter schools. Allen is president of CER, which since the early 1990s has been among the most visible proponents of a market-oriented vision of school reform. Allen argues that reform efforts consistently run "smack into federations, alliances, departments, councils, boards, commissions, panels, herds, flocks, and convoys that make up the education industrial complex," what she derisively has labeled "the blob."[27] Reflecting this, CER built into both its legislative analysis and legislative agenda a distinct preference that the responsibility for authorizing charters be assigned to a range of organizations (including the state, universities, newly established boards, and other nonprofits) rather than to traditional districts, which they presumed would be too politically indebted to teacher unions to do anything but try to suffocate the infant reform initiative in its cradle. CER's ranking of charter school laws, which has been widely utilized by researchers as well as journalists, advocacy groups, and others, grades laws as "stronger" if they allow for multiple authorizers on the basis that "states that do not have multiple authorizers create hostile environments for charters because school boards often view charter schools as competition and reject applications not based on merit, but on politics."[28]

As we have discussed, theories about public agenda setting suggest that policy changes are "more likely to occur if policy entrepreneurs can move the process out of the stable legislative subsystem where established groups and their legislative and bureaucratic supporters dominate institutional agendas to the broader and publicly visible 'macro arena' where a more diverse set of policy elites and the public can be mobilized."[29] Chapter 3 noted the connection between state legislators and the diffusion of the charter school idea. Here I take the argument further by tracing how the activation of a wider, general-purpose arena at the state level played an important role in the injection and diffusion of new ideas and new interest groups that have dramatically altered the education policy landscape. Minnesota was the first state to establish charter schools, so I start the discussion there with an account of how governors and legislators were critical in establishing public school choice as a more politically viable reform than school vouchers, which prior to then had been the preferred vehicle for advocates of market-oriented strategies for educational change.

Governors, Legislators, and the Birth of Charter Schools: The Minnesota Story

The first charter law in the nation was passed in Minnesota in 1991. By 2002, forty states had enacted charter laws, and there were roughly two thousand seven hundred charter schools. By the end of 2011, all but eight states had charter school laws, and there were an estimated five thousand six hundred schools serving roughly 2 million children.[30] Analysts consistently characterize the charter school phenomenon as extraordinary, both because of the sharpness of the change it represented and the speed with which the policy spread. It's probably fruitless to speculate what would have happened had Minnesota not taken the first step. Public school choice was already a topic of conversation at the national level, with magnet schools and controlled choice plans for school desegregation being cited as working examples; this, combined with the rapidity of the subsequent spread of charters, suggests that there may have been enough pent-up demand for an alternative to the traditional attendance-zone-based schools that something akin to the charter phenomenon would eventually have emerged in any event. But this was not a case of Minnesota just happening to be the first over the legislative line. Although the term *charter* and some of the core ideas had emerged previously, the legislative template for what we currently think of as charter schools was stamped with the Minnesota seal, so delving into the historical roots of the Minnesota story should tell us something of general import about how new policies find traction despite the anticipated indifference or resistance of a dominant subsystem.[31]

In his classic book on agenda formation, John Kingdon explains why it can be frustrating to look for the origin of a policy idea: "When we try to track down the origins of an idea or proposal we become involved in an infinite regress . . . there is no logical place to stop the process."[32] But in the case of Minnesota and charters, the particular "ground soften-ing" that occurred before the charter legislation seems highly pertinent. Before passing charter legislation, Minnesota was a leader in establish-ing other policies promoting public school choice: cross-district open enrollment policies and postsecondary options that enabled high school students to take courses at state colleges and universities for credit that would apply to their high school requirements. Others have laid out the history in greater detail; I summarize the key threads of the story here.[33]

Rather than developing within the traditional education sector, the roots of school choice in Minnesota were in elite, multi-issue civic groups combined with strong gubernatorial and legislative support-ers. Tim Mazzoni begins his chronology in 1982, when the Citizens League issued an education report calling for vouchers, the Minnesota Business Partnership established an education quality task force, and Rudy Perpich was elected governor of the state. Early efforts that still linked choice to vouchers were defeated, but by 1985 Perpich had as-sembled a coalition supportive of his open enrollment plan, which was intended to allow students to attend schools in other districts with the state's public support traveling with them. While supporters included some education-oriented groups and individuals—such as the PTA, the Secondary Principals Association, and Perpich's appointee as commis-sioner of education—lined up on the other side were the big guns of the traditional school-specific arena: the Minnesota School Boards As-sociation, the Minnesota Association of School Administrators, and the state's two major teacher unions (associated with the NEA and AFT). Perpich's own children had been denied a choice of schools when the family moved to St. Paul, and Mazzoni suggests that this personal mo-tivation gave added impetus to his efforts, as did his "obvious desires to be hailed nationally as an 'education governor.'"[34] But a proactive gov-ernor, even one with business and civic support, might not have been able to carry the day. Mazzoni credits Connie Levi, the Republican House majority leader, as having "finessed or fended off" opponents in the House in order to get the postsecondary option enacted, and "with-out this policy beachhead . . . there might well have been no choice statutes at all in subsequent legislative sessions."[35]

Minnesota went on to pass open enrollment in 1988. That same year, a group of activists who had worked on these battles got together after a conference, convened by a local foundation, at which public school choice options pioneered by District 4 in New York City had been described and AFT president Albert Shanker had spoken about his vision of teacher-led schools that could innovate outside the direct control of bureaucratic local districts. Shanker had used the term *charter*, and the Minnesota group picked up on that and added some defining elements of its own. The five core activists included two members of the Citizens League, a state senator, a program officer of the Urban Coalition, and the president of the state PTA. This group—which, with the exception of the PTA president, did not include members of the traditional school-specific interest groups—took the lead in shaping the charter school idea, using the access to elected leaders they had developed during the earlier battles to mobilize what became the successful battle to pass the charter school law.

Diffusion of the Charter School Idea

The rapid spread of charter school laws also can be understood at least in part as a consequence of the growing importance of general-purpose government and politics. Single-purpose governance was most engrained at the local level—and part of the appeal of early charter legislation was its potential to outmaneuver what were assumed to be parochial and union-intimidated school districts fundamentally hostile to new policy ideas. Charter proponents, such as the Center for Education Reform, insisted that school districts, if left to their own devices, would make the charter school approval process difficult or impossible. Accordingly they promoted state legislation that would multiply both the number and types of authorizers; as of 2010, there were nearly one thousand authorizing bodies. In addition to traditional school districts, these included state education agencies, universities and community colleges, other nonprofit organizations, mayors' offices, and independent charter boards constituted specifically to carry out the charter approval and oversight functions.[36]

Several studies have attempted to explain empirically why some states were quicker than others to embrace charter schools, to account for differences in the balance of flexibility and accountability struck by the state laws, and to examine patterns of legislative change when charter laws were revisited by legislatures after their initial adoption. Each of these studies looks at different measures of charter policy, different combinations of independent variables, and different analytical techniques. That they do not find strong patterns or clearly converge on a specific explanation may be partly a function of these differences, although it also suggests that unmeasured and state-specific factors—such as particular policy entrepreneurs, political history, and dynamics associated with noneducation issues on the agenda—may be important factors not yet taken into account.

Despite this fuzzy and still emergent set of findings, some general tendencies across the studies are relevant to our understanding of the role of general-purpose versus school-specific institutions and the ways in which they may be differentially responsive to interest groups and issues. First, state policies regarding charter schools are not determined solely by need, region, culture, or the tendency to imitate neighboring states: political factors—including governance structure, party, ideology, and interest group alignments—also play an important role. Kenneth Wong and Warren Langevin found that the chance that a state adopted charter school legislation in a given year increased by 292 percent under Republican as opposed to Democratic governors.[37] Ramona McNeal and Lisa Dotterweich found that liberal legislatures, conservative citizens, spending by the NEA, and the number of civil rights groups active in the states all were positively associated with the number of bills concerning charter schools in state legislatures from 2003 to 2006. Legislative professionalism was negatively related to charter school activity, leading McNeal and Dotterwich to speculate that more professional legislatures—those with longer sessions, higher salaries, and larger staffs—might be "less likely to simply adopt the governor's agenda."[38]

Second, the political factors influencing subsequent revision of charter school laws differ from those affecting the initial adoption. The spread of charter school legislation across the states was relatively rapid, and as states jumped on the bandwagon they tended to mimic laws from other states or adopt model legislation recommended by national charter advocacy groups. Change over time may be a better window into the assertion of each state's own values, legislative processes, and politics. Arnold Shober, Paul Manna, and John Witte looked at two dimensions of charter laws—the degree of flexibility provided to the schools (freedom from regulation plus financial and other support) and the degree of accountability to government (versus market) for outcomes. The most important factor they found was whether or not the states have revised their original charter laws; those that have revised the laws were most likely to increase both flexibility and accountability.[39] Thomas Holyoke et al. also looked at policy change as well as initial adoption. When it to came to adoption, they concluded, "governors . . . played the dominant political role in deciding whether or not there would be a new policy, but it was legislators who worked out the details."[40] When it came to change in the laws, heightened Democratic strength in the legislature, increased membership in the NEA, and a larger number of for-profit charter management organizations were associated with increased regulatory restrictiveness, while higher campaign contributions by the state's chamber of commerce was associated with less.

A third conclusion has to do with what political scientists sometimes refer to as *policy feedback*. Policy feedback refers to the fact that policy changes can spark changes in political configurations that affect the original policy in turn.[41] For example, the initiation of a social program or tax benefit may create or energize a set of beneficiaries who subsequently exert pressure to expand or deepen the original initiative. As an example of how a policy can create new interests, Eric Patashnik cites airline deregulation, which "led to the emergence of new discount carriers which have been a key force in preserving the reform."[42] The role of the testing industry in accelerating the momentum behind high-stakes testing provides an example from the world of education policy; private sector providers of testing and measurement systems and training therein were not dominant forces in the coalition that initially propelled standards and accountability onto the national and state agendas, but as the testing industry grew it became a larger, wealthier, and intensely committed element in the expansion of that movement.[43]

One study looks directly at how interest groups may selectively target general-purpose versus school-specific venues in seeking to influence charter school law and its implementation. Holyoke et al. surveyed all charter schools operating in Arizona, Michigan, and Pennsylvania in 2002, with responses from 270 (35 percent). A sizable minority (42 percent) reported that they did not do lobbying, but most reported regularly lobbying in at least one governmental venue, and about one-quarter lobbied in two or more. The survey asked about six venues: half at the state level and half local; half school-specific and half general-purpose.[44] Figure 4.4 shows the percentage of charter schools lobbying each of the six venues.

FIGURE 4.4

Percentage of charter schools lobbying in each venue

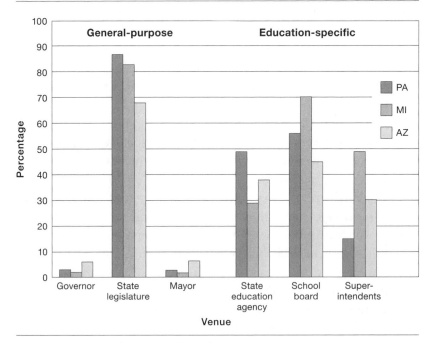

Source: Adapted from (Holyoke et al., 2012).

State legislatures, a general-purpose venue, were the most frequent target of lobbying—much more so than governors. This finding is consistent with the notion that governors get involved at the front end, but legislatures stay involved as policies are adapted over time. Other than the legislature, however, it was education-specific units that got the most lobbying attention. One way to interpret the pattern is that charter proponents focused on the state legislatures as the point of first attack: a venue less dominated by traditional public school interest groups and therefore more willing to initiate charter schools as a reform idea. But education-specific institutions still carry a lot of the load as far as implementation issues. As observed earlier, new institutions and political behaviors do not so much replace the old ones as get layered on top of them.[45] For interests with enough resources to engage in multiple venues, it makes sense to do so and even, occasionally, to play one off against the others. The politics of institution creation—in particular, the creation of new authorizing bodies—coexists with a politics of venue shopping.

Anecdotal accounts flesh out the ways in which charter proponents have used their access to general-purpose institutions—particularly state legislatures—to work around local districts and promote their interests and ideas. The *New York Times* reported, for example, on the extensive state lobbying efforts by K12, Inc., in support of its efforts to expand its business in providing online education and charter schools. One national analysis estimated that the company and its employees contributed nearly half a million dollars to candidates in state elections between 2004 and 2010. In Pennsylvania, "where K12 Inc. collects about 10 percent of its revenues, the company has spent $681,000 on lobbying since 2007," and the state's budget secretary is a former senior vice president of education and policy for the company and still holds shares of its stock.[46] In New York State, wealthy investors in charter schools worked through a nonprofit organization to orchestrate a grassroots campaign that, among other things, arranged for charter school parents to lobby state legislators to encourage them to lift the state's cap on the number of charter schools. The nonprofit, Education Reform Now, substantially outspent the New York teacher union for lobbying expenses in 2010.[47]

Accounting for State Legislative Agendas

The preceding chapter presented data on state legislative priorities based on the more than twelve thousand bills dealing with preK–12 and enacted from 1994 through 2009. We saw there that some issues, like curriculum and teaching, finance, and special populations, are steady and perennial subjects of legislative interest; some, like bills relating to federal initiatives, come and go; some, like safety, are gradually becoming less predominant; and some, like health, may be rising on the scene. I grouped the legislation broadly into categories representing *school-focused* reforms (curriculum, accountability, federal policy, and technology); *redistributive* approaches focused on the needy and nonschool factors (special populations, health, vocational, early learning, parents/community, and race and ethnicity); and more *operational* functions (logistics, facilities, and organization; safety; finance; governance). Overall, school-focused reforms and operational issues dominated, accounting for 42 percent and 38 percent of all bills, respectively, with redistributive bills accounting for 18 percent and the rest not codeable.

Is there a pattern across states? In particular, is there a pattern that might help to explain why some state legislatures might more aggressively pursue contemporary, school-focused reform initiatives while others focus more on redistributive approaches or those that consider nonschool factors?

On the one hand, it is reasonable to expect deeply etched differences across the states. There is a hot and polarized debate over whether a school-focused versus poverty- and social-focused approach has better prospects for improving educational outcomes and reducing education gaps. The latter position is generally associated with teacher unions and the progressive left in American politics; the former—manifested in emphasis on standards, high-stakes testing, and holding schools and teachers accountable—is more typically associated with the political right, although it is a position that has strong support within the New Democratic wing of the party and is generally supported by President Obama and Secretary of Education Arne Duncan and many education governors and education mayors. Based on this framing of the political tenor of school reform, we might expect greater legislative emphasis on school-focused reform priorities in more conservative states as well as those with strong governors, professional legislatures, more of a state role in funding education, weaker unions, and stronger interest groups representing constituencies (like seniors and antitax interests) that have a stake in keeping education efforts lean and focused. States' general orientation toward single-purpose versus general-purpose governance might also play a role, with those that tend to allocate authority to is-sue-specific institutions less likely to see a lot of legislative activity on these school-focused reform ideas. We might expect legislative atten-tion to redistributive policies to be more associated with states that have stronger teacher unions and where interest groups representing minori-ties and children are more prominent.

The empirical literature on state policy outputs in general has found demographic and economic characteristics of states are at least as im-portant as governance and politics. Urban states and those with higher incomes tend to be more likely to engage in redistributory policies, for example.[48] And some studies suggest that racial and ethnic characteris-tics of program recipients play a role, with programs that serve large mi-nority populations tending to be more restrictive because the targets are regarded less sympathetically by predominantly white majorities at the state level.[49] To the extent that the school-focused reform agenda is seen as imposing accountability and efficiencies on public education, that raises the possibility that it will be more prominent in states with large or growing nonwhite populations.

To get at these kinds of issues, I used exploratory regression tech-niques to determine which of an array of governance, political, and demographic variables correspond with the extent to which state legis-latures were active in school-focused, redistributive, and operational is-sues from 1994 through 2009.[50] Variables that tap aspects of statewide *governance* systems included the governor's formal powers (generally and in education), the state's historical percentage of "education governors" (as operationalized via the NGA biographies), a measure of state in-volvement (percentage of education revenue coming from the state), and an overall measure of orientation to general-purpose governance (the ratio of the number of general-purpose to issue-specific substate governments). To get at the *political environment*, I included measures of state government liberalism, the interest group effectiveness within the states (based on Hrebenar and Thomas's surveys of political scientists' expert assessments of the effectiveness of interest groups representing children, taxpayers, seniors, human services, women, and minorities in each of the states), and teacher union strength. Demographic variables included percent urban, per capita income, region (the South), the average percent minority, and a measure of change in the size of the black population between 1970 and 1990.

Table 4.2 presents the analysis in which the proportion of legislative attention to the three types of issues is regressed upon various indicators of states' demographic, political, and institutional characteristics.

Redistributive activity was highest in states with: a tradition of governmental liberalism; a smaller state share of education funding; weaker formal gubernatorial education power; increases in the black population between 1970 and 1990; weaker interest groups representing seniors and stronger ones lobbying on behalf of human services. The percentage of teachers represented by unions was modestly positively related to redistributive activity, but union influence measured by campaign donations was negatively so. The pattern for school-focused reform activity is less well defined. Somewhat intriguing are the two variables for which the signs are reversed from those for redistributive activity. States with a generally higher orientation toward general-purpose governance forms were less likely to have redistributive issues on the agenda and more likely to focus on school-focused reforms. Senior citizens' interest group influence was negatively associated with redistributive and showed a positive, albeit statistically weak, association with school-focused reform. Legislative attention to operational issues was weakly predicted overall, possibly reflecting the fact that attention to these "housekeeping" issues is relatively constant from state to state.

We need to be careful about drawing conclusions from an exploratory analysis like this one. Among the factors making interpretation tricky: that the dependent variable registers the extent to which these three types of issues were higher on the legislative agenda, not the specific legislative goals; that legislatures active on redistributive approaches may or may not have been pursuing them in progressive ways; and that legislatures emphasizing school-focused reforms may have been playing

TABLE 4.2

Relationship between redistributive, school-focused reform, and operational/logistical education legislation and select state characteristics

	Redistributive legislation	School-focused reform	Operational/ logistical
Governor's education power	−.009[b]		
Governor-to-legislature power ratio			.018[a]
Education revenue (%)	−.002[d]		
Ratio of general- to single-purpose	−.021[b]	.032[b]	−.021[a]
Liberalism	.321[c]		
Senior citizens interest group strength	−.063[b]	.103[a]	
Human services interest group strength	.061[b]		
Children's issues interest group strength		.075[b]	−.042[a]
Change in black population (%)	.015[c]	−.024[c]	
Union influence	−.844[b]		
Union membership (%)	.0011[b]		
Urban population (%)	−.001[b]		−.001[a]
Southern state	.032[b]		
Constant	.353[d]	.357[d]	.448[d]
R_	.707[d]	.340[d]	.273[c]

[a]p<.1; [b]p<.05; [c]p<.01; [d]p<.001

catch-up under federal pressure rather than expressing state-centered priorities. The three broad clusters I've highlighted, moreover, each comprise subissues that have political dynamics of their own.[51]

The results are interesting as much for what they do not show as what they do. Differences in formal governance structures in general and differences in both formal and informal power of the governor do not emerge as important differentiating factors. Rather than being driven by executive leadership, it is possible that state legislatures are setting their own course or broadly—and more or less in step with one another—responding to national factors, such as changing public views of the nature of the education reform challenge or national policy promulgated by presidents, Congress, and the courts. When the constituent subissues are analyzed separately, state variation in union strength and campaign activity rarely emerges as a significant factor and does so much less frequently than general state ideology and the influence of more general interest groups representing children, human services, seniors, and taxpayers.

The finding that formal governance structures on their own have only limited association with the shape of the state legislative education agenda should not be surprising. From the early days of empirical research on state policy outputs, there has been controversy over whether formal governance structures, informal political factors like ideology and interest group, or background factors relating to state demography, wealth, or culture are the "real" drivers of policy variation.[52] As I have argued throughout, formal institutions affect the shape of the playing field, *influencing* but not *determining* the outcome of the contest. Paul Manna and Timothy Harwood, in their recent analysis of the relationship between state governance and education policies, similarly found that governance structure alone was less consistently consequential than were variables accounting for partisan control of the state house and legislature.[53]

But there is also an affirmative finding that is important to the broader argument in this book. Within the legislative arena, variables like racial change, general ideology, and interest groups other than teacher unions alone emerge as important factors, although in ways that vary across the three kinds of policies. State legislatures, like executives, are general-purpose bodies—and therefore more open than traditional education-specific bodies to ideas and interests percolating in other areas of domestic policy. But state legislatures also represent a counterweight to governor-led reform, an institutional venue with norms of access and decision making that may nudge them to approach education in a different manner than that associated with the so-called education governors. The conventional narrative about education executives highlights them as pragmatic, rational managers, attuned to the role of education as a tool for dealing with global economic competition. Compared to governors, state legislators are elected by more localized constituencies, with more limited professional staff capacity, and more dependent for election on local party, local contributors, and appeals to local tradition. Considered in this light, the reabsorption of education into general-purpose politics promises to generate a less constrained, less predictable, and less status quo–oriented approach than might be expected from the traditional, more buffered institutions that elevated education professionals and provided favored access to teachers and parents. But at the same time, it exposes education to the kinds of pluralistic jostling, venue shopping, and institutional competition that are bemoaned by those yearning for a unified, coherent, consistent approach.

THE CHANGING CAST OF CHARACTERS ON THE LOCAL STAGE

The ways that shifting venues open doors to new political actors and new policy notions are perhaps most sharply illustrated at the local level. There, the expanded role of general-purpose institutions is intimately and iteratively intertwined with the increased influence of a new set of actors, many of which are nonlocal and many of which are drawn from the private nonprofit or for-profit sector. These interests bring with them a different view of the education challenge, a new set of ideas, and new policy instruments. These views, ideas, and instruments draw heavily on perspectives associated with corporate management and market theory. This emergence of new local governance regimes tracks closely with the adoption of mayoral control, but shows signs of spreading more broadly.

Many governors, state legislatures, and more recently the White House have encouraged mayoral control of schools in the expectation that occupants of City Hall will be more reliable partners for their visions than school boards, which they see as loyal to the "old ways" of thinking about schooling and overly responsive to parent activists and teacher unions invested in protecting the status quo. In doing so, they have joined forces with some national foundations, philanthropists, and an emerging set of private-sector education organizations that consider mayor-controlled school systems to be more open than local school boards to new ways of organizing and delivering education—charters; contracting out; portfolio management models; alternative systems of recruiting and training teachers, principals, and superintendents; and capital-intensive rather than labor-intensive technologies for delivering instruction. The causal relationship has become two-way. At the same time that the growing state and federal roles have attenuated the power of local school districts and augmented the role of local general-purpose institutions, mayors and the entrepreneurial superintendents they have appointed are actively reaching for allies outside of the local well, creating new types of local school governance regimes that include local non-education-focused groups but also outside actors who can provide legitimacy, resources, and political support.

The New Education Governance Regimes

The expansion of mayoral control of schools has been discussed primarily as a management tool: as a strategy for increasing the focus, efficiency, and coordination of local school-reform activities. This is an apolitical perspective of the phenomenon in the sense that it presumes that the fundamental goals of public education are relatively clear and consensual so that the fundamental challenges have to do with the selection of the best means to achieve them. But shifting authority from a single-purpose venue (like school boards) to a general-purpose venue (like City Hall) does more than change the tools for implementing policy decisions. It also changes the line-up of groups with favored status at the table where priorities are negotiated and policies chosen.

One way to understand both the impetus behind and the consequences stemming from mayoral control is to recognize it as part of a broad reconfiguration of the constellation of interest groups and political actors that has traditionally set the agenda for local education. Scholars who study urban politics use the concept of *governance regimes* to account for the ways in which local political arrangements—not only the formal institutions and powers of government, but also the informal yet patterned interactions among government, business, unions, the nonprofit sector, and a diverse array of interest groups—shape local policy priorities and the prospects for getting things accomplished.[54] Governance regimes are distinct from *electoral regimes*—the set of supporters who help leaders capture office in the first place. Elected leaders fashion governance regimes in order to get things done; groups that are important sources of electoral support have an advantage in gaining access to the governance regime, but others that may have stayed on the sidelines during elections or even supported opposing candidates can gain access if they bring to the table resources, skills, or connections that leaders need. Even leaders who might have campaigned on issues that appealed primarily to lower-income, minority, and community-based organizations frequently incorporate business groups into their governance regimes, both because of the financial assets and reputation for management expertise that business leaders can contribute and because failure to reassure them that their interests will be considered carries the risk that they will relocate, resulting in a critical loss of tax revenue.[55]

Elected school boards and the superintendents they appoint anchor the traditional local education governance regime. Teachers and parents have favored status within this governance arrangement partly because of the intensity and personal stake that makes them hyperattentive and readily mobilized. Political scientist James Q. Wilson decades ago noted that the distribution of benefits and costs from public policies—whether concentrated on a small and readily identifiable group or spread broadly over the public—alters the dynamic of politics. Concentrated benefits and costs generate interest groups that are more alert, reactive, and likely to maintain constant vigilance and access.[56] Such alert and intense interests can often win political battles even when their gain comes at the expense of a much larger, but diffuse, set of individuals. Within the traditional institutional framework of school-specific politics, teachers and parents typically face concentrated benefits and costs; policies that affect salary, benefits, tenure, hours worked, teacher assessment, and teaching practices are felt most immediately and directly by teachers. Parents are focused on the near-term needs of their children and the immediate practices in their children's schools. Policy changes also present costs and benefits to the broader public, but because they are spread widely and indirectly via tax bills (cost) and property values (benefits), they may not suffice to generate a mobilized constituency. This standard pay-off to intensity, moreover, receives an additional boost in traditional local school politics because school board elections—often formally nonpartisan and held off-cycle from higher-profile elections for general-purpose offices—are usually marked by low levels of attention and participation, making it easier for an active group to hold disproportionate sway.[57] Teacher unions, because of their important role in local politics but also because of their value as a partner in bringing about educational change, historically were featured in most local education governance regimes, even in cases where school boards might have been elected by Republican majorities based on promises to eliminate waste in school spending and keep taxes low.

Contracting regimes, mayoral control, and the portfolio management model

While groups like business and teacher unions are commonly incorporated into local education governance regimes, the particular configuration of regimes can vary, and because those inside the regime have disproportionate influence on establishing the agenda, these differences in regime configuration can determine the kinds of ideas, issues, and policies that get favorable attention or are pushed to the side.[58] A new type of local education regime—the *contracting regime*—is closely tied to mayoral control and the emergence of what is frequently referred to as the *portfolio management model* for urban school reform.[59] School districts that employ the portfolio approach develop a range of types of schools—including traditional public schools, charter schools, privately managed schools, and public schools with special grants of autonomy—and then actively manage that supply by closing down those that fail to perform and recruiting, nurturing, and helping to expand those that deliver the goods.[60] Portfolio management models are not necessarily limited to mayoral control, but their spread to date has coincided substantially with the imposition of mayoral control or, as in New Orleans, state interventions in local school governance, both of which substantially weaken elected school boards and open the political process to a range of new actors.[61] Those new actors include nontraditional education service providers—who are looking for new markets—along with an array of national

148

political entrepreneurs, advocacy organizations, and funders who are eager to turn the pioneering districts into laboratories for new ideas.

The emerging regimes differ from the traditional one not only in their primary actors, but also in the way they frame the relationship between the public and private sectors. Proponents of contracting regimes emphasize markets and competition as desirable alternatives to education-specific bureaucracies, in contrast to traditional regimes that portray education policy and delivery as being almost exclusively public sector activities. But contracting regimes also differ from more substantially market-oriented regimes, such as those associated with vouchers and charter schools, due to their recognition (sometimes more implicit than explicit) that local government—in the form of the school district's central offices or the mayor's office—is a major player. Government—not unconstrained supply and demand—determines priorities, establishes standards, and intervenes as necessary to ensure the desired outcomes are maximized. Considered in these terms, contemporary reformers are typically seeking to deconstruct what they consider to have been self-protective employment regimes, hoping to supplant them with market or contracting regimes that will be more receptive to them and their ideas.[62]

Table 4.3 juxtaposes the traditional education governance regime with the kinds of reform-oriented regimes that appear to be emerging in many local districts. The left side illustrates the traditional arrangement, drawing a distinction between core stakeholders—those almost always involved—and more episodic and peripheral participants such as community-based organizations, the downtown business community, civil rights organizations, and local foundations. Mayors are listed here as well, reflecting the fact that mayors do not need to have had formal authority over schools in order to interject themselves into education policy debates. The right side of the table suggests the composition of the very different form of governance regime that seems to be emerging in a number of urban districts, particularly those that have made the transition from elected school boards to mayoral control.

Parents, teachers, and school boards may at times play a role even in the newly emerging reform regimes, but that role tends to be less central and episodic. In their place, general-purpose elected officials are constructing supporting regimes that incorporate a new set of actors,

TABLE 4.3

Traditional versus emerging education governance regimes

	Traditional governance regimes	Emerging reform regimes
Core stakeholder groups	• Teacher unions • Parent organizations • School boards • Superintendents and bureaucracy	• Mayors • National foundations, venture philanthropists • Service providers (for-profit and nonprofit, local and nonlocal) • State and national advocates • Private education industry (publishing, testing, professional development, management consultants, etc.)
Episodic and variable stakeholder groups	• Mayors and councils • Youth advocates • Racial and ethnic advocacy organizations • Downtown business community • Local foundations • Parents (as voters)	• Superintendents • School boards • City councils • Teacher unions • Local business and civic groups • Parent organizations • Families as individual consumer • Nonparent citizens as voters (including advocates for lower taxes/spending)
Core values and premises	• Local control • Teacher as professional • Individualization via teacher judgment and grouping • Inputs matters —Money matters —Process matters • Class size matters • Parents (as junior partners)	• National standards • Global competitiveness • Incentives matter • Outcomes matter • Markets • Management expertise • Choice • Technology • Teacher substantive knowledge
Policy and instruments	• Professional development • Class size reduction • Higher salaries • Curriculum reform • Formative assessments	• Charter schools • School closures and turnarounds • Portfolio management • Test-based accountability • Value-added teacher assessment • Merit pay • Tenure reform • Educational technology

notably foundations and other philanthropists, private charter school operators, organizations (like Teach for America and New Leaders) that represent an alternative source of teachers and principals, and for-profit providers in the publishing and testing business.

Cleveland, one of the earlier big cities to switch to mayoral control, provides an illustration of the on-the-ground distinction between core and peripheral status. In February 2012, Mayor Frank Jackson announced a new reform plan that would rely heavily on charter schools and a portfolio management approach. As reported locally, "he did not talk to the union before coming up with his latest plan because he wanted to avoid further delay."[63] But Jackson had found time to consult with the local business, philanthropic, and charter school communities. Representatives of the Cleveland Foundation and Greater Cleveland Partnership, the city's chamber of commerce, joined him in presenting the plan with the chief executive officer of Breakthrough Schools, a charter school group working with the district, also on hand.

These new regimes often substitute a national constituency for what historically was a very localized one and emphasize expertise in management and technology in place of the traditional focus on pedagogical and instructional skills. Included in this mix are national charter management organizations; publishers and testing firms; consulting organizations such as McKinsey, Parthenon, or the Boston Consulting Group; national foundations such as the Bill & Melinda Gates Foundation, Walton Family Foundation, and Broad Foundation; and advocacy groups like StudentsFirst and Stand for Children. Jal Mehta and Steven Teles suggest, moreover, that national political leaders are self-consciously nurturing such alternative regimes at the local level, supporting new stakeholders who will promote policy change as a supplement to the federal government's traditional efforts to steer local policy more directly through top-down mandates imposed on resistant localities.[64]

The Denver case

Denver provides an interesting case, and one that shows that elements of the new-style contracting regimes can take root even in the absence of mayoral control or state takeovers. Denver has an elected school board, the majority of which is elected by ward rather than at-large. In 2005, however, a reform-minded board selected a nontraditional superintendent—Michael Bennet, a lawyer who had worked in the financial community but subsequently spent two years as chief of staff for the mayor. Bennet very quickly rose to national attention, hailed by reformers who saw him as someone willing to push for test-based accountability, to challenge the teacher union on issues relating to benefits and assessment, and to adopt key elements of the portfolio management approach, including closing low performing schools and embracing charters and other alternatives on the school delivery side. At the same time, Bennet was seen as less abrasive and more of a coalition builder than some other nontraditional superintendents such as Joel Klein or Michelle Rhee; this was likely a matter of personal style in part, but it may also have reflected the fact that he reported to an elected school board and had political ambitions beyond the education sphere.

With increasing interest from across the country, Denver school policy and politics were opened to a range of influences from outside. That Bennet's supporting coalition included key elements from the new-style education regime cut two ways. His viability and collaboration with national reformers led to his quickly being picked out for appointment to a vacated Senate seat, leaving some concerned that his initiatives would falter. But the elected board selected a replacement who pledged to follow Bennet's course. Matters came to a potential head in a 2010 school board race where union-backed candidates threatened to recapture control of the board. "The fight between the teachers union and education-reform interests for control of Denver schools is leading to one of the most expensive campaigns in district history, with more than $600,000 already donated in school-board races," the *Denver Post* reported. Campaign finance reports "indicate that union leaders have backed one slate of candidates for three seats on the board while reform interests have chosen another."[65] The state chapter of the Democrats for Education Reform issued a cry of concern: "If the Denver school board flips, you can be assured that most of this reform work, which has taken about a decade to build, could fade away within a year" and called for donors who cared about the local race or the national battles to lend a hand. "All of these reformers . . . could use any support to get over the finish line. First and foremost this is a race that will decide the direction of Denver schools in the future. But this will also be a race to decide where Colorado stacks up on education reform, and in turn, influence reform around the country."[66]

The emerging new regime held its ground, and Denver, as a result, continues to be seen as a key site for proponents of test-based account-ability, charter schools, portfolio management, and a more business—rather than union—oriented approach for changing education. In February 2012, U.S. Secretary of Education Arne Duncan told several hundred Denver residents, gathered at a campus containing both tradi-tional and charter schools, that the city's ongoing reform efforts were a key to its getting a waiver from NCLB restrictions.[67] In 2011 the Walton Family Foundation gave almost $8 million in grants to Denver schools and organi-zations, more than any city other than (the much larger) New York City and Los Angeles.[68] Districts around the country began sending delegations to Colorado to study and bring back lessons from the "Denver model."[69]

The impact of foundations and philanthropic support

Sarah Reckhow's research has helped to clarify the connections among foundations, changing educational regimes, and the promotion of may-oral control, portfolio management, and charter schools. She analyzed federal tax forms filed by the fifteen foundations that gave the most money for K–12 education in 2000 and 2005. Foundations, she found, were increasingly targeting their giving on a smaller number of dis-tricts. In 2005, five districts—New York City, Los Angeles, Oakland, Boston, and Chicago—received more foundation grants than all of the one hundred largest districts had just five years before, and those five accounted for almost two-thirds of major foundation grant dollars dis-tributed to the one hundred largest districts in 2005. And the strongest predictor of funding was the displacement or marginalization of tradi-tional school boards: "Four of the five districts receiving the most grant dollars in 2005—New York City, Oakland, Boston, and Chicago—have mayoral or state control." A regression analysis of allocations to the one hundred largest school districts found mayoral control or state takeover to be the strongest predictor—stronger, for example, than the location of the foundation, or a measure of district need: districts with mayoral or state control "received roughly ten times as much in grants per student compared to those governed by an elected school board.[70]

This alignment between philanthropic support and the erosion of school-specific arenas for governance is not coincidental. Partly out of frustration with what they have considered to be the recalcitrance or ineptitude of elected boards, some foundations have very self-consciously sought out districts where the governance arrangements and political dynamics are more favorable to the core values and premises and policy instruments that they are seeking to promote. "I don't mind telling you that I believe in mayoral control of school boards or having no school board at all," major education philanthropist Eli Broad told an assemblage of governors in 2003. "You should craft legislation that enables school board members to be appointed by the mayor. You should . . . limit the authority of school boards."[71] And, as reported in his foundation's 2009–2010 annual report, this preference for mayoral control translated into a primary criterion in giving: "Observing the frequent political turnover on school boards (and often the resulting shakeup in a school district's leadership or reform agenda) and the lack of focus on student achievement led us to conclude that a more successful governance structure than the country's 14,000 school boards was mayoral, gubernatorial or state control. So our work evolved into supporting mayors and governors in cities and states like New York, Boston, Washington, D.C., Chicago and New Orleans, where their education reform efforts are supported politically in a more sustainable way."[72]

Broad, Gates, Walton, and others among the top education givers have invested in governance change as well as supporting specific educational reform initiatives. They do this not only by supporting the districts with mayoral control, but also by funding networks of nonprofit groups within those and other districts that support mayoral control along with charter schools, alternative teacher certification and development, and portfolio management systems. While New York City's Bloomberg/Klein administration received substantial support, other funds went to nongovernmental groups—like New Visions, the Harlem Children's Zone, Democracy Prep Charters, Village Academies, Urban Assembly, and Good Shepherd Services—that were integral to the city's small schools, charter schools, and portfolio model. And in Los Angeles, almost all the giving by major foundations was to such intermediary groups, including the Knowledge Is Power Program (KIPP), Green

Dot, ASPIRE, and Pacific Charter School Development.[73] Sometimes, when the activity involved might veer too close to the kinds of partisan activity proscribed by law, these donors have dug into their own pockets. LEARN NY was a visible proponent of efforts to extend New York state law that had granted mayoral control but was scheduled to sunset in June 2009. Although publicly positioned as a homegrown, community-based organization, it was subsequently revealed that Bill Gates and Eli Broad had quietly given millions of dollars to help launch and support it.[74]

City Council Versus School Board in New York City: Who Testifies and About What Issues

Critics have suggested that mayoral control comes at the cost of diminished voice for advocacy and community-based groups representing parents, especially from minority communities.[75] Defenders of mayoral control argue that such complaints typically come from groups that previously had *too much* access: that by engaging a broader range of stakeholders, mayoral control provides a richer and more pluralistic form of democratic involvement, and that this is desirable even if it might entail shaving down the relative influence of a hyperinterested segment of the community that has gotten used to having its way. "Mayoral control promises to dilute the influence of teacher unions, by forcing them to compete alongside all other parties when it comes to shaping policy, contracts, and spending," Frederick Hess and Olivia Meeks project. "Rather than being free to dominate their own isolated, local education sphere, educational interests are brought into the larger give-and-take of municipal governance where they will have to vie for political influence alongside transportation, health services, environmental management, business development, and a number of other advocacy groups."[76]

While there are anecdotal and case study reports that support this, there is, to my knowledge, no systematic empirical evidence about the ways in which reabsorption of education decision making into general-purpose arenas alters the access by different groups at the local level. To examine this more closely, I compared information on those who have given testimony or made presentations to New York City's Panel

155

for Educational Policy (PEP), and the New York City Council's Committee on Education, as shown in figure 4.5.[77] PEP, as explained in chapter 3, is the appointed board that was initiated in 2002 as part of the New York state legislature's action granting mayoral control to Michael Bloomberg. PEP held ninety-seven sessions between September 23, 2002, and March 1, 2011. During that same period, the Committee on Education held 156 meetings, either alone or in some cases jointly with another council committee.

Some proponents of mayoral control suggest that it leads to a more disciplined and focused approach to policy making, one less subject to distracting battles among interest groups maneuvering for relative

FIGURE 4.5

Formal presenters: New York City Council versus Panel for Educational Policy, September 2002–March 2011

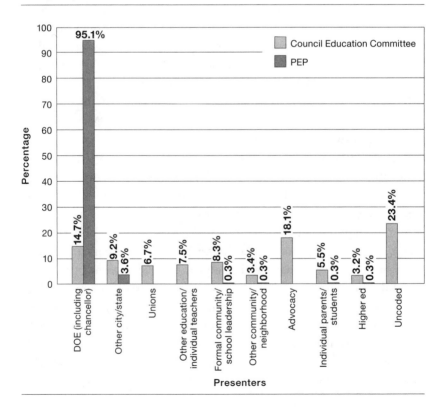

advantage at the cost of the collective good. Reflecting the Bloomberg administration's emphasis on management and control, the PEP meetings were regular (basically once a month) and tightly controlled, with few people called upon to testify, and nearly all of those being high-level officials from within the New York City Department of Education. The official minutes for the PEP meetings list as speakers those who were formally invited to make presentations; they do not include those who might be recognized from the floor for brief comments during the open discussion comments of the meeting.[78] This provides a window, then, into the formal witness agenda: a indication of whose views PEP considered important enough to formally solicit, but understating the extent to which parents, community groups, and others might gain airtime.[79]

Of the 305 presentations listed in the official minutes, all but 15 came from within the DOE (the chancellor or one of the deputy chancellors presented 127 times, accounting for 41.6 percent of all presenters).[80] Others who appeared at least ten times included the agency head responsible for Labor Policy and Implementation (twenty), the Division of Accountability and Assessment (fifteen), and the Senior Counselor to the Chancellor on education policy (eleven). The presenters who were not representing the DOE were, for the most part, also representative of organizations firmly nestled within the mayor's governance regime. Ten of the fifteen were presenters from the School Construction Authority; although nominally distinct from the DOE, changes in state law in 2002 gave the mayor power to appoint the authority's three members, with the chancellor serving as the chair.[81] Of the others, one was the head of the Leadership Academy, an organization established to train city principals. At the time he appeared (August 23, 2003), the Leadership Academy was formally separate from the DOE but funded through a nonprofit education fund deliberately established to support the DOE's efforts; it subsequently became part of the DOE budget in 2008. Two were representatives from units within the City University of New York.[82] And one was the chair of the PEP Arts Advisory Committee.[83]

The only formal presentation even remotely representing a grassroots organization outside the mayor and chancellor's orbit was a letter from parents concerned about overcrowding, safety, and programming at their school. The group had not been listed as part of the formal agenda, but after it made its concerns known during the "public comments" segment of the meeting, Klein, as chair, requested, without objection, that the letter be included in the minutes.

During the same period of time, the city council's Committee on Education held 156 meetings, at which the minutes record 2,403 people presenting testimony of some kind. Unlike PEP, the council does include in its formal minutes the names and affiliations of those who fill out forms indicating an "intent to appear and speak." This in itself reflects a more serious regard for input that is not directly solicited and managed by the incumbent officials and their staffs, but it does make the comparison across the two organizations an imperfect one. In contrast to PEP, the overwhelming majority of those officially recorded as giving testimony were from organizations outside of the DOE, indeed mostly outside of government. The chancellor appeared 30 times (1.25 percent); other DOE members, 323 (13.4 percent); other members of the mayor's office or School Construction Authority, 43 (1.79 percent); borough presidents or their reps, 36 (1.5 percent); unions representing teachers or principals and administrators, 161 (6.7 percent); and other education organizations or individual educators, 112 (4.7 percent).

What distinguishes PEP from the city council committee is the formal legitimization of different voices. Early in its history, when chaired by Klein, PEP was highly controlled and antiseptic, "a study in blandness and efficiency," as reported by the *New York Times*. "Gone were the self-aggrandizing speeches, the barbed questions meant to undermine the visibly uncomfortable schools chancellor, the verbal fisticuffs that would often follow back in the days of a powerful, unapologetically political Board of Education." Of sixty meetings from September 2002 through 2008, nearly all of which started promptly at 6:00 p.m., only three adjourned later than 8:30 and only one lasted more than three hours.[84] Later—especially after the state legislature, in extending mayoral control, toughened requirements for impact statements and public notices about school closings and proposals to move charters into public school buildings—the crowds at some PEP meetings ballooned, and meetings began to run deep into the night, with raucous commentary from the floor. Of twenty-one meetings between September 2009 and March 2011, only three lasted two hours or less; thirteen lasted until at least 9:30 p.m., and five ended at midnight or later. The official roster of witnesses, however, remained small and focused almost exclusively on school-based officials. Blocked from expressing themselves fully, critics of the administration turned more to the council, which out of habit, eagerness to flex its own muscles, and a growing confidence that it could challenge the mayor without suffering heavy retribution, became the forum where alternative visions could be recognized.[85]

———

Theories about institutional politics—about venue shopping, venue defense, and venue shaping—all predict that shifts along institutional fault lines can alter the mix and relative prominence of policy stakeholders, ideas, and instruments. There is evidence, I have argued in this chapter, that the reabsorption of education decision making into general-purpose arenas may be having this effect. School-specific institutions give favored access to those with special expertise and intense interest; teachers and parents have traditionally dominated, and ideas about accountability, performance standards, and the introduction of market forces—ideas with currency in other areas of domestic policy—have been slow to penetrate. As more and more key decisions about schools are migrating into general-purpose areas, the mix of influential actors and ideas has begun to look more similar to that involved in policy decisions about economic development, taxes, environmental protection, zoning, housing, crimes, and social services.

There is much we still do not know about the end of education exceptionalism, and much that is uncertain about how far it may proceed and how deep its eventual consequences may be. This book, overall, should be understood as a call for more research and deliberation and for expanding our understanding of institutional change beyond the important—but not *all* important—debates about privatization and centralization. Despite the curtain of uncertainty, however, it is important to begin to think about possible implications. And it is to that task that I turn in the next, and final, chapter.

CHAPTER FIVE

THE END OF EXCEPTIONALISM: IMPLICATIONS FOR THE FUTURE

AMERICANS LIKE to think about education as an issue that floats above the hurly-burly of politics and conflict. This is what Frederick Wirt and Michael Kirst labeled the *apolitical myth*: "a mutual but unspoken long-standing agreement . . . that the world of education is and should be separate from the world of politics."[1] In other arenas, Americans might be divided by contrasting values and competing material interests, but when it comes to schooling they prefer to think of themselves as united in the belief that when a child receives a good education we all benefit. Investment in education is generally thought to raise economic performance, nurture social values, build a common foundation of knowledge, and create citizens who are more tolerant, more analytical, and more capable of fulfilling their role in a healthy democracy. But conflict is endemic in complex societies, and the appearance of consensus usually means that discordant voices have been subordinated, sublimated, or pushed to the margins. As E. E. Schattschneider famously observed: "Some issues are organized into politics while others are organized out."[2]

The truth is, Americans differ in many deeply held values concerning topics that schools cannot easily avoid: nationalism, religiosity, scientific skepticisms, obedience to authority, deference to parents, acceptance of diversity, individualism versus conformity, creativity versus mastery of common material, ethnic and racial identity, civil law versus moral principle, and the nature of family, to name a few. And Americans differ in the direct material stake they hold in the system of public schooling, based on whether they have or will have children who attend public schools, whether they own property whose value is influenced by local schools' reputation, whether they have jobs in the schools, whether they work for or hold stock in private companies that compete for school system contracts, the amount and kinds of taxes they pay, and the opportunity costs they might incur if funding that goes to schooling instead came to be directed into other programs of which they are beneficiaries.

The defining elements of the traditional American system for education policy—the combination of localism and segmentation into school-specific decision-making venues—can be understood in part as an effort to give reality to the apolitical myth despite these underlying incongruities. Local control organized some potential conflicts out of politics by shrinking the geographic boundaries within which differences must be battled, negotiated, or accommodated. Given people's tendencies to cluster residentially based on shared values, common incomes, religion, race, and the like, smaller communities are more likely to be homogenous, or to create dominating majorities that keep conflict submerged. School-specific governance institutions organize out different potential conflicts by rearranging other kinds of boundaries; they attract and provide favored access to those with a direct stake, intense interest, or special expertise. While they may differ on many specifics, these actors usually share a commitment to strong public investment in education. Delegating decisions to venues in which they dominate takes off the table competing claims on the public purse, and diminishes the voice of those who might be more concerned about costs, taxes, and efficiency. These school-specific actors also have deep knowledge about education, and delegating decisions to venues in which they dominate might reduce conflicts that are based on ignorance or misinformation.

The end of education exceptionalism—the reabsorption of education policy into general-purpose arenas of governance and politics—has implications for how education is governed, which conflicts will remain latent, and which conflicts will be met head on. Changes in governance structures will not determine America's education future on their own, of course. Decisions and actions made by political leaders, education leaders, and other important stakeholders—both the substance of the choices and the skill and wisdom with which they are pursued—are critical variables also. And these are matters that institutions influence but do not dictate. Institutional rules of the game tilt the field of probabilities, however, by altering the configuration of interests, issues, and policy that influence the nation's schools. What will change is more than just the *manner* in which shared goals are pursued; what will change is *whose values and interests* will determine the goals to which policies are oriented. In the world of general-purpose politics, what Schattschneider referred to as *the scope of conflict* is expanded, new voices heard from, new options put into play. In the process, some previously influential voices will be muted, and some quiescent conflicts will reemerge.

But are the changes, overall, something to be welcomed or feared? If the former, are there things we can be doing to make the transition speedier and more complete? If the latter, is it possible to reverse course or at least put on the brakes? Making predictions is hazardous, but one way to transform it into more than an exercise in idle fantasy is to ground it in an understanding of the arc of change to date. With that in mind, I begin this chapter with an overview of the historical developments described throughout this book, and distill some general observations about the momentum and manageability of the end of education exceptionalism.

The story of education governance to date includes strong doses of path dependency, context-specific institutional politics, and unanticipated effects. There were—and still are—good reasons to sequester education policy, and the institutional realization of education exceptionalism became a powerful and deeply engrained element in American life. But much of the rationale in its favor was devised ex post facto, and its shape and the forces that protected it over time were historically contingent. Education exceptionalism, I am led to conclude, is more an anomaly than a natural realization of a sustainable institutional alternative. And just as nature abhors a vacuum, institutional politics abhors anomalies and tends to wear them down.

If the reabsorption of education into general-purpose politics and governance is here to stay, what, then, should we think and do? This chapter concludes with a discussion of both risks and opportunities. The major risks, as I explain, are that investment in public education will suffer in competition with other priorities, that education policy decisions will be driven by broader political currents in place of educational expertise. The benefits, if realized, could be substantial: a more broadly conceptualized understanding of education that incorporates schools and teachers into a multisector approach to improving learning and narrowing learning gaps, and a more inclusive constituency to project and protect the collective interest in public education and sustain those efforts over time.

PATH DEPENDENCY, INSTITUTIONAL POLITICS, AND UNANTICIPATED EFFECTS

It is easy and tempting to picture institutional choice as a deliberate process informed by political philosophy. This is an image deeply etched in Americans' understanding of the nation's founding. The precarious task of wresting power from Great Britain and the serious financial problems, security risks, and popular unrest experienced under the Articles of Confederation created a crisis atmosphere in the eighteenth century, in which it was clear that the stakes attached to making the right choices were high. The deeply thoughtful exchanges in political essays like those encapsulated in the Federalist Papers and in subsequent debates at the constitutional convention underscore that key decisions were made after smart people gave deep thought to the issues, and after clashing ideas, theories, and predictions were fully aired.

But one is hard-pressed to apply an equivalent narrative to the birthing of education exceptionalism. The full reasons for the initial separation of education governance from other general-purpose institutions are partially obscured by the passage of time and the seductive power of reconstructed rationales that make the choices appear logical and inevitable. But at least part of the explanation is that an independent path had been established before there was much self-conscious discussion of school governance at all.

Public education today is a high-stakes enterprise, both in the material terms of jobs and contracts and in its link to the collective interest of a nation wrestling with global competition and the internal tensions deriving from inequalities in wealth and well-being. The creation of separate school governance structures—with separate electoral and budgeting arrangements and with boundaries often distinct from counties, municipalities, and townships—occurred, however, when the stakes were much less clear.

The Origins and Institutionalization of Exceptionalism

During the colonial era, education was largely a family-based or informal local affair.[3] It was not until the middle of the nineteenth century that the common school movement, with champions such as Horace Mann, began to establish public schooling as a core government function. At the same time, by making education compulsory, the common school movement asserted the claim that the broad community had a stake in educating its citizens, a stake that was distinct from the one that parents held in the well-being of their own children.[4] While there were various localized skirmishes over the changes induced by the common school movement, substantial and self-conscious battles over governance issues did not emerge until around the turn of the twentieth century. In large cities, removing school decisions from general-purpose municipal school governance was part of a turn-of-the-twentieth-century effort by Progressive reformers to reduce the role of partisan politics and the power of political urban machines in all matters of local policy. For most of the nation, where schools and districts were still extremely modest institutions, the key battles were over consolidation of school districts, and largely led by professional interests who believed tiny—often one-school—districts lacked the resources, capacity, and will to meet their visions of what public education should provide. But while these battles ultimately pushed education governance to a higher level of institutionalization, they accentuated rather than erased the distinctions between the governance of schools and of other elements of domestic policy. Writing in the mid-1960s, Laurence Iannaccone argued that education governance was still "a holdover from the eighteenth and nineteenth century." While other components of domestic policy were increasingly centralized and formalized as part of the emergence of the nation's maturing welfare state, "school districts remain as the government operation most like a mid-western adaptation of the New England Town Meeting or like the operations of the *Music Man* set in *Peyton Place*."[5]

For these reasons, the anomalous status of education should be understood at least in part as a manifestation of *path dependency*, a theory constructed to account for how small initial and seemingly inconsequential divergences can accumulate into larger ones. But to serve as a real tool for understanding, path dependency must be more than an intuitively appealing metaphor. Paths in the woods, after all, do not always diverge; they can run parallel and later rejoin. To explain the mechanisms that convert small institutional differences into large and deeply embedded ones, we need to supplement the path dependency metaphor with theories about institutional defense and the roles of *iron triangles* and *supportive rationales*.[6] The initial alignment of interests might be opportunistic and contingent—for example, a school board member with ambitions for higher office might champion more spending on public education and higher salaries for teachers, creating a shared stake with the union and superintendent. But according to the theory of iron triangles, what began as opportunistic ties has a way of becoming enshrined over time, through personal relationships, sharing of ideas, and a revolving door of job succession particular among the staffs.[7] According to the theory of supportive rationales, existing institutions build ideologies that legitimate and prioritize compatible problem definitions and policy approaches over others; as a result, innovative ideas, especially those that potentially challenge the status quo, often are dismissed out of hand.[8]

Applied more specifically to the case of education exceptionalism, consideration of path dependency, iron triangles, and supportive rationales suggests that education governance developed as an anomaly through a combination of intent, happenstance, and institutional politics that—because of the decentralization that historically has characterized education decision making—played out in different places with different timing and context-specific details. Once in place, as the policy subsystem matured, it provided favored access to a limited set of interest groups with intense interest in public schools and a commitment to maintain and expand public investment in education.

At the time of path deviation—when general-purpose municipal governance moved in one direction and independent school districts in another—teachers were not a powerful force either individually or collectively. The feminization of the teaching force in the middle of the nineteenth century, in combination with dominant gender biases, marginalized teacher voices; by default, the role of defining and defending the institutional and intellectual touchstones of the emerging profession fell to leading lights within the academic education community, civic leaders, local businesspeople, and parents within more affluent communities. But the administrative apparatus of education delivery grew rapidly, fueled by growing enrollments and the consolidation movement. As this happened, superintendents and central-office bureaucracies became steadily more influential. By the 1970s, teacher unions, bolstered by newly won powers of collective bargaining, became a major—some say *the* major—element of the supporting coalition.[9]

Hyperlocalization meant that schools often were seen as extensions of dominant community norms and that investment in good schools would accrue as appreciation in local property values, expanding support for the existing arrangements beyond those who might currently have a child attending the public schools. "School systems with their legal structure of boards, administrators, and teaching staffs, increasingly tend to be encased in a network of extra-governmental friends and allies," Iannaccone observed. "A civic cocoon of advisory groups, lay committees, parent-teacher organizations, grade mothers, Girl Scout Brownies, and athletic boosters surround, politically protect, and nurture the local education leaders in school district matters."[10] Buffered from the broader interplay of party politics, frequently funded by dedicated revenue streams, and with leadership selected off-cycle in low-turnout elections dominated by parent and increasingly by teacher organizations, the school-specific governance system had little resemblance to anything that might have been envisioned when the governance path diverted a century before.

Many of the attributes that distinguished the education-specific governance system were sources of genuine strength—not simply the reflection of the raw power of an increasingly muscular professional education sector, but also a system that earned legitimacy based on performance. The strengths included a prominent place for professional expertise, and a stability of funding and support that was less vulnerable than other domestic policies to competing demands, shifting public priorities, changing political regimes, and the vicissitudes of fiscal pressure. Nonetheless, unanticipated side effects developed into problems and tensions that helped to fuel a potent backlash.

These included bureaucratic sluggishness, a lack of coordination with other agencies, selective recruitment, socialization into a narrow mind-set, and a reliance on a zealous but narrow coalition to maintain the privileged position of education insiders.

Pressures and Facilitators of Reabsorption

The so-called Great Migration, beginning roughly around 1910 and continuing through the post–World War II period, brought large numbers of African Americans out of the South and into northern cities, and the emergence of the civil rights movement in the 1950s and 1960s gave this demographic shift a political voice. The closed nature of the existing system contributed to frustrations on the part of newcomers who felt they had limited access to jobs and limited influence on policies. At the same time, the changing racial and ethnic composition of the classroom and, eventually, the teaching and leadership force, unsettled white America and put psychological distance between the schools they remembered and those that now seemed to serve "other peoples' children."[11]

When the nation's economic and political dominance on the world stage weakened, the view of America's schools as failing to compete bruised their image, opening the education profession to criticism from which it had been largely spared. Teachers had historically benefited from the fact that local parents and communities generally held them in high regard. Teacher unions, more aggressive and generally successful during the 1960s and 1970s, arguably took this support too much for granted, and failed to cultivate allies, thinking their claim to expertise put them in a position to hold off parent and community pressures to renegotiate their role from passive supporters to equal partners. This did not signal a sharp cleavage between parents and teachers—the alignment was resilient, especially in the more homogenous and affluent suburbs—but the relationship began to degrade.

The weakening of the constellation of interests and perspectives supporting the traditional system took place in the context of two additional factors that facilitated the drift toward general-purpose governance. The first involved complementary shifts along the other two critical fault lines in the institutional landscape. Separate governance arenas for education were never as sharply etched at the state and national levels as they have been locally, and because of that, the drift toward centralization within the federal system moved more of the political action to arenas where the traditional defenders of education exceptionalism had less leverage. The marked expansion of the private provider community—publishers, testing companies, education management organizations (EMOs) and charter management organizations (CMOs), supplementary education services, and the like—created new interest groups with a stake in education. These groups also had a stake in shifting decisions about education into general-purpose venues, where public officials were less likely to be beholden to education-specific interest groups and conventional norms about what education should look like.

The second broad facilitator is one that can be thought of as a rubber band effect. Since the single-purpose, buffered, and protected status of American education was always an anomaly, the reassertion of general-purpose politics and government once its vulnerabilities emerged is not really a surprise; the true surprise is that it has taken so long. Those outside the system—general-purpose politicians looking for ways to build power and influence; private companies looking for a piece of the action, the same kind of contract action they'd obtained for other public services—had long been held at bay, intimidated by the iron triangle that protected the status quo, as well as by the treacherous currents of race, religion, and family values that threatened to flare up when local equilibrium was disrupted.

The issue of race, as I discussed in chapters 2 and 3, played a critical role in making general-purpose politicians reluctant to wade into what might be rough currents of intergroup conflict. But the phenomenon might have been broader, not limited to elected politicians but incorporating important civic actors as well. Business and civic groups did not begin to coalesce into a high-profile and forceful education reform constituency until the 1980s. Most accounts explain this as a consequence of a growing sense that the nation was losing ground in an increasingly competitive global economy, and there is little doubt that this was a powerful animating force. But the business community is often gun-shy when it comes to hot-button issues. The economic interests of businesses—in hoping to cultivate a broad customer base, in making sure not to roil investors who might see social reform efforts as a distraction from pursuing the bottom line—led them to want to stay out of heated disputes on these matters.[12] But the gradual receding of flashpoints such as desegregation and mandatory busing has made business and civic groups somewhat less skittish. They have gradually become a more active constituency, one with established access to, and comfort with, general-purpose politicians. This in turn has prompted some governors, mayors, and legislatures to move to recapture the reins of education policy.

Here to Stay, but Not All the Way

We're not likely to return to the earlier era of localism and school-specific decision making. There might be pauses and backflow, but the genie is out of the bottle. If the past is prelude, however, and if lessons from political development in other areas apply to education as well, the transition will not be a complete one. General-purpose government and politics will be layered onto the preexisting array of school-specific institutions, which will have diminished authority but will not fade away.

The general history of policy reform, as well as the more specific story of the end of education exceptionalism, discounts the likelihood that we will make a clean and sharp break to a more pure and internally coherent system. Instead, the result almost certainly will be a mixed system, with new venues and actors layered onto the old, and with the degree of transformation variable across states and subject to retraction due to political backlash or reconsideration based on experience. This kind of mixed result is manifested in the historical push and pull tensions between centralization and decentralization in American federalism: an outcome that was metaphorically captured when Morton Grodzins characterized it as a marble cake (as opposed to a layer cake) as noted in chapter 1.[13] Similarly, when it comes to the public-private fault line, we have settled on a resolution that is not firmly and decisively in one sector or the other: the development of charter schools and portfolio management models as mixed systems combining elements of market choice and private delivery with public oversight and accountability. And some sort of variable and incomplete transition is what we should expect along the third fault line of institutional change as well.

The structural shifts we have been discussing are real and important, but I do not claim or believe that they are moving inexorably to a complete displacement of the traditional regime. The changes are like the slow shifting of tectonic plates, not the earthquake to end all earthquakes. Core institutions persist precisely because they are resistant to change, and once in place they develop protective mechanisms to remain in place. The groups and ideas that develop to sustain core institutions may or may not be the same as those that accounted for their original development. Teachers were not a collective influential force at the turn of the twentieth century when separate governance structures first took root, but their unions today are a primary source of their defense. The Progressives who pushed at that time to wrest education away from machine-dominated general-purpose politics were wary of ethnic identity and a role for parents in setting policies, but identity politics and parent and community engagement are themes that resonate now among those rallying around elected school boards and battling against their extinction. I do not project that special-purpose governance arrangements, education specializing institutions and venues, and single-purpose interest groups are destined for obsolescence. I expect them to be resilient, to use power and argument to resist some of the end of education exceptionalism, to adjust tactics and settle into somewhat new patterns of interaction, but to still be around for many years to come.

Just as the early development and long domination of local school districts did not make general-purpose governance and politics irrelevant for education decision making, so too the muscling up of the general-purpose venues we are witnessing now likely will stop short of displacing or even marginalizing local school districts and education-specific agencies, committees, and interest groups. The game is changing, but given the many special and political factors that enforce incrementalism, many of the familiar rules, groups, tactics, and outcomes will likely stay on the scene. The effect, as others have written about institutional change, is more like "layering" than replacement, with new institutional arrangements simply added to the mix.[14]

The result is likely to be a complex field of play, where shopping for the most hospitable venue becomes an increasingly important tactical tool.[15] The overlapping decision-making venues open more channels for new ideas, but they also have the potential to make things worse, since the lack of coherent management or clear lines of accountability is, as many argue, a central problem in public education.[16] The venue-shopping environment also opens avenues for influence by different groups with differing ideas and interests, but those with limited resources and limited mobility might be at a distinct disadvantage because of the expense of playing politics in this complicated landscape.

END OF EXCEPTIONALISM: REASONS FOR CONCERN

Critics of the contemporary shifts in education governance are derided by reformers who portray them as blind loyalists to tradition or as self-interested defenders of a regime in which they have prospered even though it has become dysfunctional and obsolete in the face of today's challenges. But there are reasons that institutions, once they take root, persist and develop strong constituencies. Prime among these reasons is that they address at least some important societal needs. As Robert Merton observed, "we should ordinarily (not invariably) expect persistent social patterns and social structures to perform positive functions which are at the time not adequately fulfilled by other existing patterns and structures."[17] In considering where we might wish to see the equilibrium set between the older school-specific institutions and the expanding general-purpose ones, it is worthwhile to consider what might be put at risk by the end of education exceptionalism.

The first risk involves the degradation of expertise in the core areas of instruction. General-purpose decision makers almost inevitably lack the detailed technical knowledge of education and curriculum held by experts. David Cohen and Susan Moffitt make a compelling case that much of the energies and resources expended in the contemporary efforts to reform education have lacked traction precisely because they were disconnected from knowledge about the aims, instruments, capabilities, and environment that shape educational practice and determine its consequences.[18] And the reform models that seek to work around the traditional model of professionalism—charter schools that depend on waves of young teachers willing to work longer hours with fewer benefits and job protections; education technology solutions that envision teachers able to handle large classrooms while students spend increasing amounts of their time doing self-paced learning—are largely untested in terms of their sustainability and scalability. It is reasonable to be suspicious of the notion that the only expertise worth valuing is steeped in the particularities of education, detailed in its understanding of curriculum and instruction, delivered through traditional institutions for training professional educators, and leavened by years in the trenches of classroom experience. Yet it is totally unreasonable to assume that these traditionally recognized forms of expertise are not important.

A second risk is that investment in public education will not fare well in the broader arena of general-purpose politics. The initial expansion of executive involvement in education and the growing role of general-purpose institutions rode in on a wave of broad enthusiasm for the importance of education as a way to leverage economic competitiveness and to narrow the inequalities associated with race, ethnicity, and socioeconomic class. It benefited as well from a relatively expansive economy through many of the key years, and strong philanthropic support that found working with mayors, governors, and the White House more appealing than working with the slow-moving traditional public school sector. To the extent that public education can deliver on these fronts, its contribution to social well-being is objectively important. But there is no guarantee that objective importance will drive the politics and policy agenda of the future. After having played a major role in the previous four presidential elections, education was not a prominent feature of the 2008 campaign or the lead-up to 2012, displaced by concerns over the economy, deficits, and federal health care reform. Within general-purpose governance arenas, calls to invest more resources into public education must compete on a head-to-head basis with other demands on governmental attention, as well as with the arguments to cut taxes and rely more on private incentives and market forces. Research on governmental agenda setting establishes both the somewhat fickle nature of public attention and the ways in which objective measures of need compete with politics, ideology, symbolism, biased perceptions about beneficiaries, external events, and serendipity as determinants of what the government chooses to focus on.[19] Advocates for public education might need to find new ways of framing their issues in order to attract and maintain allies among non-school-focused groups that share some of their aspirations but are also competing for public and philanthropic support.

A third risk concerns the weakening of what Kenneth Meier and Laurence O'Toole identify as the representative and democratic functions of bureaucracies. Although the discretion that bureaucracies often enjoy is typically presented as a threat to democratic control, Meier and O'Toole point out that "bureaucracy itself can sometimes facilitate democracy and political leaders can sometimes impede it."[20] They illustrate this with an analysis suggesting that treatment of Latino students is more supportive when there are Latino teachers, and that this is more important even than having Latinos elected onto the local school board.

Fourth, some aspects of general-purpose politics and the increased importance of venue shopping might reinforce inequities in political influence. General-purpose politics expands the scope of conflict. Under some circumstances, as Schattschneider observed, expanding the scope of conflict can benefit groups that have traditionally been outmuscled by bringing some more powerful allies into the fray.[21] But that formulation may play out differently in this case. Low-income and minority groups have benefited from some aspects of education-specific institutions. They have more clout in low-turnout and ward-based school board elections than mayoral elections that are conducted citywide, where campaign funding is more important and where older households, singles, and those committed to private schools are also engaged and likely to vote.[22] As I suggested in the previous chapter, the end of education exceptionalism has facilitated the involvement of a new set of actors from outside the local community, and while many of these profess a mission of helping low-income children, their greater influence comes at some cost to the political leverage of locally rooted groups.

Finally, even if general-purpose institutions keep education high on the policy agenda, there is no guarantee that they will offer coherent plans or deliver effective policies. Enthusiasts for stronger executive involvement portray it as a step toward more rational, comprehensive, and decisive decision making. This vision may prove naïve if, as I have suggested, the governance changes under way also include more active legislatures and courts. Each branch of general-purpose governance has its own history of dysfunction, and the clashes among them could just result in new forms of policy churn or gridlock.[23]

END OF EXCEPTIONALISM: REASONS FOR OPTIMISM

The concerns I've laid out are substantial ones. It is important, though, to realize that there are opportunities as well. Two kinds stand out. The first involves prospects for a richer and more flexible set of ideas, evidence, and policy options. Contemporary reformers have emphasized this as part of the rationale for moving power away from school-specific governments and agencies, and because the argument is probably familiar I'll give it a light treatment here. The second opportunity has to do with prospects for a broader conceptualization of what education means, and for generating a multisector approach to education reform that gives due attention to the role played by nonschool factors. This opportunity is attractive and important. While realizing the potential will be challenging, it is this aspect of the end of exceptionalism that converts it, in my own mind, from an inexorable change that must be accommodated and endured to a catalyst for a reinvigorated and more sustainable movement for genuine and progressive change.

The more all-purpose arena of governance within which education policies are shaped and implemented today means that unconventional ideas for delivering education are more likely to get a hearing. This is partly because the mix of interest groups that have access to general-purpose venues is broader than in school-specific arenas. Policy entrepreneurs who lack traditional education credentials—who have not been teachers or principals, whose academic training is in management, or law, or science and technology—are better able to make the case in the context of general-purpose governance that their different kinds of expertise are relevant and should be taken into account.

General-purpose governance and politics have also increased the emphasis upon improved data systems and high-quality empirical research. I know of no a priori reason why data and research should play more of a role in general-purpose venues. Traditional school systems, after all, have long collected scads of data about student race, absenteeism, free or reduced-price school lunch eligibility, and the like. For the most part, though, this data has been collected for administrative purposes (such as determining eligibility for certain programs or complying with federal requirements to monitor racial composition). Some large districts have an internal research capacity, but for the most part districts have not tended to use such data analytically or engaged in serious efforts to evaluate the outcomes of different types of interventions. Nor have districts embraced the idea of sharing data with outside researchers. For at least the past decade, there has been a substantial ratcheting up of the amount and quality of school data and education policy research, and there is little question that the primary momentum came from outside school districts. Some of this emanated from the federal level. The Institute for Education Science, formed within the U.S. Department of Education in 2002, described its mission as "the transformation of education into an evidence-based field," and Congress, in the No Child Left Behind legislation, included more than one hundred references to the importance of grounding educational policy decisions on scientifically based evidence.[24] Even before the federal government began explicitly supporting this, a handful of states began developing student-level longitudinal databases; in Florida, a national leader, the impetus came from the state legislature.[25] While some traditional districts have also actively developed research capacities, the emphasis has been especially prominent in large systems adopting portfolio management models that require constant monitoring of performance, with mayoral control cities typically in the lead.[26]

Along with newer ideas and evidence has come experimentation with a wider array of policy instruments, especially those involving public-private partnerships and the introduction of market forces. Here, the different backgrounds and experiences of the general-purpose officials themselves come into play. While school systems have a fair amount of experience contracting with private providers of auxiliary services like janitorial and food service provision, doing so to provide core aspects of the educational enterprise is a new and somewhat alien and threatening concept for those accustomed to the traditional public school model. But contracting out has been a major and somewhat routine experience for mayors, governors, and their associated legislative bodies for many years in areas like road and highway construction, parking enforcement, daycare provision, and the like.[27]

For those frustrated with what they consider to be complacency, lack of imagination, or self-serving bureaucracy, the changes in the institutional landscape have been welcome. There are bitter and still unresolved debates about whether the new reform elements and the initiatives they have launched in charter schooling; test-based accountability for students, teachers, and schools; portfolio management districts; new educational technologies; alternative certification; and the like are leading to better education or worse, narrowing achievement gaps or exacerbating inequalities.[28] But there are few who would deny that a system with a reputation for stasis has been opened to disruption and change.

But new is not always better. The policy approaches that have been spearheaded by general-purpose governments and the constellation of interests that have found favored access within them have yet to prove themselves on the bottom line of student performance.[29] Moreover, the history of education reform in general has suggested that sequential episodes of innovation and hot new ideas have often generated a cycle of enthusiasm followed by disillusionment.[30] More important than a greater openness and experimentation, then, might be the prospect that the end of education exceptionalism could create the conditions for a broader vision of education, one recognizing the role of both school and nonschool factors, drawing on multiple sectors of government in a more comprehensive attack on low and unequal educational achievement, and supported by a multi-issue coalition of interest groups that is more stable and less prone to infighting than is currently the case.

The chance of making genuine progress in addressing educational needs in the U.S. has been stymied by a stale and fundamentally dysfunctional stand-off between those who emphasize school-centered intervention and those calling for a broader, bolder approach that encompasses nonschool forces like concentrated poverty, public health inequities, racially and economically diverse housing and neighborhoods, social services, and social-emotional supports.[31] While both sides nod in acknowledgment of the truism that both school and nonschool factors are important, they differ fundamentally in the relative emphasis they place on the two. The "schools can do it" crowd warns that broad inequalities in wealth and living conditions are so tangled and tough to resolve that calling attention to them risks losing focus on school-based interventions that are immediately available, effective, and less divisive. The "broader, bolder" crowd argues that efforts focused just on schools have failed, and that the good things that schools can do are overwhelmed and defeated when surrounding conditions are left unaddressed.[32]

In just the last couple of years, there has been a virtual explosion of serious research that begins to map out the empirical connections between nonschool factors and educational outcomes.[33] Converting this research into a politically feasible policy agenda remains a challenge. "Sure, these things matter, is the general attitude, but they are so big, powerful, and deeply ingrained that to even acknowledge their import is to risk losing focus on things like accountability, standards, tenure reform—policy levers we know how to manipulate," as S. Paul Reville and I wrote elsewhere. "Attention to nonschool factors is feared as an excuse to let bad schools and teachers off the hook. It seems to be a call for a vast increase in spending in an era in which retrenchment is the order of the day."[34]

But several factors are combining in ways that make a more comprehensive attack on educational challenges more likely, and the end of education exceptionalism is one of these. Trade-offs and spillovers across policy domains are more visible in general-purpose government where multiple bureaucracies report to a single administration. And the levers for addressing these trade-offs and spillovers are more readily in reach. When schools do what they are supposed to do, payoffs are not limited to school performance; they include an array of human- and social-capital outcomes, including lower crime rates, greater tolerance across racial and ethnic subgroups, stronger neighborhoods, and overall economic vitality. And the causal arrow runs in the other direction as well: when neighborhoods provide stable and economically integrated housing conditions, social services, access to affordable health care, and lower levels of health-threatening environmental conditions, student mobility and absenteeism decline, and learning and educational attainment benefit. Traditional school boards might sense that school-based clinics or midnight basketball would create conditions more conducive to teaching, but governors, state legislators, mayors, and city councils are better positioned to get health departments, parks and recreation departments, and principals into the same room.

The incentive for general-purpose leaders to undertake a more comprehensive approach goes beyond abstract idealism. Faced with tight fiscal environments and the pressure to achieve measurable gains, ignoring spillover costs and benefits is a luxury they can no longer afford. Public officials need to know if a dollar spent on asthma screening generates more benefit than a dollar spent on computers in the classroom, or if a dollar devoted to in-school health care helps parents better manage family-versus-employer tensions and retain urgently needed jobs.

Being politicians, general-purpose leaders also need supportive constituencies if they are to take the risk of battling bureaucratic silos, reallocating resources, and in some instances spending money early in order to save money in the longer term.[35] That means it is also critical that there be a coalition of multi-issue groups—including but not limited to traditional advocates for public education.

A MULTI-ISSUE POLITICS TO FIT THE MULTI-ISSUE INSTITUTIONAL LANDSCAPE?

Political futures do not simply unfold; they are created. How far education exceptionalism will erode and whether that represents a good thing or a bad one will depend in large measure on political battles yet to be fought, how they are structured, and how they are resolved. Will devotees of strong public education work hard to turn the tide against the growing role of general-purpose government and politics in the effort to save an institutional arrangement that for many decades gave favored access to those with the greatest direct stake? Or, recognizing the handwriting on the wall, will they recalibrate their strategies and begin to build the kinds of arguments and coalitions that might better position them for influence in a multi-issue environment?

Teacher unions, parent groups, and other traditional public school advocacy organizations might not easily make the switch from battling within school-specific venues to joining with other interest groups to collaboratively push for public investment in human and social capital, including but not limited to schools. Nostalgia is powerful, and some will pine for the "good old days" when public belief in the superiority of American schools, dominant and protective school boards, and dedicated local property tax revenue streams meant proponents of school funding could often get what they needed without having to make the compromises necessary to win and keep allies with progressive agendas of their own.

But necessity is the mother of reinvention. The risks that the end of education exceptionalism will lead to relative disinvestment or susceptibility to policy fads will be substantial absent a broad coalition capable of defending education in a multi-issue competitive environment. And without a multi-issue coalition capable of articulating and providing pressure for a cross-sector approach to integrating school and nonschool policies, the potential for a more comprehensive approach to building education achievement and narrowing educational gaps is likely to go unrealized. As the school-specific institutions that historically served them well gradually lose relative influence and power, it will fall upon education advocates to refashion their arguments and political tactics to attract and hold allies for whom spending on schools is not necessarily the highest priority. We will be better off if they do; my expectation is that they will.

NOTES

CHAPTER 1

1. (Hess, 1998).
2. Quoted in (Riley, 2009).
3. (Bryk, Easton, Kerbow, Rollow, & Sebring, 1992): 26.
4. (Iannaccone, 1967): 99.
5. Ibid., 10.
6. This is a *re*absorption because control over school policy often was in the province of general-purpose government and politics prior to the Progressive Era's successful efforts to wrest the schools away from "professional politicians" and the urban machines that treated schools, at times, like patronage mills.
7. (Henig, 2009c).
8. (Hodgson, 2010; Lipset, 1997).
9. (Kirst & Wirt, 2009): 6; also (Tyack, 1974).
10. For example, there are also lines of cleavage among the branches of government.
11. On the centralization of education policy and the attenuation of localism, see (DeBray, McDermott, & Wohlstetter, 2005; Henig, 2009d; Kaestle, 2007; Manna, 2006; McDermott, 1999; McGuinn, 2006; M. A. Vinovskis, 2008). On the shifting relationship between public and private, see (Bulkley, Henig, & Levin, 2010; Burch, 2009; Chubb & Moe, 1990; Henig, Holyoke, Lacireno-Paquet, & Moser, 2003).
12. The legal principle that local governments are creations of the states and that any reasonable doubt concerning their power should be resolved in favor of the state is known as Dillon's Rule, after the mid–nineteenth-century judge and legal theorist John Forrest Dillon.
13. (Manna, 2006; Timar, 1997).
14. (Kirst, 2004): 18.
15. (McDermott, 1999; Reed, 2003).
16. (Timar, 1997): 237.
17. Data from the National Center for Education Statistics. Number of districts from Table 90. Number of public school districts and public and private elementary and secondary schools: Selected years, 1869–70 through 2008–09, http://nces.ed.gov/programs/digest/d10/tables/dt10_090.asp. Enrollment from Table 35. Historical

summary of public elementary and secondary school statistics: Selected years, 1869–70 through 2007–08, http://nces.ed.gov/programs/digest/d10/tables/dt10_035.asp.

18. (Hunt, 1983).

19. (Caldwell, 1985).

20. In discussing the growing federal role, Manna draws a distinction between growing federal *interest*, manifest by the early 1980s, and growing federal *involvement*, which came a decade later (Manna, 2006).

21. (Fuhrman, 1994): 83–84.

22. (McGuinn, 2006).

23. (McGuinn, 2010).

24. Critics worry that movement toward involving the private sector is part of a direct assault on traditions of democratic and collective responsibility for the nation's children (Lipman, 2011; Saltman, 2005), while proponents see resistance to private sector involvement as misguided allegiance to a failed system of indifferent and unresponsive bureaucracies backed by self-interested unions (Chubb & Moe, 1990; Lieberman, 2000). The result is a debate premised on the nation facing a stark choice between government or private control. In reality, ours is a mixed public and private system and will remain that way, with the contestation really about the particular degree and form of involvement that each sector will have (Burch, 2009; Henig, 1994, 2005, 2009b). Charter schools, as discussed shortly, are an illustration of this hybrid element—public in some sense, private in others—while vouchers, at least in some forms, can represent a more extreme diminution of the public sector role.

25. (Katz, 1970).

26. (Orfield, 1969).

27. (Oppel, 2012).

28. (Friedman, 1955).

29. (Henig, 1994).

30. (Menendez, 1999).

31. (Burch, 2009).

32. Under some circumstances these specialized agencies can operate with a great deal of autonomy, able to sidestep or directly evade efforts by general-purpose legislatures and executives to exercise oversight and control (McCubbins, Noll, & Weingast, 1987; Miller, 2005; Weingast, 1981). For this reason, it can sometimes make sense to think of the distinction between general- and single-purpose governance as a continuum, with powerful and semi-autonomous agencies occupying a middle ground between pure general-purpose and pure single-purpose governance.

33. *Special district governments*, as defined by the U.S. Census Bureau, are: "All organized local entities (other than counties, municipalities, townships, or school districts) authorized by state law to provide only one or a limited number of designated functions, and with sufficient administrative and fiscal autonomy to qualify as separate governments; known by a variety of titles, including districts, authorities, boards, and commissions," http://www.census.gov/govs/state/definitions.html#s.

34. http://www.census.gov/govs/cog/GovOrgTab03ss.html.

35. Special district employment and payroll data, 2007. Data generated by the author from the Census Bureau's Build-a-Table tool with data from the Census of Government Employment.

36. As noted previously, the general precedent establishing that substate governments are creations of the state and possess no powers other than those delegated by the state is known as Dillon's Rule, named after John Forrest Dillon, the Iowa judge in the classic 1868 case. "Municipal corporations owe their origin to, and derive their powers and rights wholly from, the legislature," Dillon wrote. "It breathes into them the breath of life, without which they cannot exist. As it creates, so may it destroy. If it may destroy, it may abridge and control." *Clinton v. Cedar Rapids and the Missouri River Railroad* (24 Iowa 455; 1868).

37. See (Hess & Kelly, 2011; McGuinn & Manna, 2012) for two recent and wide-ranging efforts to address these issues.

38. Three excellent discussions of the origin and implications of special districts are (Burns, 1994; Foster, 1997; Mullin, 2008). While each considers the broader public-regarding rationales for specialized versus generalized governance structures, they ultimately argue that the phenomenon needs to be considered as a political one in which institutions affect the likelihood that particular interests will be reflected in policy and in which organized interests, aware of this, occasionally battle for the institutional parameters that will operate in their favor. None of the three attends specifically to school districts. The arguments and evidence they present strongly suggest, though, that both the particular functional specialization and political context matter, with the implication that school districts might have different trajectories and consequences than the set of special districts they consider. The institutional politics framework I develop later in this chapter, and ultimately throughout this book, nonetheless draws on and complements their insight that group conflict is more revealing than idealized public interest as a lens for understanding choices among governance institutions.

39. This capacity to span borders of smaller general-purpose local governments leads some to imagine that most single-purpose districts are regional in scope, but fewer than one in five is countywide or larger in scope (Foster, 1997).

40. http://www.panynj.gov/port-authority-ny-nj.html.

41. http://www.mwdh2o.com/mwdh2o/pages/about/about01.html; http://lgrs.sco .ca.gov/sb282/SpecDistDetails.asp?ID=4935&FY=2001. General-purpose governments in principle might negotiate intergovernmental compacts or memos of understanding that allow them to work together to address such border-spanning problems, but in practice such arrangements can be politically tricky to work out (elected officials, sensitive to the need to protect "their" constituents and concerned that they might be accused of sacrificing local prerogatives, would sometimes prefer to cede the hot-potato issue to a special unit). Except where the boundaries run across state lines, individual states have the geographic span of authority that in principle would

let them directly manage such issues, but because they have limited knowledge and time to devote to the particulars of local governance, their favored way of meeting those responsibilities is in fact to create a single-purpose district to which they can hand off day-to-day authority.

42. "Profile of New York City Voters," *New York Times*, 2009, http://www.nytimes.com/interactive/2009/11/04/nyregion/1104-ny-exit-poll.html.

43. (Stewart & Schwartzman, 2010).

44. (Lowi, 1967): 89.

45. (Berstein, 1955).

46. (Burns, 1994; Foster, 1997).

47. (Moe, 2011).

48. For much the same reasons that James Madison argued, in *The Federalist Papers #10*, that "factions" would be less likely to dominate a large national government than was the case under the decentralized Articles of Confederation.

49. The layered presentation is just one of the ways in which this schematic presentation necessarily oversimplifies. Federalism, as Grodzins classically noted, is better likened to a marble cake than a layer cake (Grodzins & Elazar, 1966).

50. Hawaii has a single statewide school district comprising about three hundred schools. There is also only one traditional school district in the District of Columbia Public Schools, although a number of DC charter schools are formally their own systems (Local Education Agencies). The 2007 census of government lists Virginia as having one traditional school district and 134 dependent school systems.

51. (Kirst & Edelstein, 2006).

52. (Bawn, 1995; Moe, 2006). See (Meier & O'Toole Jr., 2006) for a good overview, as well as an argument that bureaucratic influence may be both stronger and of less concern than the standard presentations suggest.

53. See, for example, (McCubbins et al., 1987; McCubbins & Schwartz, 1984).

54. (Peters, Jon, & King, 2005; Pierson, 2000).

55. Using a term like *normal* is somewhat hazardous, since it may connote a bland universality that masks lots of important variation. In adopting it, I'm reaching back to three intellectual forerunners. First, and most directly apropos, is Laurence Iannaccone's use of the term to distinguish education politics from partisan politics, as quoted earlier in this chapter. Second is the concept of *normal science*, as developed by Thomas Kuhn. Kuhn used the term to refer to day-to-day science that operates within an established paradigm: a set of premises, beliefs, expectations, and established instruments that are accepted as foundational (Kuhn, 1996). The third involves the concepts of *equilibrium politics* within *endogenous institutions*, particularly as these have been developed by Frank Baumgartner and Bryan Jones (Baumgartner & Jones, 1993, 2002). "Since the major institutions of government generally may remain in place for decades or longer, and since their organization, structure, and rules of participation tend to induce a certain type of outcome," they write, "scholars are often well served by treating them as relatively fixed, exogenous" (2002: 3). The insight

that this view is incomplete, and that periods of equilibria are occasionally "punctuated" by sharp political changes that alter reigning institutions, underlies my distinction between normal politics and institutional politics.

56. My daughter, Jess Zimmerman, who knows more about this (and many other things) than I do, helped me to craft this metaphor.

57. (Burns, 1994): 7.

58. (Baumgartner & Jones, 1993; Constantelos, 2010; Holyoke, 2003; Pralle, 2003).

59. (Moe, 2011).

60. Proposition 13 was an amendment to the California constitution, passed by a 1978 initiative, that set hard limits on the level and future rates of increase of property taxes.

61. (Grodzins & Elazar, 1966).

62. The term is usually traced to (Bernstein, 1955).

63. (Pralle, 2003): 236.

64. Under some circumstances, even elite groups might see a benefit in pursuing institutional change rather than simply defending the institutional advantages they have already accrued. This is especially the case for elite groups that see their own status as precarious. Indeed, according to some accounts it was this kind of dynamic that accounted for the Progressive Reform movement and the adoption of its slate of governance reforms, including the establishment of school districts as single-purpose arenas buffered from general-purpose municipal politics. Immigration and urbanization around the turn of the twentieth century set the stage for the emergence of urban political machines, eroding the dominance of traditional upper-class elites. A sense of slipping power expressed itself sometimes in symbolic crusades, such as the Temperance Movement (Gusfield, 1963), but in many places the old-style elite sought to change governance institutions in ways that would help them reconsolidate their positions of control. Samuel Hays offers one of the clearest arguments to that effect. Reformers, he argued, "wished not simply to replace bad men with good; they proposed to change the occupational and class origins of decision makers. Toward this end they sought innovations in the formal machinery of government which would concentrate political power by sharply centralizing the processes of decision making rather than distribute it through more popular participation in public affairs" (Hays, 1964: 163).

CHAPTER 2

1. (Herszenhorn, 2004a).

2. (Robelen, 2009).

3. (Hoffman, 1988).

4. Some of the discussion in this chapter borrows and builds upon arguments I first offered in (Henig, 2009c).

5. Lawrence J. McAndrews's *The Era of Education: The Presidents and the Schools,*

1965–2001 does a nice job of recounting the evolving role of the presidency during an important time period, but has very little to say about governors and nothing about governance changes at the local level (McAndrews, 2006). Larry Sabato's *Goodbye to Good-time Charlie* recognized earlier than most the systemic changes that were altering the modern gubernatorial office, but kept its focus firmly at the state level (Sabato, 1983). My own coedited volume on mayoral control is equally vulnerable to the charge that it failed to sufficiently recognize that these changes in cities were not *sui generis* (Henig & Rich, 2004).

6. For example: (Cohen & Moffitt, 2009; Davies, 2007; DeBray, 2006; Hess & Kelly, 2011; Manna, 2006; McGuinn, 2006; Murphy, 1990; Toch, 1991; M. Vinovskis, 2008; Vinovskis, 1999).

7. (M. A. Vinovskis, 2008).

8. Alexander as secretary of education under George H. W. Bush and subsequently as a U.S. senator. Clinton, of course, as president. Riley, who had served in the Senate before becoming governor, later served as secretary of education under Clinton. Graham moved to the Senate after serving as governor of Florida, although he was known there more for his work on foreign policy issues.

9. (McDonnell, Timpane, & Benjamin, 2000; Pangle & Pangle, 1995).

10. *Clinton v. Cedar Rapids and the Missouri River Railroad* (24 Iowa 455; 1868). The rather remarkable impact—national and long-lasting—of this decision owes much to the fact that Dillon was a highly regarded legal scholar who subsequently went on to serve as a federal judge, write a widely cited text on municipal governance, teach on the law faculties of Columbia and Yale universities, and serve as president of the American Bar Association.

11. (Kingdon, 1995; Mintrom, 2000; Sheingate, 2003).

12. (Toch, 1991): 17.

13. Ibid.

14. (Davies, 2007; Manna, 2006; M. A. Vinovskis, 2008).

15. On the measurement issue, see (Dometrius, 1979; Schlesinger, 1965). A classic application is (Dye, 1969). For a pretty comprehensive set of contemporary and historical measures and their definitions, see http://www.unc.edu/~beyle/gubnewpwr .html.

16. (Barrilleaux & Berkman, 2003).

17. (Cavanagh, 2011b).

18. Historical data was gathered from various sources including (Beach & Will, 1955; Deffenbaugh, 1940; Keesecker, 1950; Fuller & Pearson, 1969; McCarthy, Langdon, & Olson, 1993). Paul Manna generously provided his codes for the selection of CSSOs and state boards of education for each year from 1975 to 2010.

19. New York's Board of Regents' initial role was to oversee colleges and academies that had been established by Britain, during the colonial era, and it was not given full control over public schools until 1904 (Keesecker, 1950).

20. Initially, many state boards were composed wholly or mostly of ex officio

members; however, during the first half of the twentieth century, most states moved away from ex officio membership (Beach & Will, 1955). In 1890, twenty state boards were made up of a majority ex officio members compared to four states in 1950, and no states in 2010 (Keesecker, 1950; Fulton, 2010). In fact, most states have moved away from having any ex officio members on the state board: in 1920, thirty-five states had at least one ex officio member, whereas in 2010, only twenty states did (Beach & Will, 1955; Fulton, 2010).

21. For up-to-date information on state governance models, see http://www.ecs.org/html/educationIssues/ECSStateNotes.asp?nIssueID=68.

22. http://www.staradvertiser.com/news/20110331_Governor_makes_his_picks.html.

23. http://www.lasvegassun.com/news/2011/jun/18/new-law-gives-governor-more-control-over-schools/.

24. (Severson, 2011).

25. (Cavanagh, 2011a).

26. (Robelen, 2009).

27. (Cavanagh, 2011a); also see http://www.katu.com/news/local/124647014.html.

28. (Cole, 2012).

29. (Robelen, 2009).

30. The bill, intended to take effect in 2013, would also shorten the terms of state board of education members, all appointed by the governor, from six to three years and reduce the power of the board to block the governor on policy issues on which they disagree (http://www.boston.com/news/local/vermont/articles/2012/03/21/vt_legislation_would_change_education_leadership/).

31. See (Toch, 1991), pp. 17–20, for some examples of governors' use of informal powers. For example, Lamar Alexander, in Tennessee, established a task force that ran a speakers bureau, set up a toll-free hotline, distributed brochures touting his education reform proposals, and "used receptions at his executive residence to encourage lobbyists from Tennessee's powerful beer, liquor, insurance, grocery, and real estate industries to work the state legislature on behalf of his education agenda" (p. 278, note #6).

32. (Fleisher, 2010). In November 2011, after resisting for a year, the Parsippany–Troy Hills school board voted to reduce Seitz's salary by $43,000 after the state threatened to withhold $3.6 million in state aid (http://nj1015.com/district-bows-to-state-pressure-cuts-leaders-pay/).

33. (Cavanagh, 2011a).

34. When state-of-the-state speeches were unavailable, they used budget addresses or inaugural speeches. They excluded ten states in which governors did not consistently offer a major agenda-setting speech (either state-of-the-state, budget, or inaugural). These were Arkansas, Kentucky, Louisiana, Massachusetts, Montana, Nevada, New Hampshire, North Carolina, Oregon, and Texas.

35. (DiLeo & Lech, 1998). Perennial issues are distinguished from *cyclical*, for which attention ebbs and grows, and *temporal* issues that flare up occasionally (Herzik, 1983).

36. This database is searchable by many criteria, including state, governor's name, time in office, number of terms, and keyword. Because the NGA does not have a historian on staff, the Office of Management Consulting and Training assumes responsibility for writing and revising the biographies. Biographies of current and new governors are reviewed and updated on an annual basis, whereas biographies of former governors are edited only upon significant career or life events, such as death. To write the biographies, NGA staff draws upon a variety of sources, including state archives, state history museums, and online databases, such as the Political Grave-yard. These biographies are intended to provide summaries of each governor's career interests and accomplishments, but are not intended to be comprehensive resources due to NGA length limitations (http://www.nga.org/cms/home/governors/past-governors-bios.html).

37. Governors who addressed only higher education or special populations (e.g., deaf children), who negatively affected education policy enactment, or who used education solely as a means of promoting segregation were coded 1 for each of these respective categories, but were coded 0 for "education governor." If the biography included an ambiguous reference to education, we conducted additional research to decide upon the coding. After serendipitously discovering some "false negatives" (cases in which our search words appeared in the biographies but were not identified through the site's search engine), we then collected all of the noneducation biographies, did a word search for *education* and *school* in Microsoft Word, and skimmed these biographies to discover and code any unidentified education governors. Lastly, we compiled word counts of all of the biographies, including the reference lists, and used these word counts to check for several possible sources of bias. The concern was whether larger, more urban states and those presumably with more media coverage would have longer bios, and therefore an artificially greater probability of mentioning education issues. We first conducted one-way analyses of variance (ANOVA) and then conducted Scheffé post-hoc tests to determine that there is no relationship between state urban population and education biography word count ($p>.05$), or between state education revenue and education biography word count ($p>.05$). However, we did find that there is a relationship between state population and education biography word count. More specifically, states in the lowest population quartile had, on average, shorter biographies than those in the third quartile ($p<.05$). Using *t*-tests, we found no relationship in the word count between regions ($p>.05$), or between "old" states (those that existed prior to the Civil War) and newer ones ($p>.05$).

38. See, for example, (Hess, 1998) for his account of why school superintendents are drawn toward—and often rewarded for—ritualistic appearance of activity, and (Manna, 2006) for his distinction between "interest" (e.g., speech making) and "involvement" (e.g., policy making). On the broader phenomenon of symbolic politics, see (Edelman, 1967, 1985).

39. The first three time periods depicted are relatively arbitrary efforts to capture half-century spans; 1983 (*A Nation at Risk*) and 1994 (the Improving America's Schools Act) provided substantively meaningful benchmarks for dividing the contemporary era.

40. On average, the post-1983 bios are about twenty words longer ($p<.05$), but this slight increase in length did not drive the proportional increase in those mentioning education. There was no difference between the two time periods in the average length of the biographies that included a mention of education. The post-1983 biographies of governors that did not include mentions of education are approximately forty words longer, on average ($p<.001$), than those for the earlier period.

41. The p-value for the difference in averages is less than .001.

42. One of these, New Mexico, strengthened the role of the governor in selecting the CSSO at the same time that it reduced the governor's role in selecting the state board of education, reverting to an elected board as it had had prior to 1987.

43. States strengthening the formal power to appoint the CSSO also had higher minority populations and greater increases in the black population between 1970 and 1990. There was no relationship with 1975 formal power. States that already had stronger gubernatorial power over the state board of education were more likely to increase it further; there was no relationship with the race variables or history of an active education governor.

44. Washington did not have a post-reform governor because the governor in office at the time of the change was the last one included in the NGA database.

45. (Berube, 1991): 17.

46. (McAndrews, 2006).

47. (Mittelstadt, 2007). "Once again," Johnson declared to Congress in 1965, "we must start where men would improve their society have always known they must begin—with an educational system restudied, reinforced, and revitalized." Special Message to Congress: "Toward Full Educational Opportunity" (http://www.lbjlib .utexas.edu/johnson/lbjforkids/edu_quotes.shtm).

48. Eisenhower's address to the nation is available at http://www.teachervision .fen.com/civil-rights/resource/4316.html#ixzz19hVKULJp.

49. (McAndrews, 2006): 16.

50. (Stephens, 1984).

51. (Manna, 2006; Radin & Hawley, 1988).

52. (Stephens, 1984). See also (McAndrews, 2006).

53. (Bell, 1988; Davies, 2007; Manna, 2006).

54. Finn's assessment of the Reagan administration's education accomplishments might be buoyed by the fact that he served as assistant secretary of education during Reagan's second term in office (Finn, 2004).

55. (Manna, 2006): 80–81.

56. (McGuinn, 2006): 149.

57. The Policy Agendas Project used "quasi sentences" to account for the fact

that a single sentence sometimes included more than one policy idea. The analysis further distinguished offhand or ritualistic mentions of education from those with "policy content." The length of a speech is not necessarily a determination of how much policy content there was. The presidents with the highest percentage of their speeches devoted to statements with policy content were Jimmy Carter (95.2 percent) and Dwight D. Eisenhower (90.2 percent).

58. http://blog.lib.umn.edu/cspg/smartpolitics/2011/01/a_content_analysis_of_barack_o.php.

59. The ongoing pressures of responding to 9/11, terrorism, the invasion of Iran, and similar foreign policy events likely led Bush to talk less about NCLB and education in general as a president than he had as a governor or presidential candidate.

60. (McGuinn, 2010).

61. Because competitive grants by their nature are selective both in who applies and who wins the award, Congress tends to get less involved in stipulating the conditions than do the executive agencies that run the competitions or than it does with formula grants that affect a far larger number of local districts.

62. Frederick Hess, foreword to (McGuinn, 2010). With Johnson's ESEA and Bush's NCLB as competitors, it is an open question whether Hess's characterization of the relative importance of RTTT will stand up to scrutiny in decades to come. The short-term impact—in terms of changing state laws and policies—was remarkable, to be sure.

63. (Finn, 1977): 104.

64. Parts of this section draw directly on some of my earlier writing about mayoral control. See (Henig, 2009a; Henig & Fraser, 2009; Henig & Rich, 2004).

65. Washington, DC, gave its mayor partial control in 2000 and adopted a stronger form of mayoral control in 2007. Some districts (e.g., Detroit; Oakland, California; Prince George's County, Maryland) adopted (or had imposed) mayoral control but then reverted to elected school boards during this same time period.

66. http://rockrivertimes.com/2011/03/11/state-of-the-city-mayor-blasts-school-district-read-the-full-text-of-his-speech/.

67. Indianapolis already has one form of formal mayoral involvement as the first major city in which the mayor has the direct authority to create charter schools.

68. (Moore, 2009).

69. (Orr, 2004).

70. (Shipps, 2003).

71. (Kirst & Edelstein, 2006).

72. (Wong, Shen, Anagnostopolous, & Rutledge, 2007). The Richmond story took an odd turn in September 2007. The mayor had instructed the school board to move its offices out of City Hall to make room for his economic development department. Backed by the council, the school board refused, and Wilder evicted them in the middle of the night, dismantling their offices and moving the contents into moving vans. A school board member attributed Wilder's act to his resentment

of the fact that they had refused his request to cede to him the power to hire and fire the superintendent. See Lisa A. Bacon, "Famous Mayor Under Fire in Virginia," *New York Times*, October 21, 2006, p. 25.

73. At least as long as the mayor selected someone with a minimal threshold of educational training and experience. State law did set some formal limits by stipulating that school superintendents must meet certain certification requirements relating to their educational background, training, and teaching or leadership experience. By choice, Mayor Bloomberg twice chose to appoint candidates with almost no educational background, which required a waiver from the requirement by the New York State Commissioner of Education. In both cases this waiver was granted. In the case of his appointment of Joel Klein, whose background was primarily as an antitrust lawyer but who had taught in public school much earlier in his career, the waiver was granted with relatively little fuss. In the case of Cathleen Black, who had no experience with public school education as a teacher or leader or in graduate-level education, the waiver came after considerable controversy and only on the condition, agreed to by the mayor, that Black appoint a second-in-command who had the requisite background. While this represents a formal check, it is a relatively minor one, made even more minor in practice by the informal political power and authority that Bloomberg added to his formal position.

74. (Winerip, 2004).

75. (Herszenhorn, 2004a).

76. (Gold, Henig, Silander, & Simon, 2010; Gyurko & Henig, 2010).

77. (Cavanagh, 2011b). For a non-education-focused discussion of the need to understand how state governments act within local politics, including specifically through the creation of single-purpose governments, see (Smith, 2010).

78. Mayoral control was renewed, but not without a lengthy battle and some modest concessions to parent and community groups that had strongly objected to what they considered to be the administration's authoritative and nonresponsive regime (Gold et al., 2010).

79. (Campanile, 2006).

80. (Richards, 2010).

81. (Quaid, 2009).

82. (Bergquist & Marley, 2009).

83. On the education-specific story, see (McGuinn, 2006). On the general tendency of contemporary presidents to seek to expand their power, see (Savage, 2012).

84. (Kirst & Bulkley, 2000).

85. (Henig, 2009c).

86. Elisabeth Thurston Fraser and I first made this argument, as applied to mayoral control, in (Henig & Fraser, 2009).

87. For the edited volume, *Besieged*, see (Howell, 2005; Miller, 2008); for the *Atlantic Monthly* article, see Miller (2008).

88. http://www.nj.com/news/index.ssf/2011/05/nj_school_board_members_now_re.html.

89. Reagan had famously promised to eliminate the U.S. Department of Education, but animus toward the agency faded until reemerging in the 2012 presidential primary campaigns. In mid-April 2012, Mitt Romney, by then the clear frontrunner for the Republican nomination, indicated that his preference would be to "either consolidate with another agency, or perhaps make it a heck of a lot smaller" (Weiner, 2012). Two things are especially interesting about this position, which he expressed at a private fundraiser. First, his views about the U.S. Department of Education were part of a general proclamation about the need to rein in domestic policy agencies—he took aim, for example, at Housing and Urban Development as well—and a supporting example of my argument that education politics is increasingly being subsumed within the broader envelope of general-purpose politics. Second, Romney very clearly indicated that he did not want to eliminate the agency so much as he hoped to bend it to his control and turn it against the teacher unions that he felt had gained too much power.

90. (Majone, 1977). Contracting out is often presented as a market-oriented strategy, and in that way a rival to the stronger and more interventionist public sector associated with the regulatory state. When the executive branch has the capacity to define its goals, select the best providers, exercise informed oversight, and terminate contracts based on nonperformance, contracting regimes can extend the reach of the public sector, providing flexibility of response and making it more feasible to undertake new areas of activity (Henig, 2010a).

91. (Henig, Hula, Orr, & Pedescleaux, 1999): chapter 6.

92. The Milwaukee voucher experiment was launched in 1990. Minnesota passed the first charter school law in 1991. For *Fortune*'s declaration, see http://money.cnn.com/magazines/fortune/fortune_archive/1990/05/28/73586/index.htm.

93. (Mayhew, 1974).

94. (Edelman, 1967, 1985, 1988).

95. (U.S. Census, 2011): Table 1. States collected 46.7 percent, localities 43.8 percent, and the federal government 9.5 percent.

96. (Moe, 2001).

97. (Peterson, 1981). Peterson suggests that this developmental function of education can be overridden in large, heterogeneous cities if school politics and policy get pulled away from an orientation on growth in favor of a redistributive agenda of aiding lower-income students or closing racial and economic achievement gaps. I come back to this point a bit later in this section.

98. The text of the complete report can be found at http://www2.ed.gov/pubs/NatAtRisk/risk.html.

99. (McAndrews, 2006): 54. The quote is from Peter Libassi, as special assistant for civil rights in the Department of Health Education and Welfare.

100. (McAndrews, 2006): 979.

101. (Henig et al., 1999).

102. (Henig et al., 1999; Orr, 2000; Stone, 1989).

103. (Browning, Marshall, & Tabb, 2002).

CHAPTER 3

1. (Chen & Hernandez, 2011).

2. Ibid.

3. (Santos, 2011c).

4. (Santos, 2011b).

5. (Sheingate, 2003): 185.

6. (Kingdon, 1995).

7. (Rhodes, 2012): 9.

8. (Rhodes, 2012): 13–17.

9. (Hess, 1998).

10. For an account of the selection process in each state, see http://www.judicial selection.us/.

11. Even in states that formally rely on elections, judges often retire before the end of their terms, giving the sitting governor the ability to appoint their successor; since incumbent judges are so rarely defeated for reelection, this can effectively give the governor the ability to shape the judiciary. For a discussion of this as it plays out in Texas, see http://www.nytimes.com/2011/08/12/us/12ttperry.html?_r=1&emc=. While it is certainly the exception, judicial elections occasionally do get embroiled in ideologically charged issues, including in education policy. In 1997, for example, voucher supporters from around the country funneled campaign support to buck up a Wisconsin supreme court justice who was seen as a critical vote likely to support the expansion of Milwaukee's voucher program. The state election board sued the judge's campaign organization, charging that a blitz of postcards sent to voters represented an illegal contribution (Walsh, 2000).

12. Thanks to Paul Manna for reminding me of the importance of standing and limited agenda space as constraints on courts' responsiveness.

13. (Superfine, 2010): 112.

14. On the argument that the decision ought to be considered a *product, rather than a cause,* of social change, see (Klarman, 1994). On the argument that its impact has been severely overstated, see (Rosenberg, 1991). For a rebuttal, see (Garrow, 2004).

15. (Orfield, 1995).

16. (Armor, 1995; Clotfelter, 2004; Crain, 1969; Hochschild, 1984; Orfield, 1969; Orfield & Eaton, 1996).

17. (Crain, 1969).

18. For the story of Judge Arthur Garrity's involvement in the Boston case, see (Lukas, 1985). On the courts' uses of special masters in desegregation cases, see (Aronow, 1980; Chayes, 1976; Kirp & Babcock, 1981).

19. (Superfine, 2010): 114.

20. On the difficulty of talking about race within schools, see (Pollock, 2004). On the tensions—overt and nuanced—around race and schools on a more collective level, see (Baum, 2010; Henig, Hula, Orr, & Pedescleaux, 1999; Hochschild, 1984). On American attitudes about race generally, see (Kinder & Sanders, 1996; Schuman, Steeh, Bobo, & Krysan, 1998).

21. On the dynamic of legislative recalcitrance and how it forced the courts to become more prescriptive, see (Lehne, 1978).On the empirical literature demonstrating the centralization consequence, see (Levin & Koski, 2000).

22. 62 N.J. at 499–501, as cited in (Lehne, 1978).

23. (Lehne, 1978): 51.

24. (Lehne, 1978): 53. While leaving the legislature in charge of developing the details of a response, the court "did, however, provide some significant guidelines" (Tractenberg, 1974): 323.

25. Lehne, 1978: 122–123.

26. Although not, by any measure, putting a final period on school finance litigation in New Jersey where, the successor case to *Robinson v. Cahill*—Abbott—remains the center of controversy and continued judicial involvement thirty-five years after the legislature acted.

27. http://www.time.com/time/magazine/article/0,9171,879595,00.html.

28. Garrity's initial decision contained 148 pages of legal and factual analysis but only 4 pages discussing possible remedies (see Orfield, 1978: 145, fn 84). (Lukas, 1985) observes: "Some of the fifteen months which Garrity had spent crafting his immaculate 'liability' finding, his critics contended, might better have been spent beginning the search for an appropriate remedy" (239). See also (Dentler, 1978).

29. (Lukas, 1985): 245.

30. (Sandler & Schoenbrod, 2003): 16–17.

31. (Melnick, 2009): 25. Melnick also quotes Paul Gewirtz ("Remedies and resistance," *Yale Law Journal*, 1983: 588) "to effect that it was the massive southern resistance 'that required the courts to intrude with such coercion, with such detail, with such stubborn patience and courage, and with the strategic and managerial preoccupations that strained the boundaries of the transitional judicial functions.'"

32. *San Antonio v. Rodriguez*, 411 U.S. 1 (1973).

33. (Superfine, 2010): 118. See also (Umpstead, 2007).

34. (Superfine, 2010): 118. See also (Superfine & Goddard, 2009).

35. (Wilson, 1989): 288.

36. (Rebell, 2005).

37. Liebman and Sabel discuss this, for example, as it relates to some of the successes in Kentucky's effort to move from a judicial ruling about shortcomings in the existing system to genuine reform (Liebman & Sabel, 2003).

38. (Rebell & Block, 1982): 215.

39. (Rebell, 2009): 55. In commenting on a draft of this chapter, Michael Rebell

emphasized the need to distinguish among particular types of cases in predicting how expansive and sustained judicial involvement is likely to be. The prediction that it will be self-limited seems more probable in cases of discrimination (particularly when looked at in the context of the current U.S. Supreme Court), but may not hold in all areas. "Courts seem to have a more sustained permanent role in areas like special education, where the congressional statute has given them an important on-going role," he observed in a personal communication, and in areas like fiscal equity and education adequacy, where there is strong pressure on legislatures to recreate the advantages previously enjoyed by voters within their own districts. Citing Metzler, Rebell suggests that even if equity reforms are enacted at a certain point in time, judicial oversight, at least on a periodic basis, is probably necessary to counter a basic tendency toward disequilibrium in equity terms (Metzler, 2003).

40. (Mayhew, 1974).

41. (Mayhew, 1974).

42. (Roza, forthcoming 2012).

43. On the general argument that "culture war" issues have their own political dynamics, see (Meier, 1994; Sharp, 1999). On specific applications to education, see (Hunter, 1992; Ravitch, 2003; Sharp, 1999).

44. The incumbency advantage to state legislators is estimated to be about 5 percentage points. This is lower than the incumbency advantage enjoyed by many other offices, including Congress, but is substantial and is steady or mildly increasing over time (Ansolabehere & Snyder, 2002).

45. (Baum, 2010): 141.

46. (Orr, 2004).

47. (Cannato, 2001): chapter 9.

48. (Marschall, Ruhil, & Shah, 2010; Meier, Juenke, Wrinkle, & Polinard, 2005).

49. (McAndrews, 2006); see also chapter 2 of this work.

50. http://www.lbjlib.utexas.edu/johnson/lbjforkids/edu_timeline.shtm.

51. (Davies, 2007): chapter 2.

52. Manna (2011): 57.

53. (Hess & Petrilli, 2006), 20; see also (Rudalevige, 2003).

54. (DeBray, 2006): 82–83.

55. Manna's recounting of the Highly Qualified Teacher provisions of NCLB suggests this as another example of how Congress often inserts key elements into laws even when popular credit is dominated by the president, who signs the final legislation. Bush's initial NCLB blueprint said nothing about teacher standards, reflecting the administration's greater interest in testing and school accountability. Congressman Miller, rather, was the instigating force (Manna, 2010).

56. The dominant role of these education-focused committees did not diminish over time; despite fluctuations from year to year, overall the two major committees accounted for exactly the same proportion of the education hearings before 1980 as they have since.

57. (Fico, 1983; Graber, 1993; Lynch, 2000).

58. (Mintrom, 2000).

59. I started with a spreadsheet provided by the Education Commission of the States to Elizabeth Rigby of George Washington University's Trachtenberg School of Public Policy. (Thanks to Professor Rigby for sharing this spreadsheet and to JoAnne Wilkins and Kathy Christie from ECS.) The data included 30,327 education-related laws coded into 435 topic categories and including information on their title, status, and a brief summary. Through an iterative process, we aggregated and recoded the topics, referencing titles and summaries for additional information in cases in which the original topic code was insufficiently clear. For the analysis presented here, we use sixteen categories (including a category "other," comprising less than 1 percent, which we've excluded from the tables), and include only bills focusing on preK–12 and that have been signed into law.

60. Massachusetts's lower level of activity may reflect the fact that it had passed a comprehensive education reform bill in 1993, just before this data series commenced.

61. The grouping of issues into these three broad types and the labels I attach to them are subjective on my part, but informed by my understanding of the shifting national policy debates.

62. http://www.boldapproach.org/index.php?id=01.

63. Contributing also to the increase in school-focused reforms was a sharp one-year blip in technology-related bills in 1997. Separate figures showing the trend lines for each of the fifteen issue types is available from the author upon request. I am unable to determine from this data whether the sharp increase from 1994 to 1997 was a continuation of a preexisting trend, although I suspect that it likely was so.

64. (Hess, 1998).

65. (Christensen, Johnson, & Horn, 2008; Moe & Chubb, 2009).

66. As quoted in (Hess & Meeks, forthcoming 2012).

67. In cities with populations over two hundred thousand, about 46 percent elect all of their council members from wards, 16 percent elect all of their councils on an at-large basis; and 38 percent rely on a mix of the two (http://www.nlc.org/build-skills-networks/resources/cities-101/municipal-elections).

68. (Henig, 2004).

69. David Nakamura, "Fenty Reverses On Schools; Mayor-Elect Now Supports Takeover," *Washington Post*, December 8, 2006, B1.

70. David Nakamura and V. Dion Haynes, "Fenty to Name Ally To Lead Turn-around," *Washington Post*, November 16, 2006, B04.

71. Gary Emerling, "City lawmakers slam Fenty plan to seize schools; system's independence a concern," *Washington Times*, January 19, 2007, 01.

72. V. Dion Haynes and Theola Labb, "As Parents Fight School Closings, D.C. Chancellor Says Input Matters," *Washington Post*, January 17, 2008, B01.

73. Theola Labb and V. Dion Haynes, "Rhee Has Ambitious Plans But Still No School Budget," *Washington Post*, February 23, 2008, B10.

74. V. Dion Haynes and Yolanda Woodlee, "D.C. Schools Chief Fires 98 Workers: Largest System Dismissal in a Decade Is Part of Pledge to Improve Efficiency," *Washington Post*, March 8, 2008, A01.

75. http://voices.washingtonpost.com/dcschools/2011/03/evans_considers_bill_to_return.html.

76. Interview conducted in person by the author in council member's office, July 24, 2008. The identity of the respondent is being protected, because the interview was conducted as part of a different project.

77. Interview conducted in person by the author in the former official's personal residence, July 15, 2007. The identity of the respondent is being protected, because the interview was conducted as part of a different project.

78. (Herszenhorn, 2004b).

79. (Cardwell, 2007).

80. Zita Allen, "Unions and City Council applaud mayor on restoring $1.3 billion to school capital budget," *New York Amsterdam News*, March 31, 2005, 3.

81. (Quinn, 2006).

82. http://schools.nyc.gov/FundForPublicSchools/AboutUs/PressKits/default.htm.

83. In June 2008, the Leadership Academy was chosen—in what was described as a competitive multibidder procurement process—to become the New York City Department of Education's primary provider of principal training, moving about $10 million per year (for five years) of its operating budget onto the public balance sheet (Gyurko & Henig, 2010).

84. (Herszenhorn, 2004b).

85. Ibid. Along with charter schools and school closings, discussed shortly, the DOE's use of contractors became a prime and continuing source of council-mayor confrontation. A series of contracting missteps and scandals made it easier for council members to publicly criticize the administration. One of the first involved the firm of Alvarez and Marsal, which was hired on a "no bid over $15 million" contract to help the department find cost efficiencies; their recommended midyear redesign of school bus routes turned into a public relations debacle when many children had to stand out in midwinter waiting for buses that never showed up (Gootman & Herzenhorn, 2007). Another high-profile blow-up involved an $80 million contract with IBM to develop a data system to allow parents and teachers to access student-specific information. Initially, it was the high cost, followed by glitches in implementation, that proved controversial (Gootman, 2008). Later IBM was drawn into a much broader controversy over contracting, with charges of fraud leveled at a contractor on a major project that included but extended beyond the city schools (Santos, 2011a).

86. In addition to the mayor, the law, which had twice been supported by public referenda, applied to the public advocate, comptroller, borough presidents, and council members.

87. (Saul, 2011).

CHAPTER 4

1. http://www.washingtonpost.com/blogs/answer-sheet/post/president-obamas-unusual-education-roundtable/2011/07/18/gIQAf3UJMI_blog.html.

2. (Conlan, 2006).

3. (Hatry & Durman, 1985; Heinrich, 2002; Henig, 1989/90; Wholey & Hatry, 1992).

4. (Abramson, Salamon, & Steurle, 1999; Salamon, 1995; Smith & Lipsky, 1993).

5. (Donahue, 1989; Feigenbaum, Henig, & Hamnett, 1998; Kamerman & Kahn, 1989; Savas, 2000; Sclar, 2000).

6. (Moe, 2011): 6, 8.

7. (Debray-Pelot, 2007). On the changing constellation of interest groups at the national level, see also (DeBray-Pelot & McGuinn, 2009; Kaestle, 2007).

8. (Manna, 2006): 161.

9. (Sawchuk, 2012). For a broad overview, see the series of articles at http://www.edweek.org/ew/collections/education-advocacy/index.html.

10. (Meier, Wrinkle, & Polinard, 1999; Viteritti, 2004).

11. (Coleman et al., 1966).

12. The analysis is based on those hearings ($n=1977$) and State of the Union mentions ($n=702$) with a major code=6 (education) as coded within the Policy Agendas Project data set.

13. (Davies, 2007; McGuinn, 2006).

14. For a full description of each of the categories, see http://www.policyagendas.org/page/topic-codebook#6.

15. (Kingdon, 1995; Mintrom, 2000).

16. Congress, for example, held twenty hearings with a focus on the underprivileged from 1997 through 1999, and the 2000 State of the Union address had seven distinct mentions of the underprivileged.

17. (Baumgartner & Jones, 1993).

18. (Baumgartner & Jones, 1993).

19. (Jochim, 2009).

20. The names of the two core committees have changed at various times, including during the years covered here; I use the current names. The most active of the noncore committees was the House Science Committee, with nine hearings.

21. The House Committee on Science was the source of a number of hearings relating to math, science, and computing education in which excellence was a dominant theme.

22. Paul Manna and Michael Petrilli find a somewhat similar pattern of marginalization of traditional education voices in their analysis of the affiliations of 1,169 witness appearances in 155 hearings leading up to NCLB. In particular, of the eight most frequently appearing witnesses, only one (Diane Ravitch) had an affiliation with an education school (and that affiliation is as a research professor rather than a tenured member of the regular faculty), and only two had advanced degrees from education

schools (Manna & Petrilli, 2008). They generously shared with me their data, which groups together all advocacy groups and associations. Based on my recoding of the 163 witnesses from associations, I find that just over three-quarters (76.1 percent) were from education-focused organizations; in other words, one in four was from an organization with a multi-issue focus. And just a bit under one in four (22.6 percent) of those with an education-specific focus were from groups outside the traditional pro-public education spending coalition (this includes, for example, charter schools, private schools, and education committees of business organizations). Only 11 percent in all were from teacher unions.

23. This could occur through either or both of two mechanisms. One might be via a change in view by the members of Congress who had long-term roles within the key committees. Accounts of the politics around NCLB, for example, suggest that Ted Kennedy, George Miller, and other influential Democrats may have grown increasingly frustrated with what they came to see as rigidity on the part of teacher unions who had been their party's traditional allies. The second might be via deliberate efforts by theretofore outsiders to capture those committees. After the 1994 elections, for instance, Richard Armey worked to stack the House committee with conservatives (DeBray, 2006). Both of these possibilities serve as useful reminders that the tactical importance of these venues can make them targets of takeover by challenging groups (and not bypassing of these venues as emphasized by Baumgartner and Jones).

24. (Jencks, 1964).

25. (Citizens Conference on State Legislatures, 1971).

26. (Hrebenar & Thomas, 2004; Moe, 2011).

27. I'm not certain when she began using the term "the blob," but it was no later than March 1996 (Innerst, 1996). The quote here is a more recent one (Stossell, 2011).

28. http://www.edreform.com/wp-content/uploads/2012/05/CERPrimer MultipleAuthorizersDec2011.pdf.

29. McDonnell in Cohen, Fuhrman (2007): b22. Referencing (Mazzoni, 1991).

30. See http://www.edreform.com/issues/choice-charter-schools/facts/. In December 2011, the National Alliance for Public Charter Schools released a report estimating that the number of charter school students had surpassed 2 million (http://www .publiccharters.org/pressreleasepublic/default.aspx?id=643).

31. The "origin story" behind charter schools has become the focus of political jostling. Richard Kahlenberg and others credit teacher union leader Albert Shanker with bringing the idea into broader public awareness. Massachusetts educator Ray Budde had originated the term, but Shanker saw in Budde's plan a way to realize some of his ideas about a more diverse and teacher-driven form of education delivery, less handcuffed by bureaucratic constraints (Kahlenberg, 2007). Paul Peterson sees the effort by teacher unions to claim contributing authorship of the idea as opportunistic on their part—an attempt to blur what he considers to be their fundamental opposition to any but the mildest forms of choice and reform—and argues that it was the

Minnesota originators who introduced the more "radical" vision, including, significantly, the insistence that responsibility for charter authorization be placed outside the traditional school districts (Peterson, 2010).

32. (Kingdon, 1995): 77.

33. (Mazzoni, 1991; Mintrom, 2000; Nathan, 1999; Roberts & King, 1996).

34. (Mazzoni, 1991): 121.

35. Ibid., 122.

36. Fears that local districts would never approve charters proved overdrawn; today, districts account for over half of charters. Local school districts (LEAs) account for 89 percent of chartering bodies and oversee 53 percent of charter schools. Higher education institutions account for 5 percent of authorizers and 8 percent of schools. Figures for the others are: not for profits (2 percent; 4 percent); state education agencies (2 percent; 20 percent); independent charter boards(<1 percent; 14 percent); and municipalities (<1 percent; <1 percent).(National Alliance of Charter School Authorizers, 2010).

37. (Wong & Langevin, 2007).

38. (McNeal & Dotterweich, 2007): 19.

39. (Shober, Manna, & Witte, 2006).

40. (Holyoke, Henig, Brown, & Lacireno-Paquet, 2009): 46.

41. (McDonnell, 2009; Mettler, 2002; Mettler & Soss, 2004; Pierson, 1993).

42. (Patashnik, 2008).

43. (Burch, 2009; McDonnell, 2004).

44. (Holyoke, Brown, & Henig, 2012).

45. Others have observed this layering phenomenon as a characteristic of institutional development (Orren & Skowronek, 2004; Thelen, 2003; van der Heijden, 2011). I return to this layering issue in the concluding chapter.

46. http://www.nytimes.com/2011/12/13/education/online-schools-score-better-on-wall-street-than-in-classrooms.html?_r=1&pagewanted=

47. (Manno, 2012): 47.

48. Classic studies include (Dawson & Robinson, 1963; Dye, 1966; Fry & Winters, 1970).

49. (Hero & Preuhs, 2007; Schneider & Ingram, 1993; Soss, Schram, Vartanian, & O'Brien, 2001).

50. I characterize this as an *exploratory* analysis because it is not driven by a set of well-defined and well-defended hypotheses. Rather, this is an inductive exercise, albeit with special attention to some variables that bear more directly on the governance and political attributes that have been the focus of the discussion. It is important not to overinterpret the results, as I note, but to treat them more as suggestive of avenues that future empirical studies might more directly explore.

51. Separate analysis of the constituent issues reinforces the finding that there are multiple types of factors at play. In general, redistributive issues—particularly those related to race and equity, parent and community participation, and health—are more

likely to reflect ideology and interest group alignments. School-focused reforms—and in particular choice and technology-related legislation—are more associated with urban states and more conservative ones, with interest group influence and formal structure not playing a major role. Operational issues—particularly those related to governance—are more correlated with formal structures, especially a governor's power *relative* to the legislature. Interestingly, variation in teacher unions is less notable as a determinant of legislative priorities than activities by other interest groups.

52. For an overview, see (Dye, 1979).

53. (Manna & Harwood, 2011).

54. (Stone, 1989).

55. On the constraining role of the threat of business exit, see (Peterson, 1981). On mayoral power and interest group access in non–school-related decision making, see (Lubell, Feiock, & Cruz, 2009).

56. (Wilson, 1973).

57. (Moe, 2011).

58. Dorothy Shipps, for example, distinguishes among four types of educational governance regimes. *Performance* regimes are focused on improving the pedagogy, practice, and culture of schools in order to improve educational outcomes. *Empowerment* regimes seek to bring new, often previously marginalized, groups into the decision-making process in order to promote innovation and diminish longstanding political inequalities in power. *Employment* regimes emphasize the protection of jobs and patronage and the self-interest of those who have benefited from the ways those have been allocated among individuals and groups. And *market* regimes focus on restructuring education to maximize efficiency and effectiveness by expanding parental choice and private sector delivery (Shipps, 2003).

59. (Henig, 2010a).

60. (Bulkley, 2007; Bulkley, Henig, & Levin, 2010; Hill et al., 2009; Hill, Pierce, & Guthrie, 1997).

61. The overlap between portfolio management models and mayoral control and state takeovers is partly attributable to the fact that both kinds of governance reform are being promoted by the same set of interests, including influential foundations (Reckhow, 2010).

62. Local educators typically argue that theirs is not an employment regime but a performance regime, in which, rather than reflexively resisting change, they are battling to maintain sufficient autonomy to apply their professional knowledge and judgment to the learning process. Minority and community-based organizations sometimes pursue an empowerment regime, arguing that both employment and performance regimes are dominated by teachers but that market-oriented reformers displace teachers with outside experts, consultants, foundations, and nonlocal charter operators who are equally unresponsive to their interests and needs.

63. (O'Donnell, 2012).

64. (Mehta & Teles, 2011).

65. http://www.dfer.org/2011/10/denvers_moment.php.

66. Ibid.

67. http://www.9news.com/rss/story.aspx?storyid=252484.

68. http://www.denverpost.com/news/ci_20249547/walton-family-foundation-awards-denver-8m-school-reform.

69. http://www.phillytrib.com/newsarticles/item/2226-nutter-goes-to-denver-to-study-school-reform.html; http://www.memphisdailynews.com/news/2012/mar/30/schools-planning-group-looks-at-denver-blueprint/.

70. (Reckhow, forthcoming). Reckhow's work also is available in (Reckhow, 2008a, 2008b).

71. Eli Broad, address, National Governors Association Education Policy Advisors Institute, Marina del Rey, California, April 4, 2003), http://beepdf.com/doc/133219/national_governors_association_education_policy_advisors_institute.html.

72. As cited in (Reckhow, forthcoming).

73. Ibid., figures 3.2 and 3.4.

74. (Campanile, 2009).

75. (Chambers, 2006; Gold, Henig, Silander, & Simon, 2010; Henig, 2009a; Henig & Rich, 2004; Viteritti, 2009).

76. (Hess & Meeks, 2012).

77. To tally the witnesses who appeared at New York City Council education meetings, we downloaded the hearing transcripts made available at the New York City committee legislation website (http://legistar.council.nyc.gov/DepartmentDetail.aspx?ID=6903&GUID=5D939F6A-A26A-456C-BF68-2FE3903139C8&Search=). All individuals listed under Appearances were used in the data set, even when the Committee on Education held a joint meeting (with a noneducation committee). Minutes for the Panel on Educational Policy are available at http://schools.nyc.gov/AboutUs/leadership/PEP/meetings/MinutesofAction/default.htm.

78. Elected officials who wish to speak get to do so first, followed by members of the Citywide and Community Education Councils (CECs), which are formal bodies comprising parents (the majority) and some appointed civic and community members. After that, comments are made on a first come, first served basis.

79. In extending mayoral control in 2009, the New York state legislature made some changes designed to require the New York City Department of Education to provide more information to parents and the public and to provide more opportunities for public comment. Since then, PEP meetings have been more visible and highly attended, especially those dealing with school closings. These meetings have often lasted much longer, as discussed in this chapter, in order to accommodate the many attendees who wished to speak. The state requires the DOE to provide PEP members with a summary of those comments, but these still are not incorporated into the publicly available minutes. Those speaking from the floor are expected to limit their comments to no more than two minutes (although, according to a sitting PEP member, this is sometimes extended when the speaker is a public official).

80. The chancellor accounted for forty-nine.

81. "The School Construction Authority (SCA) was established by the New York state legislature in December 1988 to build new public schools and manage the design, construction, and renovation of capital projects in New York City's more than twelve hundred public school buildings, half of which were constructed prior to 1949.

Following changes in school governance law in October 2002, management of the New York City Department of Education's Capital Program was consolidated under one agency, the SCA, and the mayor became responsible for appointing the three SCA trustees (http://www.nycsca.org/AboutUs/Pages/default.aspx).

82. The Gotham Center, which had received a $2 million federal grant for teaching history of the United States and New York City, and the New York City Partnership for Teacher Excellence, which worked with the DOE in a professional development initiative for aspiring teachers.

83. As characterized in a blog post by Patrick Sullivan, PEP's most outspoken critic of the mayor, the "membership of this committee is chosen by the PEP, which means by the Bloomberg administration as the mayoral appointees voted in a bloc for their preferred candidates." When Sullivan asked the committee chairman a question, "Chancellor Walcott interrupted and called on a DOE staffer to respond" (http://nycpublicschoolparents.blogspot.com/2011/07/arts-advisory-committee-calls-for-more.html).

84. In addition to these sixty, there were thirteen meetings for which the minutes, without explanation, fail to record a closing time. Of the three meetings that lasted past 8:30, two finished by 8:35. The very first meeting also was long; it started at 4:30 and lasted until 7:10.

85. (Goodnough, 2002).

CHAPTER 5

1. (Wirt & Kirst, 2001): 30.
2. (Schattschneider, 1960).
3. (Kaestle, 1983).
4. (Iannaccone, 1967; Kaestle, 1983; Wirt & Kirst, 2001).
5. (Iannaccone, 1967): 8–9.
6. Theories about iron triangles and supportive ideologies developed primarily to explain the stickiness of *programs and policies* once enacted, but there are reasons to expect them to be even more potent when applied to *governance structures*. Policies and programs develop sustaining coalitions and rationales because they allocate benefits—direct material payoffs to interest groups, larger and more secure budgets to bureaucracies, and status and support for political sponsors. Governance institutions also allocate benefits—positions to those in authority; jobs and contracts—but they have additional dimensions that drive their roots deeper and embed them more deeply into the accepted status quo. Compared to governance institutions, policies and programs are more discrete and the distribution of winners and losers more visible and

direct. Governance institutions are more apt to be taken as fixed elements; accepted as givens; and protected by a mantle of perceived legitimacy, bias of habit and tradition, and deference to precedent. Building problem definitions and beliefs that support programs and policies can require a deliberate and sustained campaign of public relations. The ideas that support broad governance arrangements are more likely to become deeply integrated with institutionalized forms of political socialization, such as the media and schools, shaping expectations earlier, more subtly, and in a more sustainable manner.

7. A complementary set of notions—about subgovernments, subsystems, advocacy coalitions—differs in the particulars but shares in common the expectation that reigning policies and programs develop protective mechanisms that make them difficult to dislodge. (Jenkins-Smith, Clair, & Woods, 1991; McCool, 1990; Wood, 1992).

8. (Baumgartner & Jones, 1993).

9. Terry Moe argues that states' adoption of laws providing collective bargaining rights to public sector unions—many of which occurred between the mid-1960s and the mid-1970s—were critical to the development of teacher unions as powerful interest groups (Moe, 2011).

10. (Iannaccone, 1967): 10.

11. For a vivid account of shifting demographics, see (Lemann, 1992); on "other peoples' children," see (Delpit, 1996).

12. For a discussion of how racial politics can lead business to pull back to the sidelines of urban school reform, see (Henig, Hula, Orr, & Pedescleaux, 1999): chapter 6.

13. On federalism as a marble cake, see (Grodzins & Elazar, 1966). On portfolio management systems as mixed public-private systems, see (Henig, 2010a).

14. (Orren & Skowronek, 2004; Thelen, 2003; van der Heijden, 2011). The term *layer cake* as applied to federalism has a very different connotation than the term *layering* as it has been used by students of American political development, and this can admittedly cause some confusion. The layer cake metaphor is associated with the idea that governmental authority is cleanly assigned to distinct levels of government. The layering phenomenon refers to the tendency for new institutional arrangements to be added to an existing array without any clear reassignment of purpose and function. When Grodzins rejected the layer cake image in favor of the marble cake characterization of federalism, then, he was, in effect, making an argument consistent with the ideas about layering subsequently developed by Orren and Skowronek, among others.

15. (Baumgartner & Jones, 1993).

16. Thanks to Paul Manna for suggesting this point.

17. (Merton, 1968): 125.

18. (Cohen & Moffitt, 2009).

19. (Downs, 1972; Baumgartner & Jones, 1993; Kingdon, 1995; McCombs & Shaw, 1972; Pierson, 1993; Rochefort & Cobb, 1994; Schneider & Ingram, 1993).

20. (Meier & O'Toole Jr, 2006): 6.

21. See also (Lipsky, 1968).

22. For a fuller elaboration of the ways in which low-income and community-based groups are disadvantaged in competing on the new, multivenue education politics landscape, see (Henig, 2010b).

23. On both the institutional strengths and limitations of Congress to engage in education reform leadership, see (Barone & DeBray, 2011).

24. For discussions about the contemporary emphasis on evidence and scientific research, see (Henig, forthcoming; Hess, 2008; Mosteller & Boruch, 2002; Walters, Lareau, & Ranis, 2009).

25. http://www.dataqualitycampaign.org/files/State_Specific-Florida_2006_Site_Visit.pdf.

26. (Hill et al., 2009; Honig & DeArmond, 2010).

27. (Henig, 2010a).

28. For a full-bore critique of the new reformers, see (Ravitch, 2010).

29. While the research is controversial and still evolving, findings have been mixed, disappointing, or untested regarding such favored instruments as vouchers, charter schools, portfolio management models, cash incentives to motivate students, and small schools.

30. (Hess, 1998; Stone, Henig, Jones, & Pierranunzi, 2001).

31. The "schools can do it" side of the debate initially was championed by the Education Equality Project (EEP), under the leadership of Joel Klein and, for a while, the Reverend Al Sharpton. In November 2001, EEP was subsumed into another group, Stand for Children (http://stand.org/national/about). The case for a broader, comprehensive approach to education has been spearheaded by Broader, Bolder Approach (BBA; http://www.boldapproach.org/).

32. I am a signatory to the BBA mission statement.

33. Important collections of this research include (Duncan, 2009; Kahlenberg, 2012; Smeeding, Erikson, & Janntti, 2011; Tate, 2012).

34. (Henig & Reville, 2011).

35. In (Henig, Malone, & Reville, 2012), my coauthors and I discuss scenarios that might lead to a more comprehensive approach to education quality—including executive branch leadership, grassroots pressure, and judicial mandates.

REFERENCES

Abramson, A. J., Salamon, L., & Steurle, C. E. (1999). *The Nonprofit Sector and the Federal Budget: Recent History and Future Directions*. In E. Boris & C. E. Steurle (Eds.), *Nonprofits and Government* (pp. 99–139). Washington, DC: Urban Institute Press.

Ansolabehere, S., & Snyder, J. M. (2002). The Incumbency Advantage in U.S. Elections: An Analysis of State and Federal Offices, 1942–2000. *Education Law Journal, 1*(3), 315–338.

Armor, D. (1995). *Forced Justice: School Desegregation and the Law*. New York: Oxford University Press.

Aronow, G. F. (1980). The Special Master in School Desegregation Cases: The Evolution of Roles in the Reformation of Public Institutions Through Litigation. *Hastings Constitutional Law Quarterly, 7*, 739–782.

Barone, C., & DeBray, E. (2012). *Education Policy in Congress*. In F. M. Hess & A. Kelly (Eds.), *Carrots, Sticks, and the Bully Pulpit: Lessons from a Half-Century of Federal Efforts to Improve America's Schools*. Cambridge, MA: Harvard Education Press.

Barrilleaux, C., & Berkman, M. (2003). Do Governors Matter? Budgeting Rules and the Politics of State Policymaking. *Political Research Quarterly, 56*(4), 409–417.

Baum, H. (2010). *Brown in Baltimore: School Desegregation and the Limits of Liberalism*. Ithaca, NY: Cornell University Press.

Baumgartner, F. R., & Jones, B. D. (1993). *Agendas and Instability in American Politics*. Chicago, IL: University of Chicago Press.

Baumgartner, F. R., & Jones, B. D. (2002). *Policy Dynamics*. Chicago, IL: University of Chicago Press.

Bawn, K. (1995). Political Control Versus Expertise: Congressional Choices about Administrative Procedures. *American Political Science Review, 89*(1), 62–73.

Beach, F. F., & Will, R. F. (1955). *The State and Education: The Structure and Control of Public Education at the State Level*. Washington, DC: United States Government Printing Office.

Bell, T. H. (1988). *The Thirteenth Man*. New York, NY: Free Press.

Bergquist, L., & Marley, P. (2009, December 16). State lawmakers decline to act on mayoral control of MPS. *Milwaukee Journal Sentinel*. Retrieved from http://www.jsonline.com/news/milwaukee/79445957.html.

Bernstein, M. H. (1955). *Regulating Business by Independent Commission*. Princeton, NJ: Princeton University Press.

Berube, M. R. (1991). *American Presidents and Education*. Westport, CT: Greenwood Press.

Browning, R. P., Marshall, D. R., & Tabb, D. H. (Eds.). (2002). *Racial Politics in American Cities* (3rd ed.). New York, NY: Longman.

Bryk, A. S., Easton, J., Kerbow, D., Rollow, S., & Sebring, P. (1992). *A View from the Elementary Schools: The State of Reform in Chicago*. Chicago, IL: Consortium on Chicago School Research.

Bulkley, K. E. (2007). Bringing the Private into the Public: Changing the Rules of the Game and New Regime Politics in Philadelphia Public Education. *Educational Policy, 21*(1), 155–184.

Bulkley, K. E., Henig, J. R., & Levin, H. M. (Eds.). (2010). *Between Public and Private: Politics, Governance, and the New Portfolio Models for Urban School Reform*. Cambridge, MA: Harvard Education Press.

Burch, P. (2009). *Hidden Markets: The New Education Privatization*. New York, NY: Routledge.

Burns, N. (1994). *The Formation of American Local Governments: Private Values in Public Institutions*. New York, NY: Oxford University Press.

Caldwell, P. (1985, February 6). Governors: No Longer Simply Patrons, They Are Policy Chiefs. *Education Week, 4*(20), 1.

Campanile, C. (2006, March 30). Bam Backs Mike School Rule. *New York Post*. Retrieved from http://www.nypost.com/p/news/politics/item_oL38ZA3Nwxxo WnBELBhPXP.

Campanile, C. C. (2009, August 18). Gates' $4 Million Lesson. *New York Post*. Retrieved from http://www.nypost.com/p/news/regional/item_ekjA6OeXIrxZj DATHPbkuJ.

Cannato, V. J. (2001). *The Ungovernable City: John Lindsay and His Struggle to Save New York*. New York, NY: Basic Books.

Cardwell, D. (2007, September 17). Under Bloomberg, Budget and Revenues Swell. *New York Times*. Retrieved from http://www.nytimes.com/2007/09/17/ nyregion/17bloomberg.html.

Cavanagh, S. (2011a, July 1). New Governors Squeezing State Ed. Boards' Authority. *Education Week*. Retrieved from http://blogs.edweek.org/edweek/state_edwatch/ 2011/07/state_boards_squeezed_in_many_states.html.

Cavanagh, S. (2011b, January 21). Stage Set for Fresh Tussling on Control of K–12 Direction. *Education Week*. Retrieved from http://www.edweek.org/ew/articles/ 2011/01/20/18control.h30.html.

Chambers, S. (2006). *Mayors and Schools: Minority Voices and Democratic Tensions in Urban Education*. Philadelphia, PA: Temple University Press.

Chayes, A. (1976). The Role of the Judiciary in Public Law Litigation. *Harvard Law Review, 89*, 1281–1316.

Chen, D. W., & Hernandez, J. C. (2011, May 5). Bloomberg to Lay Off Thousands of Teachers. *New York Times*. Retrieved from http://www.nytimes.com/2011/05/06/nyregion/bloomberg-budget-will-seek-400-million-more-in-cuts.html.

Christensen, C., Johnson, C. W., & Horn, M. B. (2008). *Disrupting Class: How Disruptive Innovation Will Change the Way the World Learns*. New York: McGraw-Hill.

Chubb, J. E., & Moe, T. M. (1990). *Politics, Markets, and America's Schools*. Washington, DC: Brookings Institution Press.

Citizens Conference on State Legislatures, The. (1971). *The Sometime Governments: A Critical Study of the 50 American Legislatures*. New York, NY: Bantam.

Clotfelter, C. T. (2004). *After Brown: The Rise and Retreat of School Desegregation*. Princeton, NJ: Princeton University Press.

Cohen, D. K., & Moffitt, S. L. (2009). *The Ordeal of Equality: Did Federal Regulation Fix the Schools?* Cambridge, MA: Harvard University Press.

Cole, M. (2012, June 4). Oregon's state schools superintendent resigns, leaving the governor in charge of education. *The Oregonian*. Retrieved from http://www.oregonlive.com/politics/index.ssf/2012/06/oregons_schools_superintendent.html.

Coleman, J. S., Campbell, E., Hobson, C., McPartland, J., Mood, A., Weinfeld, F., and York, R. (1966). *Equality of Educational Opportunity*. Washington, DC: U.S. Government Printing Office.

Conlan, T. (2006). From Cooperative to Opportunistic Federalism: Reflections on the Half-Century Anniversary of the Commission on Intergovernmental Relations. *Public Administration Review, 66*(5), 663–676.

Constantelos, J. (2010). Playing the Field: Federalism and the Politics of Venue Shopping in the United States and Canada. *Publius, 40*(3), 460–483.

Crain, R. L. (1969). *The Politics of School Desegregation*. Garden City, NY: Anchor Books.

Davies, G. (2007). *See Government Grow: Education Politics from Johnson to Reagan*. Lawrence, KS: University Press of Kansas.

Dawson, R. E., & Robinson, J. A. (1963). Inter-Party Competition, Economic Variables, and Welfare Policies in the American States. *The Journal of Politics, 25*(2), 265–289.

DeBray, E. H. (2006). *Politics, Ideology, & Education: Federal Policy During the Clinton and Bush Administrations*. New York, NY: Teachers College Press.

DeBray, E. H., McDermott, K. A., & Wohlstetter, P. (2005). Federalism Reconsidered: The Case of the No Child Left Behind Act. *Peabody Journal of Education, 80*(2), 1–18.

Debray-Pelot, E. (2007). Dismantling Education's 'Iron Triangle': Institutional Relationships in the Formation of Federal Education Policy between 1998 and 2001. In C. F. Kaestle & A. E. Lodewick (Eds.), *To Educate a Nation: Federal and National Strategies of School Reform* (pp. 64–89). Lawrence, KS: University Press of Kansas.

DeBray-Pelot, E., & McGuinn, P. (2009). The New Politics of Education: Analyzing the Federal Education Policy Landscape in the Post-NCLB Era. *Educational Policy, 23*(1), 15–42.

Deffenbaugh, W. S., & Keesecker, W. W. (1940). *State Boards of Education and Chief State School Officers: Their Status and Legal Powers.* Washington, DC: United States Government Printing Office.

Delpit, L. D. (1996). *Other People's Children: Cultural Conflict in the Classroom.* New York, NY: New Press.

Dentler, R. A. (1978). Desegregation Planning and Implementation in Boston. *Theory into Practice, 17*(1), 72–77.

DiLeo, D., & Lech, J. C. (1998). Governors' Issues: A Typology Revisisted. *Comparative State Politics, 19*(6), 9–20.

Dometrius, N. C. (1979). Measuring Gubernatorial Power. *The Journal of Politics, 41*(2), 589–610.

Donahue, J. D. (1989). *The Privatization Decision.* New York, NY: Basic Books.

Downs, A. (1972). Up and Down with the Ecology: The Issue Attention Cycle. *The Public Interest, 28*, 28–50.

Duncan, A. (2009). Turning Around the Bottom Five Percent. Secretary Arne Duncan's Remarks at the National Alliance for Public Charter Schools Conference, Washington, DC, June 22.

Dye, T. R. (1966). *Politics, Economics, and the Public.* Chicago, IL: Rand McNally.

Dye, T. R. (1969). Executive Power and Public Policy in the States. *The Western Political Quarterly, 22*(4), 926–939.

Dye, T. R. (1979). Politics Versus Economics: The Development of the Literature on Policy Determination. *Policy Studies Journal, 7*(4), 652–662.

Edelman, M. J. (1967, 1985). *The Symbolic Uses of Politics.* Champaign-Urbana, IL: University of Illinois Press.

Edelman, M. J. (1988). *Constructing the Political Spectacle.* Chicago, IL: University of Chicago Press.

Feigenbaum, H., Henig, J. R., & Hamnett, C. (1998). *Shrinking the State: The Political Underpinnings of Privatization.* Cambridge, UK: Cambridge University Press.

Fico, F. (1983). Search for the statehouse spokesman: Coverage of the governor and lawmakers. *Journalism Quarterly, 62*(1), 74–80, 90.

Finn, C. E. (1977). *Education and the Presidency.* Lexington, MA: Lexington Books.

Finn, C. E. (2004, June 9). The Original Education President: Reagan's ABCs. *National Review Online.* Retrieved from http://www.nationalreview.com/articles/211015/original-education-president/chester-e-finn-jr.

Fleisher, L. (2010, November 16). School Chiefs' Pay Frozen. *Wall Street Journal.* Retrieved from http://online.wsj.com/article/SB10001424052748703326204575616913225018040.html.

Foster, K. A. (1997). *The Political Economy of Special-Purpose Government.* Washington, DC: Georgetown University Press.

REFERENCES

Friedman, M. (1955). The Role of Government in Education. In R. A. Solo (Ed.), *Economics and the Public Interest*. New Brunswick, NJ: Rutgers University Press.

Fry, B. R., & Winters, R. F. (1970). The Politics of Redistribution. *American Political Science Review, 64*(2), 508–522.

Fuhrman, S. H. (1994). Clinton's Education Policy and Intergovernmental Relations in the 1990s. *Publius, 24*(3), 83–97.

Fuller, E., & Pearson, J. B. (Eds.). (1969). *Education in the States: Nationwide Development Since 1900*. Washington, DC: National Education Association.

Fulton, M. (2010). *State education governance models*. Denver, CO: Education Commission of the States.

Garrow, D. J. (2004). Review: "Happy" Birthday, Brown v. Board of Education? Brown's Fiftieth Anniversary and the New Critics of Supreme Court Muscularity. *Virginia Law Review, 90*(2), 693–729.

Gold, E., Henig, J. R., Silander, M., & Simon, E. (2010). *Bringing a Public Voice to the School Governance Debate: The Campaign for Better Schools and Mayoral Control in New York City*. Philadelphia, PA: Research for Action.

Goodnough, A. (2002, September 24). A New Sort of School Board, Bland and Calm. *New York Times*. Retrieved from http://www.nytimes.com/2002/09/24/nyregion/a-new-sort-of-school-board-bland-and-calm.html.

Gootman, E. (2008, October 23). As Schools Face Cuts, Delays on Data System Bring More Frustration. *New York Times*. Retrieved from http://www.nytimes.com/2008/10/24/education/24aris.html.

Gootman, E., & Herzenhorn, D. M. (2007, February 3). Consultants Draw Fire in Bus Woes. *New York Times*. Retrieved from http://www.nytimes.com/2007/02/03/nyregion/03bus.html.

Graber, D. (1993). Swiss Cheese Journalism. *State Government News, 36*, 19–21.

Grodzins, M., & Elazar, D. J. (1966). *The American System*. New York, NY: Rand McNally.

Gusfield, J. R. (1963). *Symbolic Crusade: Status Politics and the American Temperance Movement*. Champaign, IL: University of Illinois Press.

Gyurko, J., & Henig, J. R. (2010). NYC: Strong Vision, Learning by Doing, or the Politics of Muddling Through? In K. E. Bulkley, J. R. Henig & H. M. Levin (Eds.), *Between Public and Private: Politics, Governance, and the New Portfolio Models for Urban School Reform* (pp. 91–126). Cambridge, MA: Harvard Education Press.

Hatry, H. P., & Durman, E. (1985). *Issues in Competitive Contracting for Social Services*. Falls Church, VA: National Institute of Governmental Purchasing, Inc.

Hays, S. P. (1964). The Politics of Reform in Municipal Government in the Progressive Era. *Pacific Northwest Quarterly, 55*, 157–169.

Heinrich, C. J. (2002). Outcomes-Based Performance Management in the Public Sector: Implications for Government Accountability and Effectiveness. *Public Administration Review, 62*(6), 712–725.

Henig, J. R. (1989/90). Privatization in the United States: Theory and Practice. *Political Science Quarterly, 104*(4), 649–670.

Henig, J. R. (1994). *Rethinking School Choice: Limits of the Market Metaphor*. Princeton, NJ: Princeton University Press.

Henig, J. R. (2004). Washington, DC: Race, Issue Definition, and School Board Restructuring. In J. R. Henig & W. C. Rich (Eds.), *Mayors in the Middle: Politics, Race and Mayoral Control of Urban Schools*. Princeton, NJ: Princeton University Press.

Henig, J. R. (2005). Understanding the Political Conflict over School Choice. In J. R. Betts & T. Loveless (Eds.), *How School Choice Affects Students and Families Who Do Not Choose*. Washington, DC: Brookings.

Henig, J. R. (2009a). Mayoral Control: What We Can and Cannot Learn from Other Cities. In J. P. Viteritti (Ed.), *When Mayors Take Charge School Governance in the City*. Washington, DC: Brookings Institution Press.

Henig, J. R. (2009b). Education Policy and the Politics of Privatization Since 1980. In B. J. Glenn & S. M. Teles (Eds.), *Conservativism and American Political Development* (pp. 291–323.). New York, NY: Oxford University Press.

Henig, J. R. (2009c). Mayors, Governors, and Presidents: The New Education Executives and the End of Educational Exceptionalism. *Peabody Journal of Education, 84*(3), 283–299.

Henig, J. R. (2009d). The Politics of Localism in an Era of Centralization, Privatization, and Choice. In R. L. Crowson & E. B. Goldring (Eds.), *Yearbook of the National Society for the Study of Education, Volume 108: The New Localism in American Education*. New York, NY: Teachers College.

Henig, J. R. (2010a). Portfolio Management Models and the Political Economy of Contracting Regimes. In K. E. Bulkley, J. R. Henig, & H. M. Levin (Eds.), *Between Public and Private: Politics, Governance, and the New Portfolio Models for Urban School Reform* (pp. 27–52). Cambridge, MA: Harvard Education Press.

Henig, J. R. (2010b). The Contemporary Context of Public Engagement: The New Political Grid. In M. Orr & J. Rogers (Eds.), *Public Engagement for Public Education*. Palo Alto, CA: Stanford University Press.

Henig, J. R. (forthcoming). The Politics of Data Use. In A. Bueschel & C. Coburn (Eds.), *Teachers College Record*, special issue on data use.

Henig, J. R., & Fraser, E. T. (2009). Correlates of Mayoral Takeovers in City School Systems. In N. Pindus, H. Wial & H. Wolman (Eds.), *Urban and Regional Policy and Its Effects: Volume 2* (pp. 69–123). Washington, DC: Brookings Institution Press.

Henig, J. R., & Reville, S. P. (2011, May 25). Outside-In School Reform: Why Attention Will Return to Non-School Factors. *Education Week*. Retrieved from http://www.edweek.org/ew/articles/2011/05/25/32henig_ep.h30.html.

Henig, J. R., & Rich, W. C. (Eds.). (2004). *Mayors in the Middle: Politics, Race, and Mayoral Control of Urban Schools*. Princeton, NJ: Princeton University Press.

Henig, J. R., Holyoke, T. T., Lacireno-Paquet, N., & Moser, M. M. (2003). Privatization, Politics, and Urban Services: The Political Behavior of Charter Schools. *Journal of Urban Affairs, 25*(1), 37–54.

Henig, J. R., Hula, R. C., Orr, M., and Pedescleaux, D. S. (1999). *The Color of School Reform.* Princeton, NJ: Princeton University Press.

Henig, J. R., Malone, H. J., & Reville, S. P. (2012). Addressing the Disadvantages of Poverty: Why Ignore the Most Important Challenge of the Post-Standards Era? In J. Mehta, R. Schwartz, & F.M. Hess (Eds.), *The Futures of School Reform.* Cambridge, MA: Harvard Education Press.

Hero, R. E., & Preuhs, R. R. (2007). Immigration and the Evolving American Welfare State: Examining Policies in the U.S. States. *American Journal of Political Science, 51*(3), 498–517.

Herszenhorn, D. M. (2004a, March 16). Bloomberg Wins on School Tests After Firing Foes *New York Times.* Retrieved from http://www.nytimes.com/2004/03/16/nyregion/bloomberg-wins-on-school-tests-after-firing-foes.html.

Herszenhorn, D. M. (2004b, March 29). Council Sends Loud Message on Schools. *New York Times.* Retrieved from http://www.nytimes.com/2004/03/29/nyregion/council-sends-loud-message-on-schools.html.

Herzik, E. B. (1983). Governors and Issues: A Typology of Concerns. *State Government, 54*(3), 58–64.

Hess, F. M. (1998). *Spinning Wheels: The Politics of Urban School Reform.* Washington, DC: Brookings Institution.

Hess, F. M. (Ed.). (2008). *When Research Matters: How Scholarship Influences Education Policy.* Cambridge, MA: Harvard Education Press.

Hess, F. M., & Kelly, A. (Eds.). (2011). *Carrots, Sticks, and the Bully Pulpit: Lessons from a Half-Century of Federal Efforts to Improve America's Schools.* Cambridge, MA: Harvard Education Press.

Hess, F. M., & Meeks, O. (forthcoming 2012). More Than the Mantra of "Mayoral Control": Rethinking District Governance for the 21st Century. In P. Manna & P. McGuinn (Eds.), *Education Governance for the Twenty-First Century: Overcoming the Structural Barriers to School Reform.* Washington, DC: Brookings Institution.

Hess, F. M., & Petrilli, M. J. (2006). *No Child Left Behind: A Primer.* New York, NY: Peter Lang.

Hill, P., Campbell, C., Menefee-Libey, D., Dusseault, B., DeArmond, M., & Gross, B. (2009). *Portfolio School Districts for Big Cities: An Interim Report.* Seattle, WA: Center on Reinventing Public Education.

Hill, P., Pierce, L. C., & Guthrie, J. W. (1997). *Reinventing Public Education: How Contracting Can Transform America's Schools.* Chicago, IL: University of Chicago Press.

Hochschild, J. L. (1984). *The New American Dilemma: Liberal Democracy and School Desegregation.* New Haven, CT: Yale University Press.

Hodgson, G. (2010). *The Myth of American Exceptionalism.* New Haven, CT: Yale University Press.

Hoffman, D. (1988, February 28). Bush Returns To Pre-Iowa Stump Speech; Attacks on Dole Dropped in South. *Washington Post,* p. A09.

Holyoke, T. T. (2003). Choosing Battlegrounds: Interest Group Lobbying across Multiple Venues. *Political Research Quarterly, 56*(3), 325–336.

Holyoke, T. T., Henig, J. R., Brown, H., & Lacireno-Paquet, N. (2009). Policy Dynamics and the Evolution of State Charter School Laws. *Policy Sciences, 42*(1), 33–55.

Holyoke, T. T., Brown, H., & Henig, J. R. (2012). Shopping in the Political Arena: Strategic State and Local Venue Selection by Advocates. *State and Local Government Review 44*, 9–20.

Honig, M. I., & DeArmond, M. (2010). Where's the Management in Portfolio Management? In K. E. Bulkley, J. R. Henig & H. M. Levin (Eds.), *Between Public and Private: Politics, Governance, and the New Portfolio Models for Urban School Reform* (pp. 195–216). Cambridge, MA: Harvard Education Press.

Howell, W. G. (Ed.). (2005). *Besieged: School Boards and the Future of Education Politics.* Washington, DC: Brookings.

Hrebenar, R. J., & Thomas, C. S. (2004). Interest Groups in the States. In V. Gray & R. L. Hanson (Eds.), *Politics in the American States* (pp. 100–128), Washington, DC: CQ Press.

Hunt, J. (1983). Address by Governor James Hunt. Paper presented at the National Governors Association, Portland, Maine, July 31.

Hunter, J. D. (1992). *Culture Wars: The Struggle to Control the Family, Art, Education, Law, and Politics in America.* New York, NY: Basic Books.

Iannaccone, L. (1967). *Politics in Education.* New York, NY: The Center for Applied Research in Education.

Innerst, C. (1996, March 11). Conservatives wary of slant in education summit agenda. *Washington Times,* p. A3.

Jencks, C. (1964, December 12). Why Bail Out the States? *New Republic,* 8–10.

Jenkins-Smith, H. C., Clair, G. K. S., & Woods, B. (1991). Explaining Change in Policy Subsystems: Analysis of Coalition Stability and Defection over Time. *American Journal of Political Science, 35*(4), 851–880.

Jochim, A. E. (2009). Ideas, Interests, and the Evolution of Federal Education Policy. Paper presented at the Annual Meeting of the Midwest Political Science Association, Chicago, IL, April 2–5.

Kaestle, C. F. (1983). *Pillars of the Republic: Common Schools and American Society, 1780–1860.* New York, NY: Hill & Wang.

Kaestle, C. F. (2007). Federal Education Policy and the Changing National Polity for Education, 1957–2007. In C. F. Kaestle & A. E. Lodewick (Eds.), *To Education a Nation.* Lawrence, KS: University Press of Kansas.

Kahlenberg, R. (2007). *Tough Liberal: Albert Shanker and the Battles Over Schools, Unions, Race, and Democracy.* New York, NY: Columbia University Press.

Kahlenberg, R. D. (Ed.). (2012). *The Future of School Integration: Socioeconomic Diversity as an Education Reform Strategy.* New York, NY: Century Foundation.

Kamerman, S. B., & Kahn, A. J. (Eds.). (1989). *Privatization and the Welfare State.* Princeton, NJ: Princeton University Press.

214

REFERENCES

Katz, M. (1970). *The Irony of Early School Reform: Educational Innovation in Mid-Nineteenth Century Massachusetts*. Boston, MA: Beacon Press.

Keesecker, W. W. (1950). State Boards of Education and Chief State School Officers: Their Status and Legal Powers. Washington, DC: Federal Security Agency, Office of Education.

Kinder, D. R., & Sanders, L. M. (1996). *Divided by Color: Racial Politics and Democratic Ideals*. Chicago, IL: University of Chicago Press.

Kingdon, J. W. (1995). *Agendas, Alternatives, and Public Policies* (2nd ed.). Boston, MA: Little, Brown and Company.

Kirp, D. L., & Babcock, G. (1981). Judge and Company: Court-Appointed Masters, School Desegregation, and Institutional Reform. *Alabama Law Review, 32*, 313–397.

Kirst, M. W. (2004). Turning Points: A History of American School Governance. In N. Epstein (Ed.), *Who's in Charge Here?: The Tangles Web of School Governance and Policy*. Washington, DC: Brookings.

Kirst, M. W., & Edelstein, F. (2006). The Maturing Mayoral Role in Education. *Harvard Educational Review, 76*(6), 152–164.

Kirst, M. W., & Wirt, F. M. (2009). *The Political Dynamics of American Education* (4th ed.). Richmond, CA: McCutchan Publishing.

Kirst, M., & Bulkley, K. (2000). "New, Improved" Mayors Take Over City Schools. *Phi Delta Kappan, 81*(7), 538–546.

Klarman, M. J. (1994). Reply: *Brown v. Board of Education*: Facts and Political Correctness. *Virginia Law Review, 80*(1), 185–199.

Kuhn, T. S. (1996). *The Structure of Scientific Revolution* (3rd ed.). Chicago, IL: University of Chicago Press.

Lehne, R. (1978). *The Quest for Justice: The Politics of School Finance Reform*. New York, NY: Longman.

Lemann, N. (1992). *The Promised Land: The Great Black Migration and How It Changed America*. New York, NY: Vintage.

Levin, H. M., & Koski, W. S. (2000). Twenty-Five Years After Rodriguez: What Have We Learned? *Teachers College Record, 102*, 480–513.

Lieberman, M. (2000). *The Teacher Unions: How They Sabotage Educational Reform and Why*. New York, NY: Encounter Books.

Liebman, J. S., & Sabel, C. F. (2003). Changing Schools: A Public Laboratory Dewey Barely Imagined: The Emerging Model of School Governance and Legal Reform. *New York University School of Law Review of Law and Social Change, 28*, 183–304.

Lipman, P. (2011). *The New Political Economy of Urban Education: Neoliberalism, Race, and the Right to the City*. New York, NY: Routledge.

Lipset, S. M. (1997). *American Exceptionalism: A Double-Edged Sword*. New York, NY: W. W. Norton.

Lipsky, M. (1968). Protest as a Political Resource. *American Political Science Review, 62*(4), 1144–1158.

Lowi, T. J. (1967). Machine Politics: Old and New. *Public Interest, 9*, 83–92.

Lubell, M., Feiock, R. C., & Cruz, E. E. R. d. l. (2009). Local Institutions and the Politics of Urban Growth. *American Journal of Political Science, 53*(3), 649–665.

Lukas, J. A. (1985). *Common Ground: A Turbulent Decade in the Lives of Three American Families*. New York, NY: Alfred Knopf.

Lynch, G. P. (2000). A Little Knowledge is a Dangerous Thing: What We Know about the Role of the Media in State Politics. *Perspectives on Political Science, 29*(2), 93–97.

Majone, G. (1977). From the Positive to the Regulatory State: Causes and Consequences of Changes in the Mode of Governance. *Journal of Public Policy, 17*(2), 139–167.

Manna, P. (2006). *School's In: Federalism and the National Education Agenda*. Washington, DC: Georgetown University Press.

Manna, P. (2010). *Collision Course: Federal Education Policy Meets State and Local Realities*. Washington, DC: CQ Press.

Manna, P., & Harwood, T. (2011). Governance and Educational Expectations in the U.S. States. *State Politics & Policy Quarterly, 11*(4), 483–509.

Manna, P., & Petrilli, M. J. (2008). Double Standard? 'Scientifically Based Research' and the No Child Left Behind Act. In F. M. Hess (Ed.), *When Research Matters: How Scholarship Influences Education Policy*. Cambridge, MA: Harvard Education Press.

Manno, B. V. (2012). Not Your Mother's PTA: Advocacy Groups Raise Money, Voices, Hopes. *Education Next, 12*(1), 43–50.

Marschall, M. J., Ruhil, A. V. S., & Shah, P. R. (2010). The New Racial Calculus: Electoral Institutions and Black Representation in Local Legislatures. *American Journal of Political Science, 54*(1), 107–124.

Mayhew, D. (1974). *Congress: The Electoral Connection*. New Haven, CT: Yale University Press.

Mazzoni, T. L. (1991). Analyzing State School Policymaking: An Arena Model. *Educational Evaluation and Policy Analysis, 13*(2), 115–138.

McAndrews, L. J. (2006). *The Era of Education: The Presidents and the Schools, 1965–2001*. Champaign, IL: University of Illinois Press.

McCarthy, M., Langdon, C., & Olson, J. (1993). *State Education Governance Structures*. Denver, CO: Education Commission of the States.

McCombs, M. E., & Shaw, D. L. (1972). The Agenda-Setting Function of Mass Media. *Public Opinion Quarterly, 36*, 176–187.

McCool, D. (1990). Subgovernments as Determinants of Political Viability. *Political Science Quarterly, 105*(2), 269–293.

McCubbins, M. D., & Schwartz, T. (1984). Congressional Oversight Overlooked: Police Patrols versus Fire Alarms. *American Journal of Political Science, 28*(1), 165–179.

McCubbins, M. D., Noll, R., & Weingast, B. R. (1987). Administrative Procedures as Instruments of Political Control." *Journal of Law, Economics, and Organization, 3*, 243–277.

McDermott, K. (1999). *Controlling Public Education: Localism Versus Equity*. Lawrence, KS: University Press of Kansas.

McDonnell, L. M. (2004). *Politics, Persuasion, and Educational Testing.* Cambridge, MA: Harvard University Press.

McDonnell, L. M. (2007). The Politics of Education: Influencing Policy and Beyond. In D. K. Cohen, S. H. Fuhrman, and F. Mosher (Eds.), *The State of Education Policy Research.* Mahwah, NJ: Lawrence Erlbaum Associates.

McDonnell, L. M. (2009). 2009 Presidential Address: Repositioning Politics in Education's Circle of Knowledge. *Educational Researcher, 38*(6), 417–427.

McDonnell, L. M., Timpane, P. M., & Benjamin, R. (Eds.). (2000). *Rediscovering the Democratic Purposes of Education.* Lawrence, KS: University Press of Kansas.

McGuinn, P. (2006). *No Child Left Behind and the Transformation of Federal Education Policy 1965–2005.* Lawrence, KS: University Press of Kansas.

McGuinn, P. (2010). Creating Cover and Constructing Capacity: Assessing the Origins, Evolution, and Impact of Race to the Top. Washington, DC: American Enterprise Institute.

McGuinn, P. J., & Manna, P. (Eds.). (2012). *Education Governance for the Twenty-First Century: Overcoming the Structural Barriers to School Reform.* Washington, DC: Brookings.

McNeal, R., & Dotterweich, L. (2007). Legislative Activity on Charter Schools: The Beginning of Policy Change? Unpublished working paper. New York, NY: National Center for the Study of Privatization and Education, Teachers College, Columbia University.

Mehta, J., & Teles, S. (2011). Jurisdictional Politics: A New Federal Role. In F. M. Hess & A. Kelly (Eds.), *Carrots, Sticks, and the Bully Pulpit: Lessons from a Half-Century of Federal Efforts to Improve America's Schools* (pp. 197–216). Cambridge, MA: Harvard Education Press.

Meier, K. J. (1994). *The Politics of Sin: Drugs, Alcohol, and Public Policy.* New York, NY: M. E. Sharpe.

Meier, K. J., & O'Toole Jr, L. J. (2006). *Bureaucracy in a Democratic State: A Governance Perspective.* Baltimore, MD: Johns Hopkins University.

Meier, K. J., Juenke, E. G., Wrinkle, R. D., & Polinard, J. L. (2005). Structural Choices and Representational Biases: The Post-Election Color of Representation. *American Journal of Political Science, 49*(4), 758–768.

Meier, K. J., Wrinkle, R. D., & Polinard, J. L. (1999). Equity Versus Excellence in Organizations: A Substantively Weighted Least Squares Analysis. *American Review of Public Administration, 29,* 5–18.

Melnick, R. S. (2009). Taking Remedies Seriously: Can Courts Control Schools? In J. M. Dunn & M. R. West (Eds.), *From Schoolhouse to Courthouse: The Judiciary's Role in American Education* (pp. 17–48). Washington, DC: Brookings.

Menendez, A. J. (1999). Voters versus Vouchers: An Analysis of Referendum Data. *Phi Delta Kappan, 81*(1), 76–80.

Merton, R. K. (1968). *Social Theory and Social Structure.* New York, NY: The Free Press.

Mettler, S. (2002). Bringing the State Back in to Civic Engagement: Policy Feedback Effects of the G.I. Bill for World War II Veterans. *American Political Science Review, 96*(2), 351–365.

Mettler, S., & Soss, J. (2004). The Consequences of Public Policy for Democratic Citizenship: Bridging Policy Studies and Mass Politics. *Perspectives on Politics, 2*(1), 55–73.

Metzler, J. (2003). Inequitable Equilibrium: School Finance in the United States. *Indiana Law Review, 36*(3), 561–608.

Miller, G. J. (2005). The Political Evolution of Principal-Agent Models. *Annual Review of Political Science, 8*, 203–225.

Miller, M. (2008, January/February). First, Kill All the School Boards. *The Atlantic Monthly.* Retrieved from http://www.theatlantic.com/magazine/archive/2008/01/first-kill-all-the-school-boards/6579/.

Mintrom, M. (2000). *Policy Entrepreneurs and School Choice.* Washington, DC: Georgetown University Press.

Mittelstadt, M. (2007, March 7). House OKs Texans' bill honoring LBJ. *Houston Chronicle.* Retrieved from http://www.chron.com/news/nation-world/article/House-OKs-Texans-bill-honoring-LBJ-1626647.php.

Moe, T. M. (2001). *Schools, Vouchers, and the American Public.* Washington, DC: Brookings Institution.

Moe, T. M. (2006). Political Control and the Power of the Agent. *Journal of Law, Economics, and Organization, 22*(1), 1–29.

Moe, T. M. (2011). *Special Interest: Teachers Unions and America's Public Schools.* Washington, DC: Brookings Institution Press.

Moe, T. M., & Chubb, J. E. (2009). *Liberating Learning: Technology, Politics, and the Future of American Education.* New York, NY: Jossey-Bass.

Moore, S. (2009, December 19). Can Detroit Be Saved? *Wall Street Journal.* Retrieved from http://online.wsj.com/article/SB10001424052748703558004574581650636077732.html.

Mosteller, F., & Boruch, R. (Eds.). (2002). *Evidence Matters: Randomized Trials in Education Research.* Washington, DC: Brookings Institution Press.

Mullin, M. (2008). The Conditional Effect of Specialized Governance on Public Policy. *American Journal of Political Science, 52*(1), 125–141.

Murphy, J. (Ed.). (1990). *The Educational Reform Movement of the 1980s: Perspectives and Cases.* Berkeley, CA: McCutchan Publishers.

Nathan, J. (1999). *Charter Schools: Creating Hope and Opportunity for American Education.* San Francisco, CA: Jossey-Bass Publishers.

National Alliance of Charter School Authorizers. (2010). The State of Charter School Authorizing: A Report on NACSA's Authorizer Survey. Chicago, IL: NACSA.

O'Donnell, P. (2012, February 07). Cleveland Mayor Frank Jackson proposes sweeping plan to improve education for city students. *Cleveland Plain Dealer.* Retrieved from http://blog.cleveland.com/metro/2012/02/cleveland_mayor_frank_jackson_26.html.

Oppel, R. A., Jr. (2012). "Santorum Questions Education System; Criticizes Obama." *New York Times*, February 18. http://www.nytimes.com/2012/02/19/us/politics/santorum-criticizes-education-system-and-obama.html.

Orfield, G. (1969). *The Reconstruction of Southern Education.* New York, NY: John Wiley & Sons.

Orfield, G. (1978). *Must We Bus? Segregated Schools and National Policy.* Washington, DC: Brookings.

Orfield, G. (1995). Public Opinion and School Desegregation. *Teachers College Record, 96*(4), 654–670.

Orfield, G., & Eaton, S. (1996). *Dismantling Desegregation.* New York, NY: The New Press.

Orr, M. (2000). *Black Social Capital: The Politics of School Reform in Baltimore, 1986–1998.* Lawrence, KS: University Press of Kansas.

Orr, M. (2004). Baltimore: The Limits of Mayoral Control. In J. R. Henig & W. C. Rich (Eds.), *Mayors in the Middle: Politics, Race and Mayoral Control of Urban Schools* (pp. 27–58). Princeton, NJ: Princeton University Press.

Orren, K., & Skowronek, S. (2004). *The Search for American Political Development.* New York, NY: Cambridge University Press.

Pangle, L. S., & Pangle, T. L. (1995). *The Learning of Liberty: The Educational Ideas of the Founding Fathers.* Lawrence, KS: University Press of Kansas.

Patashnik, E. M. (2008). *Reforms at Risk: What Happens After Major Policy Changes Are Enacted.* Princeton, NJ: Princeton University Press.

Peters, B. G., Pierre, J., & King, D. S. (2005). The Politics of Path Dependency: Political Conflict in Historical Institutionalism. *Journal of Politics, 67*(4), 1275–1300.

Peterson, P. (2010, July 21). No, Al Shanker Did Not Invent the Charter School. *Education Next.* Retrieved from http://educationnext.org/no-al-shanker-did-not-invent-the-charter-school/.

Peterson, P. E. (1981). *City Limits.* Chicago, IL: University of Chicago Press.

Pierson, P. (1993). Review: When Effect Becomes Cause: Policy Feedback and Political Change. *World Politics, 45*(4), 595–628.

Pierson, P. (2000). Increasing Returns, Path Dependence, and the Study of Politics. *American Political Science Review, 94*(2), 251–267.

Pollock, M. (2004). *Colormute: Race Talk Dilemmas in an American School.* Princeton, NJ: Princeton University Press.

Pralle, S. B. (2003). Venue Shopping, Political Strategy, and Policy Change: The Internationalization of Canadian Forest Advocacy. *Journal of Public Policy, 23,* 233–260.

Quaid, L. (2009, March 31). School chief: Mayors need control of urban schools. *Associated Press.*

Quinn, C. (2006). New York City Council Speaker Quinn's Budget Response. Remarks as delivered April 6, 2006, http://council.nyc.gov/html/soc/2010/docs/04_06_06_SOCBudgetResponse.pdf.

Radin, B. A., & Hawley, W. D. (1988). *The Politics of Federal Reorganization: Creating the U.S. Department of Education.* New York, NY: Pergamon Press.

Ravitch, D. (2003). *The Language Police: How Pressure Groups Restrict What Students Learn*. New York, NY: Alfred A. Knopf.

Ravitch, D. (2010). *The Death and Life of the Great American School System*. New York, NY: Perseus.

Rebell, M. A. (2005). Adequacy Litigations: A New Path to Equity? In J. Petrovich & A. S. Wells (Eds.), *Bringing Equity Back: Research for a New Era in American Educational Policy* (pp. 291–323). New York, NY: Teachers College Press.

Rebell, M. A. (2009). *Courts & Kids: Pursuing Educational Equity Through the State Courts*. Chicago, IL: University of Chicago Press.

Rebell, M., & Block, A. R. (1982). *Educational Policy Making and the Courts: An Empirical Study of Judicial Activism*. Chicago, IL: University of Chicago.

Reckhow, S. (2008a). A Shadow Bureaucracy: How Foundations Circumvent Politics to Reform Schools. Paper presented at the American Political Science Association, Boston, MA, August 28–30.

Reckhow, S. (2008b). Waiting for Bill Gates: Following the Money Trail from Foundations to Urban School Districts. Paper presented at the Annual Meeting of the Midwest Political Science Association, Chicago, IL, April 3.

Reckhow, S. (2010). Disseminating and Legitimating a New Approach: The Role of Foundations. In K. E. Bulkley, J. R. Henig & H. M. Levin (Eds.), *Between Public and Private: Politics, Governance, and the New Portfolio Models for Urban School Reform* (pp. 277–304). Cambridge, MA: Harvard Education Press.

Reckhow, S. E. (forthcoming). *Follow the Money: How Foundation Dollars Change Public School Politics*. New York, NY: Oxford University Press.

Reed, D. S. (2003). *On Equal Terms: The Constitutional Politics of Educational Opportunity*. Princeton, NJ: Princeton University Press.

Rhodes, J. H. (2012). *An Education in Politics: The Origin and Evolution of No Child Left Behind*. Ithaca, NY: Cornell University Press.

Richards, E. (2010, January 19). Race to the Top program extended; mayoral control won't determine winners, Duncan says. *Milwaukee Journal Sentinel*. Retrieved from http://www.jsonline.com/blogs/news/82110382.html?sort=most+thumbs+up.

Riley, N. S. (2009). An Interview with Philanthropist Eli Broad: "We're In the Venture Philanthropy Business." *Wall Street Journal*. Retrieved from http://online.wsj.com/article/SB10001424052970204251404574342693329347698.html#printMode.

Robelen, E. W. (2009, October 12 [online], October 14 [print]). At State Level, Power Over Schools a Contentious Issue. *Education Week*. Retrieved from http://www.edweek.org/ew/articles/2009/10/14/07wallace-states.h29.html.

Roberts, N. C., & King, P. J. (1996). *Transforming Public Policy: Dynamics of Policy Entrepreneurship and Innovation*. San Francisco, CA: Jossey-Bass.

Rochefort, D. A., & Cobb, R. W. (Eds.). (1994). *The Politics of Problem Definition: Shaping the Policy Agenda*. Lawrence, KS: University Press of Kansas.

Rosenberg, G. N. (1991). *The Hollow Hope: Can Courts Bring About Social Change?* Chicago, IL: University of Chicago Press.

Roza, M. (forthcoming 2012). The Machinery That Drives Education-Spending Decisions Inhibits Better Uses of Resources. In P. Manna & P. McGuinn (Eds.), *Education Governance for the Twenty-First Century: Overcoming the Structural Barriers to School Reform*. Washington, DC: Brookings Institution.

Rudalevige, A. (2003). The Politics of No Child Left Behind. *Education Next*, 62–69.

Sabato, L. (1983). *Goodbye to Good-Time Charlie: The American Governorship Transformed*. Washington, DC: CQ Press.

Salamon, L. (1995). *Partners in Public Service: Government-Nonprofit Relations in the Modern Welfare State*. Baltimore, MD: Johns Hopkins University Press.

Saltman, K. J. (2005). *The Edison Schools: Corporate Schooling and the Assault on Public Education*. New York, NY: Routledge.

Sandler, R., and Schoenbrod, D. (2003). *Democracy by Decree: What Happens When Courts Run Government*. New Haven, CT: Yale University Press.

Santos, F. (2011a, April 28). Consultant to the Schools Stole Millions, Officials Say. *New York Times*. Retrieved from http://www.nytimes.com/2011/04/29/nyregion/consultant-to-schools-stole-millions-officials-say.html.

Santos, F. (2011b, June 24). Deal Will Avert Plan to Lay Off City Teachers. *New York Times*. Retrieved from http://www.nytimes.com/2011/06/25/nyregion/deal-reached-to-avert-new-york-teacher-layoffs.html?_r=2.

Santos, F. (2011c, June 1). Quinn Offers Cuts as Alternative to Widespread Layoffs. *New York Times*. Retrieved from http://www.nytimes.com/2011/06/02/nyregion/council-speaker-quinn-proposes-alternate-education-cuts-to-save-teaching-jobs.html?_r=1.

Saul, M. H. (2011, December 9). City Council Bucks Mayor on Contractor Legislation. *Wall Street Journal*. Retrieved from http://blogs.wsj.com/metropolis/2011/12/09/city-council-bucks-mayor-on-contractor-legislation/?mod=WSJBlog&mod=WSJ_NY_NY_Blog.

Savage, C. (2012, April 22). Shift on Executive Power Lets Obama Bypass Rivals. *New York Times*. Retrieved from http://www.nytimes.com/2012/04/23/us/politics/shift-on-executive-powers-let-obama-bypass-congress.html?_r=1.

Savas, E. S. (2000). *Privatization and Public-Private Partnerships*. New York, NY: Chatham House.

Sawchuk, S. (2012, May 16). New Advocacy Groups Shaking Up Education Field. *Education Week*. Retrieved from http://www.edweek.org/ew/articles/2012/05/16/31adv-overview_ep.h31.html.

Schattschneider, E. E. (1960). *The Semi-Sovereign People: A Realist's View of Democracy in America*. Chicago, IL: Holt, Rinehart & Winston.

Schlesinger, J. A. (1965). The Politics of the Executive. In H. Jacob & K. N. Vines (Eds.), *Politics in the American States* (pp. 207–238). Boston, MA: Little, Brown and Company.

Schneider, A., & Ingram, H. (1993). Social Construction of Target Populations: Implications for Politics and Policy. *The American Political Science Review, 87*(2), 334–347.

Schuman, H., Steeh, C., Bobo, L. D., & Krysan, M. (Eds.). (1998). *Racial Attitudes in America: Trends and Interpretations, Revised Edition.* Cambridge, MA: Harvard University Press.

Sclar, E. (2000). *You Don't Always Get What You Pay For: The Economics of Privatization.* Ithaca, NY: Cornell University Press.

Severson, K. (2011, June 6). S. Carolina Supreme Court Rules Against Governor. *New York Times.* Retrieved from http://www.nytimes.com/2011/06/07/us/07carolina.html.

Sharp, E. B. (Ed.). (1999). *Culture Wars and Local Politics.* Lawrence, KS: University Press of Kansas.

Sheingate, A. D. (2003). Political Entrepreneurship, Institutional Change, and American Political Development. *Studies in American Political Development, 17*(02), 185–203.

Shipps, D. (2003). Pulling together: Civic capacity and urban school reform. *American Educational Research Journal, 40*(4), 841–878.

Shober, A. F., Manna, P. & Witte, J. F. (2006). Analyzing State Charter School Laws and the Formation of Charter Schools in the United States. *Policy Studies Journal, 34*(4, November), 263–287.

Smeeding, T., Erikson, R., & Janntti, M. (Eds.). (2011). *Persistence, Privilege, and Parenting: The Comparative Study of Intergenerational Mobility.* New York, NY: Russell Sage Foundation.

Smith, J. M. (2010). 'Re-Stating' Theories of Urban Development: The Politics of Authority Creation and Intergovernmental Triads in Postindustrial Chicago. *Journal of Urban Affairs, 32*(4), 425–448.

Smith, S. R., & Lipsky, M. (1993). *Nonprofits for Hire: The Welfare State in the Age of Contracting.* Cambridge, MA: Harvard University Press.

Soss, J., Schram, S., Vartanian, T., & O'Brien, E. (2001). Setting the Terms of Relief: Explaining State Policy Choices in the Devolution Revolution. *American Journal of Political Science, 45*(2), 378–395.

Stephens, D. (1984). President Carter, the Congress, and NEA: Creating the Department of Education. *Political Science Quarterly, 98*(4), 641–663.

Stewart, N., & Schwartzman, P. (2010, September 16). How Adrian Fenty lost his reelection bid for D.C. mayor. *Washington Post.* Retrieved from http://www.washingtonpost.com/wp-dyn/content/article/2010/09/15/AR2010091500834.html.

Stone, C. E. (1989). *Regime Politics: Governing Atlanta, 1946–1988.* Lawrence, KS: University Press of Kansas.

Stone, C., Henig, J. R., Jones, B. D., & Pierranunzi, C. (2001). *Building Civic Capacity: Toward a New Politics of Urban School Reform.* Lawrence, KS: University Press of Kansas.

Stossell, J. (2011, September 16). Stupid In America. FoxNews.com. Retrieved from http://www.foxnews.com/opinion/2011/09/16/stupid-in-america/.

Superfine, B. M. (2010). Court-Driven Reform and Educational Opportunity: Centralization, Decentralization, and the Shifting Judicial Role. *Review of Educational Research, 80*(1), 108–137.

Superfine, B. M., & Goddard, R. D. (2009). The Expanding Role of the Courts in Education Policy: The Preschool Remedy and an Adequate Education. *Teachers College Record, 111*(7), 1796–1833.

Tate, W. F. (Ed.). (2012). *Research on Schools, Neighborhoods, and Communities.* Lanham, MD: American Educational Research Association/Rowman & Littlefield.

Thelen, K. (2003). How Institutions Evolve: Insights from Comparative Historical Analysis. In J. Mahoney & D. Rueschmeijer (Eds.), *Comparative Historical Analysis in the Social Sciences* (pp. 208–240). Cambridge, UK: Cambridge University Press.

Timar, T. B. (1997). The Institutional Role of State Education Departments: A Historical Perspective. *American Journal of Education, 105*(3), 231–260.

Toch, T. (1991). *In the Name of Excellence: The Struggle to Reform the Nation's Schools, Why It's Failing, and What Should Be Done.* New York, NY: Oxford University Press.

Tractenberg, P. L. (1974). New Jersey: *Robinson v. Cahill*: The "Thorough and Efficient" Clause. *Law and Contemporary Problems, 38*(3), 312–332.

Tyack, D. (1974). *The One Best System.* Cambridge, MA: Harvard University Press.

U.S. Census Bureau. (2011). Public Education Finances: 2009. Retrieved from http://www.census.gov/prod/2011pubs/g09-aspef.pdf.

Umpstead, R. R. (2007). Determining Adequacy: How Courts Are Redefining State Responsibility for Educational Finance, Goals, and Accountability. *Brigham Young University Education and Law Journal, 2007,* 281–316.

van der Heijden, J. (2011). Institutional Layering: A Review of the Use of the Concept. *Politics, 31*(1), 9–18.

Vinovskis, M. (2008). *From a Nation at Risk to No Child Left Behind: National Education Goals and the Creation of Federal Education Policy.* New York, NY: Teachers College Press.

Vinovskis, M. A. (1999). *The Road to Charlottesville: The 1989 Education Summit.* Washington, DC: GPO.

Vinovskis, M. A. (2008). Gubernatorial Leadership and American K–12 Educational Reform. In E. G. Sribnick (Ed.), *A Legacy of Innovation: Governors and Public Policy.* Philadelphia, PA: University of Pennsylvania Press.

Viteritti, J. P. (2004). From excellence to equity: Observations on politics, history, and policy. *Peabody Journal of Education, 79*(1), 64–86.

Viteritti, J. P. (Ed.). (2009). *When Mayors Take Charge: School Governance in the City.* Washington, DC: Brookings Institution.

Walsh, M. (2000, May 24). Campaign Cash From Voucher Backers At Issue in Wisconsin. *Education Week.* Retrieved from http://www.edweek.org/ew/articles/2000/05/24/37judge.h19.html.

Walters, P. B., Lareau, A., & Ranis, S. H. (Eds.). (2009). *Education Research on Trial: Policy Reform and the Call for Scientific Rigor.* New York, NY: Routledge.

Weiner, R. (2012, April 16). Mitt Romney at private fundraiser: I might eliminate HUD. *Washington Post*. Retrieved from http://www.washingtonpost.com/blogs/the-fix/post/mitt-romney-at-private-fundraiser-i-might-eliminate-hud/2012/04/16/gIQA5QuKLT_blog.html.

Weingast, B. R. (1981). Regulation, Reregulation, and Deregulation: The Political Foundations of Agency Clientele Relationships. *Law and Contemporary Problems, 44*(1), 147–177.

Wholey, J. S., & Hatry, H. P. (1992). The Case for Performance Monitoring. *Public Administration Review, 52*(6), 604–610.

Wilson, J. Q. (1973). *Political Organizations*. New York, NY: Basic Books.

Wilson, J. Q. (1989). *Bureaucracy*. New York, NY: Basic Books.

Winerip, M. (2004, March 24). ON EDUCATION; Fired for Disagreeing, Ex-Panelist Fears the Mayor Is Discouraging Advice He Needs to Hear. *New York Times*. Retrieved from http://www.nytimes.com/2004/03/24/nyregion/education-fired-for-disagreeing-ex-panelist-fears-mayor-discouraging-advice-he.html.

Wirt, F. M., & Kirst, M. W. (2001). *The Political Dynamics of American Education* (2nd ed.). Richmond, CA: McCutchan Publishing.

Wong, K. K., & Langevin, W. E. (2007). Policy Expansion of School Choice in the American States. *Peabody Journal of Education, 82*(2–3), 440–472.

Wong, K. K., Shen, F. X., Anagnostopolous, D., & Rutledge, S. (2007). *The Education Mayor: Improving America's Schools*. Washington, DC: Georgetown University Press.

Wood, B. D. (1992). Modeling Federal Implementation as a System: The Clean Air Case. *American Journal of Political Science, 36*(1), 40–67.

ACKNOWLEDGMENTS

No author can finish a book like this without accumulating debts in the form of financial, intellectual, and moral support. Things are supposed to get easier over time, I thought, but I came out of the writing of this book feeling that I had distributed more IOUs than in my previous books.

The Spencer Foundation has always treated me generously, and did so again in this instance by granting a contract that gave me some additional writing time and research assistance. Thanks to Spencer and program officer Andrea Bueschel.

I began the writing during a sabbatical spent in Princeton as the Roger W. Ferguson Jr. and Annette L. Nazareth Member of the School of Social Science at the Institute for Advanced Studies (IAS). While there, I got to learn from and try out ideas on a diverse group of visiting scholars assembled by IAS faculty member Danielle Allen. There were lots of illuminating exchanges, but I especially benefited from the chance to trade ideas with Patrick McGuinn and David Karen, who were working on complementary issues.

One former Teachers College colleague and one current one deserve mention. Dorothy Shipps, after she had left TC, asked me to contribute an article to a journal issue she was coediting; the topic she assigned me—a look at education mayors, education governors, and education presidents—was the catalyst for my thinking about the end of education exceptionalism. Michael Rebell, a lawyer and legal scholar and my current colleague, read sections of the manuscript that dealt with the role of the judiciary; he saved me from some errors and, by not laughing me out of court, gave me a little more confidence that my characterization was at the least defensible. At an important juncture, Michael Kirst, of Stanford University, offered very helpful feedback and pointed me to some important sources that I had overlooked.

225

External reviewers can be the bane of an author's existence, but in this case Harvard Education Press did me the favor of sending the manuscript to a dream reviewer, Paul Manna. Beyond the nice things he said, which of course I welcomed, Paul contributed about twenty-five pages of comments on specific items in the text: some of them corrections, some suggestions for clarification, and some detailed ideas about implications or qualifications that had eluded me. He also shared data he had collected and generally went above and beyond the call of duty in all respects.

I was very fortunate on the research assistant front. Elizabeth "Liz" Chu, an education policy doctoral candidate in the Teachers College Department of Education Policy and Social Analysis, was patient, reliable, dogged in following up on what were sometimes vague notions on my part, and a great sounding board, willing to tell me when I was overreaching in my interpretation of the evidence. James Morgano also provided helpful assistance before he completed his master's in politics and education and moved on to better things.

Caroline Chauncey, my editor at Harvard Education Press, was enthusiastic from the day I mentioned the project. That she maintained that enthusiasm after seeing the manuscript was a huge relief. But what really made her a great editor for this project was that she knew enough and cared enough about the issues to suggest well-targeted revisions at a couple of stages along the way.

Finally, I'd like to thank my wife, Robin Marantz Henig. It's common—almost a cliché—to thank one's family for being tolerant of long absences and personal disengagement in the course of getting a book done. But Robin is herself a writer, and the joke in our family is that it's she who often pulls away as her deadlines loom, while I'm so compartmentalized about my writing that neither she nor Jess and Sam, our two (now grown) daughters, are aware I'm even working on a book until it's nearly done. So while there are plenty of things about which I could ask her forbearance, toleration of my book-induced absences is not high on the list. Even though she certainly did provide helpful feedback—as an editor and a sounding board—I'll use this opportunity to thank her instead for her support in all other aspects of my life.

ABOUT THE AUTHOR

Jeffrey R. Henig is a professor of political science and education and chair of the Department of Education Policy and Social Analysis at Teachers College, Columbia University. He is also a professor of political science at Columbia University.

He is the author or coauthor of ten books, including *The Color of School Reform: Race, Politics, and the Challenge of Urban Education* (Princeton University Press, 1999) and *Building Civic Capacity: The Politics of Reforming Urban Schools* (University Press of Kansas, 2001), both of which were named—in 1999 and 2001, respectively—the best book written on urban politics by the Urban Politics Section of the American Political Science Association. *Spin Cycle: How Research Is Used in Policy Debates: The Case of Charter Schools* (Russell Sage Foundation, 2008) won the American Educational Research Association's (AERA) Outstanding Book Award, 2010. Most recently, Henig coedited and contributed to *Between Public and Private: Politics, Governance, and the New Portfolio Models for Urban School Reform* (Harvard Education Press, 2010), winner of the Districts in Research and Reform SIG Best Book Award, 2012.

INDEX

Abercrombie, Neal, 41
academic excellence, 32
accountability, 15, 19, 56, 65, 90, 106, 172
adequacy issues, 91, 93
African Americans, 75–76, 168
Alexander, Lamar, 36
Allen, Jeanne, 132
American exceptionalism, 4
American Federation of Teachers (AFT), 120
apolitical myth, of education, 161
at-risk students, 107

Baltimore, 60, 62
Bennet, Michael, 152
blame avoidance, by politicians, 93–94
Bloomberg, Michael, 16, 33, 63–65, 79–80, 109–110, 113–118
Boehner, John, 99–100
Boston
  mayoral control in, 59, 60
  public school system, 88–89
Broad, Eli, 2
Brown v. Board of Education, 74, 84–87
bureaucracies, 17, 21–22, 168
  antipathy toward, 68–69
  weakening of, 174
Bush, George H. W., 33, 54–56
Bush, George W., 7, 56, 98
business, 71, 147, 170

California, Proposition 13 in, 29
Campaign for Fiscal Equity (CFE), 115–116
Carter, Jimmy, 52–53
Center for Education Reform (CER), 132, 135
centralization
  vs. decentralization, 5–7, 25, 27, 170–171
  shift to, 19–20, 77
charter management organizations (CMOs), 169
charter schools, 8, 10, 32, 102–103, 131–139, 149, 173
Chicago, 2, 60, 62–63
Chief Executive Officer (CEO), 71
chief state school officers (CSSOs), 38–41, 47–49
Christie, Chris, 43
city councils, 79, 97, 108–118, 155–159
civil rights movement, 74–75
civil society, 8, 25, 120
class politics, 76, 94–95
Cleveland, 60, 151
Clinton, Bill, 36, 56
colonial era, 6, 165
competing priorities, 18
Congress, 98–102, 123–126
congressional committees, 126–130
congressional districts, 96–97
congressional hearings, 124, 126–128
contracting regimes, 148–153
corporate management, 145

corporate metaphor, 71
courts, 20, 31, 80–92
  coalition building by, 91–92
  desegregation and, 84–90
  education policy and, 82–93
  effects on legislatures of, 92–95
  school funding and, 87–88
  self-limited role of, 92–95
credit claiming, by politicians, 93
CSSOs. *See* chief state school officers
  (CSSOs)
culture wars, 94
curriculum, 105–106

decentralization, vs. centralization, 5–7,
  25, 27, 170–171
democracy-bureaucracy problem, 21–22
Denver, 151–153
Department of Education, U.S., 52–53,
  69, 77, 176
departments of education, state, 5
desegregation, 8–9, 46, 51–52, 74–75,
  84–89, 95, 170
Detroit, 60
Dillon's Rule, 36–37
District of Columbia. *See* Washington, DC
domestic policy, 3, 4, 28, 119–120,
  165–166
Duncan, Arne, 140, 153

education. *See also* public education/
  schools
  apolitical myth of, 161
  centralization vs. decentralization in,
  5–7
  institutional landscape of, 4–14
  investment in, 161, 174
  reabsorption of, in general-purpose
  governance, 3–4, 7, 162–180
  reframing, as economic issue, 73

educational adequacy, 91, 93
educational decision-making
  centralization vs. decentralization in,
  5–7, 25, 27, 170–171
  public vs. private sector, 8–10
  spheres of, 24–30
educational reform, 1–4
  adequacy issues and, 91
  charter schools and, 131–139
  courts and, 82–92
  at local level, 11–12
  in Progressive Era, 165, 171
  school-focused, 140–143, 146, 178
  state legislatures and, 103–104
educational technology, 106, 173
education bureaucracies, 68–69
education exceptionalism. *See also*
  single-purpose government
  defined, 4
  end of, 4, 18, 28, 59, 81, 93, 121, 159,
  161–180
  origins and institutionalization of, 23,
  164–168
  risks of ending, 172–175
  sway of, 19–20
education executives, 31, 33–77
  facilitating factors for, 72–76
  governors, 3, 6–7, 24, 31, 34, 36–51,
  144–145
  level-specific explanations of, 65–68
  mayors, 3, 16–17, 20–21, 31–34, 58–
  65, 73, 79–80, 109–111, 145–151
  personality-based explanation of,
  65–66
  presidents, 3, 7, 31, 34, 51–58, 73–74, 98
  pull factors for, 67, 69–72
  push factors for, 67–69
education-focused interest groups, 120–
  121, 129–130, 148, 167–168, 180
education governance regimes, 146–155
education governors. *See* governors
education lobby, 34–35

education management organizations
(EMOs), 169
education policy
changes in, 1–4, 119–122
city councils and, 108–118
Congress and, 98–102
courts and, 82–92
elected officials and, 93–95
evidence-based, 176
"excellence" agenda, 122–130
executive control of, 33–77
federal role in, 5, 7, 11, 35, 51–58
interest groups influencing, 120–121
legislatures and, 96–118
traditional elements of, 162
value differences and, 161–162
education presidents. See presidents
Eisenhower, Dwight, 51, 74–75
elected officials. See also governors;
mayors/mayoral control; presidents
education policy and, 93–95
electoral districts, 96–97
electoral regimes, 147
Elementary and Secondary Education
Act (ESEA), 98–99, 123, 125
empirical research, 176, 178
equity, 32, 87–88, 94–95, 122
evidence-based practices, 176
"excellence" agenda, 34–35, 122–130
executive branch, 70–71. See also
education executives
executive leadership, 81–82, 118
executive privilege, 70
expertise, 85, 168, 172–173

Fallin, Mary, 43
family control, 8–9
federal government. See national
government
federalism, 5–11, 21, 29, 34–35, 85, 87,
120

Federalist Papers, 164
Fenty, Adrian, 16–17, 109–111
fiscal equity issues, 21, 87–88, 94–95,
122
Florio, James, 94–95
Ford, Gerald, 56, 75
for-profit education sector, 8, 10, 27
foundations, 153–155
Friedman, Milton, 9

Garrity, W. Arthur, Jr., 88–89
general-purpose government/
institutions
charter schools and, 131–132
city councils, 108–118
courts and, 82–95
defined, 11
elected executives in, 33–77
employment by, 12–14
legislatures, 96–118
optimism about, 175–179
rationale for, 17–19
reabsorption of education into, 3–4,
7, 162–180
vs. single-purpose, 10–30
global competitiveness, 34–35, 37,
73–74, 170
globalization, 73
Goodling, Bill, 99–100
governance change, 119–120
governance regimes, 146–155
government, 21, 24. See also general-
purpose government; national
government; single-purpose
government
levels of, 11–12
vs. private sector, 8–10
governors
charter schools and, 137
education, 3, 6–7, 20, 21, 34, 36–51
electoral coalitions and, 97

231

governors, *continued*
    emergence of education, 37–38
    formal powers of, 38–43, 47–51
    high profile of, 31
    informal powers of, 43–51
    leadership by, on education, 45
    normal politics and, 24
    selection of CSSOs by, 38–41, 47–49
    state legislatures and, 144–145
    state-of-the-state speeches by, 44
Graham, Bob, 36
"great man perspective," 65–66, 81
Great Migration, 168
Gregoire, Christine, 39

Haley, Nikki, 43
Harrisburg, PA, 60
Hartford, CT, 61
Higher Education Facilities Bill, 98
home schooling, 9
human capital, 73
Hunt, James, 6–7, 36, 47
hyperlocalization, 167

incumbent advantage, 94
individualism, 6
inequalities, 173, 174
institutional change, 30
institutional choices, 26–28
institutional landscape, 4–14, 121–122
institutional politics, 24–30, 164–172
institution creation, 139
interest groups, 22–26, 29, 97, 107,
    120–122, 126, 129–130
    education-specific, 120–121, 129–
        130, 148, 167–168, 180
    reconfiguration of, 146–147
iron triangles, 29, 94, 122, 166
issue-specific agencies, 21–22

Jackson, Frank, 151
Jackson, MS, 61
Jefferson, Thomas, 51
Johnson, Lyndon, 51, 75, 98–99
judges, 82, 83, 92. *See also* courts
judiciary, 4, 82–92. *See also* courts

K12, Inc., 139
Kean, Thomas, 36
Kennedy, John F., 52, 75
Kirst, Michael, 33
Kitzhaber, John, 43
Klein, Joel, 16, 64, 109–110, 113–118

legal precedent, 83, 92
legislatures
    agendas of, 140–145
    capacity and expertise of, 97–98
    changing role of, 20, 31, 81
    city councils, 108–118
    Congress, 98–102
    education policy and, 96–118
    effects of courts on, 92–95
    electoral districts, 96–97
    funding and, 28–29, 106–107
    principle-agent relationship and, 22
    state, 80, 87–88, 102–107, 139–145
level-specific perspective, 65–68
Lindsay, John, 95
local government, 5–6, 11–12, 37
    courts and, 87
    mayoral control and, 58–65, 145–151
localism, 5, 6, 8, 85, 131, 162, 170
local politics, 147–148
local school boards. *See* school boards
local school districts. *See* school districts
Long Beach, CA, 63
Los Angeles, 154–155
low-income students, 174–175

magnet schools, 10
Mann, Horace, 8
market forces, 9–10, 74, 177
market theory, 145, 149
mayors/mayoral control
  electoral coalitions and, 97
  in New York City, 16, 61, 63–65,
    79–80, 109–110, 113–118, 155–159
  philanthropic support and, 153–155
  of public schools, 3, 16–17, 20–21, 31,
    33–34, 58–65, 73, 79–80, 109–111,
    145–151
  in Washington, DC, 109–111
media, 102
Minnesota, charter schools in, 133–135
minority students, 174–175
Mississippi, 49
mixed governance systems, 170–172
multi-issue politics, 179–180

National Education Association (NEA),
  52, 120
national government, 7, 11
  Congress, 98–102, 123–126
  education presidents and, 51–58
  role of, 5, 35
National Governors Association (NGA),
  6–7, 38, 45, 131
national standards, 56
A Nation at Risk, 7, 9, 37, 39, 46, 53,
  73–74, 123
New Haven, CT, 61
New York City
  city council involvement in, 79, 113–
    118, 155–159
  legislature, 80
  mayoral control in, 16, 61, 63–65,
    79–80, 109–110, 113–118, 155–159
  philanthropic support for, 154
  school board, 155–159

Nixon, Richard, 52
No Child Left Behind (NCLB) Act, 7,
  34, 56–58, 65, 98–100, 106, 123, 176
nonprofits education sector, 8, 10, 27
nonschool factors, in educational
  outcomes, 178
normal politics, 24–30

Oakland, CA, 61
Obama, Barack, 7, 56, 57, 65, 119, 140
operational issues, 106, 140, 141, 143
overcentralization, 82

Panel for Education Policy (PEP),
  155–159
parents, 8–9, 147, 149, 168–169, 180
partisan politics, 18
path dependency, 23–24, 164–167
Patrick, Deval, 43
performance-based management, 120
Perpich, Rudy, 134
personalities, emphasis on, 65–66
Philadelphia, 61
philanthropic support, 153–155
policy entrepreneurs, 37, 125, 132
policy feedback, 137
political coalition building, 91–92
political distortion, 18–19
political entrepreneurs, 81
political environment, 141–142
politics
  class, 76, 94–95
  interest group, 22–26, 29, 97
  local, 147–148
  multi-issue, 179–180
  normal vs. institutional, 24–30
  partisan, 18
  presidential, 7, 173–174
  racial, 74–76, 86, 94–95, 131, 169–170

portfolio management model, 148–153
presidential politics, 7, 173–174
presidents
    focus on education by, 3, 7, 20, 31,
        34, 51–58, 73–74, 98, 123–125
    power of, 21
    State of the Union speeches, 55–56,
        124, 125
Prince George's County, MD, 61
principal-agent dilemma, 21–22
private foundations, 153–155
private sector, 8–10, 25, 27, 71, 146, 169
privatization, 9–11, 25, 74, 120
professionalism, 85, 168, 172–173
Progressive Era, 59, 165, 171
property taxes, 87–88
Providence, 61
public education/schools, 8, 164–165
    in colonial era, 6, 165
    desegregation of, 8–9, 46, 51–52,
        74–75, 84–89, 95, 170
    mayoral control of, 3, 16–17, 20–21,
        31, 33–34, 58–65, 79–80, 109–111,
        145–151
    negative portrayals of, 168–169
    state authority over, 36–37
    support for, 72–73
public-private partnerships, 176–177
public sector, 8–10, 27
public sector employees, by government
    type, 12–14
pull factors, for executive leadership, 67,
    69–72
push factors, for executive leadership,
    67–69

Race to the Top program, 7, 57, 58
racial discrimination, 89–90
racial politics, 74–76, 86, 94–95, 131,
    169–170
Reagan, Ronald, 10, 53, 56, 74

redistributive policies, 76, 106, 140–143
regulatory state, 70
religion, 9
Rhee, Michelle, 17, 109–110, 111–113
Riley, Bob, 45
Riley, Richard, 36
Robinson v. Cahill, 87–88

Sandoval, Brian, 42–43
Santorum, Rick, 9
scale of governance, 6
Schaeffer, William Donald, 62, 95
Schmoke, Kurt, 95
school boards, 21, 59, 145, 149
    antipathy toward, 68–69
    elections, 148
    legislatures and, 97
    New York City, 155–159
    reduced role of, 84–85
    traditional governance regimes and, 147
school choice, 10, 106, 131–134
school committees, 4
school desegregation, 8–9, 46, 51–52,
    74–75, 84–89, 95, 170
school districts, 11, 130, 171–172
    autonomy of local, 4
    charter schools and, 131–132, 135
    decision making by, 5–6
    dependent, on general government, 21
    elections, 19
    mayoral control of, 16–17, 21, 31,
        33–34, 58–65, 109–111, 145–151
    number and size of, 6
    resistance by, to school desegregation,
        85–86
    state authority over, 36–37
school-focused reform, 140–143, 146, 178
school funding
    courts and, 87–88, 90
    equity, 32, 87–88, 94–95, 122
    state legislatures and, 28–29, 106–107

school principals, 28
school reform. *See* educational reform
schools. *See also* public education/
      schools
   charter, 8, 10, 32, 102–103, 131–139,
      149, 173
   magnet, 10
   private, 8
school superintendents, 21, 147, 167
secretary of education, 21
self-paced learning, 173
single-purpose government. *See also*
      education exceptionalism
   employment by, 12–14
   vs. general-purpose, 10–30
   origins of, 14
   rationales for and against, 14–18
   at substate level, 11–12
   types of, 12
Smith, George, 45
societal values, competing, 18, 94
special needs populations, 107
standards-based education, 39, 90
standards movement, 131
state boards of education, 21, 38–41,
      47–49
state courts, 83
state government, 5–7, 11, 35, 36. *See*
      also governors
   authority of, over public education,
      36–37
   mediocrity of, 130–131
   venue shopping and, 130–145
state legislatures, 80, 87–88, 102–107
   agendas of, 140–145
   charter school lobbying of, 139
   governors and, 144–145
   school funding and, 28–29, 106–107
state-of-the-state speeches, 44
State of the Union speeches, 55–56, 124,
      125
states' rights, 8, 10, 56, 131

Strickland, Ted, 43
student performance, 177–179
substate government, 11–14. *See also*
      local government
summer vacation, 2
supportive rationales, 166
Supreme Court, 83–87

teachers, 147, 149, 167–169, 171
teacher unions, 28, 97, 115, 120–122,
      130, 148, 155, 167–168, 180
technology, 106, 173
think tanks, 120–121
Trenton, NJ, 62

United Federation of Teachers (UTF), 115
urban school systems, 2, 59, 95
U.S. Congress, 98–102, 123–126
U.S. Constitution, 36
U.S. education system. *See also*
      education; public education/
      schools
   exceptionalism of, 4, 23, 164–168
   institutional landscape of, 4–14
   negative portrayals of, 9

venue capture, 130
venue defense, 29
venue shopping, 29–30, 129–145, 172, 174
vouchers, 8, 9, 10, 134, 149

Washington, DC, 62
   city council involvement in, 110–113
   mayoral control in, 16–17, 109–111
White House. *See* presidents
Winter, William, 36, 49

Yonkers, NY, 62